PERSONAL MATURITY

PERSONAL MATURITY
The Existential Dimension

BERNARD J. BOELEN

A Continuum Book

THE SEABURY PRESS · NEW YORK

1978
The Seabury Press
815 Second Avenue
New York, N.Y. 10017

Printed in the United States of America

Library of Congress Cataloging in Publication Data
Boelen, Bernard Jacques Marie, 1916–   Personal maturity.
(A Continuum book)
Bibliography: p.
Includes index.
1. Emotional maturity. 2. Developmental psychology.
3. Existential psychology. I. Title.
BF710.B63   155   78–19196   ISBN 0–8164–9348–0

CONTENTS

FOREWORD

A foreword is actually a postscript of the author placed at the beginning of the book for the benefit of the reader. This book is concerned with the difficult, but fascinating and all-important question "What does it mean to be mature?"

Some people will wonder why we raise the question of maturity at all. For to them the meaning of maturity seems "obvious." Doesn't "everyone" know what maturity is? Others hesitate to even ask the question for fear of finding the answer. For if the answer confirms our common conception of maturity in terms of "perfect adjustment," it takes the adventure out of life. Who wants to live a dull and unexciting existence? If the answer implies that we ourselves are not really mature, it takes the pride out of life. Who wants to be called childish or immature? And if the answer shows that maturity itself is a questionable phenomenon, the security is taken out of life. Who wants to live life without a solid ground wherein to anchor his hopes for self-identity and happiness, for mental health and social peace? Then, there are those who do ask the question of maturity, but whose very attempt to answer the question gets bogged down by bewildering complexities. It seems that every answer gets entangled in unsolvable antinomies, evaporates in a mist of method, and fails to define maturity in a strictly scientific concept. No wonder that, although childhood and adolescence have been the subject of extensive and authoritative treatment, the mature personality has received very little professional attention.

This is the situation today, and this was the situation shortly after World War II when I first began to reflect on the question of maturity. But one thing has changed during the second half of this century. People are no longer indifferent to the question of maturity. On the contrary, the meaning of maturity has become a problem which haunts each of us, whether we are aware of it or not. Today we can no longer dodge the question or ignore its importance. For, there is a growing awareness that the one-dimensional world of science and technology alone cannot give meaning or fulfillment to human existence; and that whatever makes life truly worth living derives from the transcending dimension of authentic humanness. Our future and even our survival may very well depend on the achievement of authentic humanness or personal maturity. The question of maturity is no longer experienced as a threat, but rather as a challenge. The present volume was conceived to meet this challenge.

My analysis of traditional questions about maturity reveals not only the complexity of the problem, but also the inadequacy of the questions. If the traditional approaches remain unsuccessful in their attempt to deal with the question of maturity, it is not so much because "more research has to be done," but because the research is not done within *the proper perspective.* Every psychological theory presupposes at least an implicit philosophy of man. This philosophy itself is not among the data that emerge from the psychologist's research, but is decided upon even before his research gets started, and co-determines its depth and scope. The reason why traditional psychology has not been successful with regard to the question of maturity is its uncritical acceptance of a dualistic philosophy of man and his world. The psychologist who remains unconcerned with the truth of his own philosophical presuppositions runs the risk of doing his research within a distorted perspective. All this points to the need for a new dimension in our search for maturity. This new dimension is the depth-dimension of man's existential openness to the whole of Being, which both in thinking and in action transcends the subject-object dichotomy.

Although prominent psychologists, particularly those of the so-called "Third Force," have provided the search for maturity with a wealth of psychological data, and although existential thinkers have presented us with the underlying philosophical perspective, no one has as yet explicitly viewed the psychological data in the light of this new dimension. It is the purpose of the present volume to initiate this necessary and long-overdue dialogue between psychology and philosophy in their common attempt to understand the mature personality.

My existential analysis of the psychological data, within the cosmic context of their meaningful relationships to the whole of Being, elucidates their fundamental significance and original unity in the mature personality. Within this new dimension one sees things in a new light, finds new answers for old questions, and even discovers data which were hitherto unnoticed. I am, of course, aware that every individual develops in accord with a unique pattern of growth, and is subject to considerable individual variations due to differences in cultural, socio-economic, sexual, educational and hereditary factors. This unique pattern, however, is always a variation of a "fundamental" pattern which is characteristic of every individual as a human being. Because of the shift of emphasis from objectifying thinking to existential thinking, it is with this *fundamental pattern* that this book is primarily concerned. I say "primarily" because the human personality is always an interplay of both patterns, and in the search for maturity philosophy and psychology have to be synergetic.

It goes without saying that this new dimension brings about considerable changes in the traditional understanding of the mature personality. For instance, when the psychological data are viewed in their meaningful relationship to the Being-process, one realizes that "the whole of human life," including the period of personal maturity, is a process of birth and development. The "developmental stages and crises" are not merely biological and psychological phenomena terminating at the age of twenty-one. On the contrary, they are philosophical and existential phases in the birth-process of Being continuing throughout life. Fundamentally speaking, we do not understand maturity in the light of the developmental years, but rather the other way around. We do not "outgrow" the developmental stages (the road *to* maturity), but we integrate them as constituent elements into our personal maturity which is not the end of growing, but rather the full-grown way of growing (the road *of* maturity).

Similarly, the "formative years" cannot be restricted to the developmental years, and even less to the first five years of life. The first five years "determine" only what is more or less mechanistic in our existence, the "fixed" behavior patterns (character) and the "fixated" behavior patterns (illness) of "adulthood." The phenomenon of "maturity," however, is precisely that dimension in the personality which prevents one from being completely "fixed" or "fixated," and which transcends any sort of causal determinism. This is not to say that the first five years of life do not influence the mature personality. This influence, however, is not one of deterministic causality, but rather one of partnership in an existential dialogue. For the mature personality is a "person incarnate," and essentially involved in a living dialogue with his own immaturity, with the child in himself, with the fixity of his character, and the fixation of some measure of disorder. Immaturity is an essential constituent of maturity. We have to reject the usual perfectionist conception of maturity.

The new dimension in our search for maturity affects even the very *question* of maturity. The shift from objectifying to existential thinking entails a shift from reductive analysis to existential analysis, and from the traditional questions *about* maturity as an object to the *self-questioning* nature of the mature personality. The true question of maturity remains always and essentially an open-ended task for future research. No person ever has his maturity safely determined. We don't achieve maturity in a once-and-for-all decision. We can't encapsulate maturity in the fixity of a static definition. Maturity is a process rather than a state of being, a way of Being rather than a property, a response to a gift rather than an object to be controlled. Maturity is a fascinating and awesome adventure, and a creative response to an overwhelming gift; it is also a risk.

It goes without saying that all this cannot be justified in a foreword. Maturity is "self-justifying," and a book on maturity has to speak for itself. I hope that the present volume speaks meaningfully to all those for whom it was written, those who, for any reason at all, are genuinely concerned with the meaning of maturity.

I would like to acknowledge my indebtedness to DePaul University for lessening my academic duties during a period of several years. I wish to express my special gratitude to the Kavir Institute of Paris for its generous Grant-in-Aid. And, finally, I owe special thanks to all those who through their genuine interest and creative participation in my courses, lectures, and seminars on the subject have contributed so much to the inspiration of this study.

BERNARD J. BOELEN
Chicago
May 22, 1977

1

INTRODUCTION

This book is about "mature adulthood," about its genesis, its nature, its dynamism, its structural characteristics, and its significance for the crisis of our age. But just what is meant by mature adulthood? The answer to this question is the subject of this book. However, in order to arrive at a meaningful answering of this question, it is necessary to start from a genuine asking of the question. This too, is the subject of the present volume.

Today "maturity" is a curiously powerful word, a word about which people feel strongly and deeply. Yet, when asked to voice their opinion as to the "real meaning" of maturity, most people seem to feel some sort of cosmic dizziness, and often throw their hands up in despair. Things become so mysteriously intricate and all-encompassing as to defy accurate definition or even adequate description.

To some people "to be mature" and "to be adult" are synonymous, and mean "to be a grownup." But, then, there are mature and immature adults. Consequently, the terms "adulthood" and "maturity" are not synonymous. "Adulthood" denotes the end point of the process of growth and development, or a fixed, plateau-like state of being. "Maturity," on the other hand, denotes the achievement of one's full potentialities, ripeness, self-actualization. Maturity connotes "fulfillment," is non-quantifiable and cannot be measured with mathematical accuracy. Adulthood connotes a fixed point in time and space, and is more accessible to quantifying thinking and scientific verification.

However, the fact that "personal maturity" cannot become the object of observation, measurement, and scientific verification does not mean that it is a merely subjective or even meaningless phenomenon. It only means that this phenomenon is inaccessible to natural science. There are other ways and methods to reflect on the truth and meaning of non-quantifiable phenomena. To deny this is not science, but "scien-

1

tism," pseudo-philosophical belief in the absolute supremacy of natural science and its methods. It claims that whatever cannot be the object of exact observation, of reductive analysis, of mathematical measurement and experimental verification is merely subjective or even meaningless. I have exposed elsewhere the contradictions of this dogmatic pseudo-philosophy. (19, 13–25)

Yet, scientism has also affected psychology and induced many psychologists to pattern their science exclusively after the model of the natural sciences. They reduce the human personality to an "object," analyze the object into "simple elements," and call the resulting "statistical average" the "normal" man. "It seems more and more clear," says Abraham Maslow, "that what we call 'normal' in psychology is really a psycho-pathology of the average, so undramatic and so widely spread that we don't even notice it ordinarily." (150, 15) These psychologists prefer the clarity of mathematical precision to the chiaroscuro of fundamental reflection, even if this means a falsification of their very object. They remind one of the man who had lost his watch on 23rd Street, but kept looking for it on Main Street because the light was so much better there.

Another related factor which accounts for the paucity of psychological studies on maturity is the all-pervasive influence of Cartesian dualism on Western thought. Dualism has been the implicit philosophy underlying the entire history of psychology. Dualism dichotomizes the unity of the human personality into two independent substances: the mind and the body. As a result, the psychologist has for all practical purposes to proceed on the assumption that there are two irreducible worlds: the "outer" world of objective facts (observable data) ruled by physical laws, and the "inner" world of subjective facts (introspective data) controlled by psychic laws. "This assumption," says Maslow, "is acted upon by *many* or *most* psychologists, even though they are perfectly willing to admit that it is an insoluble philosophical problem." (150, 188)

Whether the psychologist studies man in the context of the outer world of observable data, or in the context of the inner world of introspective data, does not depend on his psychological research, but on his tacitly accepted philosophy of man and reality. This dualistic philosophy is decided upon even before he begins his psychological research. Yet this dualism prevents him from doing his research in the proper perspective, for it dichotomizes the human personality and contradicts the primary data of human existence. Consequently, the psychologists' research is not based on the facts as they are originally given, but on a "mental construct." No amount of research within the dualistic perspective of two irreconcilable worlds will ever reveal the original unity of the human and mature personality. For the maturity concept, more than any other concept about man, impels one to grasp the human person as a whole, and to understand his very nature in the cosmic context of his meaningful relationships to the whole of Being.

It is, therefore, imperative that the psychologist examine his uncritically accepted philosophical assumptions, and look for a philosophy which is holistic and cuts across any artificial dichotomies by turning to "the original data themselves" (Husserl). This is precisely the basic inspiration of "existential thinking" or "existential phenomenology" (19; 139), or as it is popularly called "existentialism," which Rollo May defines as "the endeavor to understand man by cutting below the cleavage between subject and object which has bedeviled Western thought and science since shortly after the Renaissance." (153, 11) This is why, as Maslow states, "it is extremely important for psychologists that the existentialists may supply psychology with the underlying philosophy which it now lacks." (150, 10)

Psychology unaided by philosophy cannot describe the mature personality. On the other hand, a philosophy which is authentic and open to experience is constantly nourished by its living contact with psychology. My approach to the problem of maturity will be to establish a dialogue between a philosophy and a psychology that don't distort the primary data of human existence, and that meet one another in the same pre-reflective immediacy of our "life-world" (Husserl).

Every psychological theory has among its often unexamined presuppositions at least an implicit philosophy regarding the nature of man. In considering the problem of maturity, it is essential to make this implicit philosophy explicit. For, if man is a robot, a mature person is a perfectly functioning robot; if man is an aggregate of personality traits, a mature person is an aggregate of fully developed personality traits; if man is a rational animal, a mature person is one who is in full possession of his rational powers, etc. Consequently, in order to deal successfully with the problem of maturity, the psychologist has to do his thinking and research within an explicit philosophical perspective. This philosophy has to be a thinking that reflects on the essence of man, without distorting its primary data by fragmentizing its original unity and freezing the flux of its basic dynamism.

It is precisely under the influence of scientism and dualism that traditional psychology believes reality, including human reality, to be made up out of "simple elements" or "fundamental units." Its reductive analysis decomposes the original unity of the personality into a "sum-total" of fundamental elements: traits, faculties, factors, characteristics, attitudes, drives, values or sentiments. As to the nature, number, or interdependence of these so-called "fundamental elements," no agreement has ever been reached. Having fragmentized man into a heap of static and disconnected fragments, the psychologist wonders if in a final chapter he couldn't put the pieces together again. Yet his attempts are in vain. For no combination of discrete elements will ever yield the original unity of the personality. Gordon Allport is right when he states that "philosophical sophistication is needed in order to reach a completely satisfactory theory of the nature of unification in the personal life." (4, 380)

The existential philosopher, on the other hand, does not arrive at this unity; rather, he starts from it on the basis of an accurate phenomenological description of human existence. He takes as his point of departure the original unity of man, the unitary but structured phenomenon of man's "co-Being-in-the-world." The analysis employed by the existential thinker is not reductive but rather existential. Whereas reductive analysis begins with breaking up the human personality into isolated elements, existential analysis examines from the very beginning its structural characteristics within the context of the original unity of man's existence. The fact that most traditional psychologists ignore the philosophical dimension of the problem of maturity explains why they are practically silent on the subject. It also explains why they complain that not a single over-all criterion for maturity is in evidence, why the various schools don't agree on the subject (2, 215), and why the traditional approach raises more questions than it answers.

According to the traditional approach, the human personality consists in a sum-total of various areas of behavior. An adult who is mature in only one or some areas is an immature adult; a mature adult is one who is mature in all areas of behavior. At first, this approach seems perfectly adequate. On closer examination, however, it leaves one with several unanswered questions. For instance, there is no agreement on the number and nature of these areas of behavior. How can it ever be known that a person is mature in all areas?

Moreover, how can it be known what maturity means in any given area? Does it mean the cessation of growth and development in this area? With the exception of physiological development, this criterion would contradict contemporary understanding of man and maturity as a process. But does man, if maturity is essentially a process, ever reach a "maximum," does he ever arrive at a peak, at full-grownness? Is any

one ever fully mature? Furthermore, doesn't the traditional classification of the mature personality into separate characteristics or criteria
contradict the facts? Both everyday experience and an unbiased
phenomenological description reveal that the characteristics of maturity are partaking of one another and of the whole, that they are
overlapping, interacting, and interdependent. Isn't this interdepen-
dency or integration itself a fundamental characteristic of maturity
rooted in the very essence of man? Couldn't this be the single over-all
criterion of maturity the psychologists have been looking for in vain?
And if this is so, wouldn't it explain why no isolated characteristic can
function as a criterion for maturity, and why the traditional sum-total
definition, which merely enumerates isolated criteria, fails to define the
mature personality? The answer to these questions hinges on the answer
to the fundamental question, "What is it that constitutes the essence
and unifying principle of our human existence?" But this is a philosophical question. Without this philosophical perspective, the whole problem of maturity would be out of focus.

The present volume, therefore, is fundamentally a philosophical
work. It has been written in the existentialist tradition, and its theoretical premises are based on my earlier book *Existential Thinking* (19).
For, as already indicated, it is existential phenomenology that rejects
dualism, and rethinks philosophy as related to the actual human condition. However, the novelty of the existential way of thinking may
prevent the uninitiated reader from understanding its terminology and
its major themes. Some concise statements concerning the meaning of
important terms and insights underlying these reflections on maturity
would therefore be appropriate.

The primary concern here, of course, is the phenomenon of man.
What is the essence of man? What does it fundamentally mean to be
a human being? Although man always has a certain understanding of
himself, this understanding is seldom fundamental. Usually he lives in
the matter-of-factness of the workaday world where self-awareness is
unquestioning and taken for granted. This world is the world of useful
values, of social functions, of human labor, and the satisfaction of
human needs. Somehow man understands himself as the sum total of
all the particulars in the public records, of the predictable behavior
patterns that are the outcome of heredity and past experiences. Underlying all this is the "I," which is some kind of permanent and unchanging core of his being, and which listens to his own proper name. For
example, the question "Who are you?" is usually answered by giving
one's name and social function: "I am Joe Smith, the president of the

First National Bank." Somehow man is a thinking or functioning "thing" among other "things" in this world.

On this usual self-interpretation of man is based the traditional definition of man as a "rational animal." Heidegger rightly states that this definition is fundamentally a zoological one (89, 142), for zoological definitions are the product of classifying thinking and belong to the logical art of defining things in terms of their proximate genus and specific difference. Man becomes a biological species, a mammal endowed with logical reason. Logic, however, deals with things and objects, but never with persons. The traditional definition fails to define the essence of man, for it fails to think what is most fundamentally human in man. Or, as Heschel puts it, "In the characteristics of man as a tool-maker or thinking animal reference is made to the functions, not to the being of man. Is it not conceivable that our entire civilization is built upon a misinterpretation of man?" (92, 5)

Man does not begin to reveal his essence until he begins to experience primordial wonder. Wonder is not only the beginning of philosophy but also of authentic humanness (119, 17). When man experiences primordial wonder, he is suddenly overwhelmed by the global and undifferentiated awareness of the radical mysteriousness of all that is insofar as it *is*. A fascinating and awe-inspiring experience makes him transcend the obviousness and matter-of-factness of his everyday world. A new world of cosmic translucency and inexhaustible depth reveals that even the familiar is unfamiliar, and that even the usual is "different" and unusual. Wonder reveals that the world of work and functions is not man's entire world, and not even his most significant world. Wonder is not concerned with particular beings in their particularity, but with the all-encompassing phenomenon of Being, and with particular beings only in the light of this primordial phenomenon. (The word *Being* is written with a capital "B" to signify the all-encompassing phenomenon of primordial wonder, whereas *being* with a small "b" stands for particular beings.)

As I have shown in *Existential Thinking*, the "all-encompassing universality" of primordial wonder has several important implications. (19, 38–51) There is no particular reason or motive that explains wonder—wonder is not functional; man does not wonder "in order that." The phenomenon of wonder is self-justifying, and cannot be perceived or validated in terms of anything other than itself. Moreover, wonder is not the prerogative of experts or special talents, but of man as the participant in Being. Its manifestation does not restrict itself to any particular human faculty, but it only reveals itself in the total openness of the personality in its entirety. Wonder is not a question man *has,* but a question he *is.* It is a lived astonishment, rather than an asked question; it is a question and a quest in undivided unity.

Furthermore, since wonder is all-inclusive universality, it cannot manifest itself as an "object," as something standing-over-against man as a human subject (L. *objicere*—to throw in one's way). And since wonder cannot be an object, it cannot be "observed" (L. *observere*—to hold at a distance). Consequently, wonder is non-quantifiable, unpredictable, and not subject to human control. Primordial wonder is an overwhelming experience, a gift, an inspiration. Wonder does not reveal itself to man as a mere "outsider," as an observer or spectator, but only to man as a participant in the event of Being. As a participant in this all-inclusive event of Being, man is essentially more than he is. This is why it is impossible for him to be the complete "possessor" of his authentic existence, or to control the dynamism of its emergence. Consequently, man's most authentic activities are not entirely his. This is why artistic creativity, philosophical reflection, authentic love, personal maturity, etc. are characterized by: ecstacy (Gr. *ek* and *stasis*—standing out, being beside oneself), enthusiasm (Gr. *en* and *theos*—being in a supreme Being), inspiration (L. *in* and *spirare*—to breathe into), and gratuitousness (L. *gratuitus*—spontaneous, given free, not of our making).

Since wonder, as an all-encompassing question, cannot be an object, it cannot be a "problem" either. For a problem (Gr. *pro*—over against; *balloo*—to throw) is a questioned object standing over against the questioner, and leaving his status unquestioned. Solving a problem is dissolving the question. Once the answer has been found, the problem can be dispensed with. Primordial wonder, on the other hand, as an all-encompassing question encompasses the questioner and the question as well. (141, 11) Wonder is a mystery. The philosophical meaning of mystery is not to be equated with an unsolvable problem or with sheer ignorance (Gr. *muoo*—to see the unseen, to participate in the super-intelligible source of intelligibility). On the contrary, what constitutes the essence of mystery is that it is a question in which the content recoils upon the questioning itself: a mystery is a self-questioning question, a problem which encroaches upon its own data, and thereby transcends itself as a problem or "questioned object" (141, 8). Wonder transcends the subject-object dichotomy. This is why every genuine answer to wonder as the self-questioning mystery of Being returns as a deeper question, as an enriched experience of wonder. Wonder can never be dispensed with, it can never be answered with complete finality' or crystallized into the fixity of a closed system. Wonder is not a problem to be solved, but a mystery to be lived.

And, finally, since wonder places man in the presence of the all-pervasive mystery of Being, it opens him up to his authentic "Selfhood" (Gr. *authentes*—"Self-doing," authoritative). For wonder *frees* man *from* merely external determinations by *freeing* him *for* his Self-determination, his Self-consciousness, and the Self-doing of his participation in Being. Philosophically speaking, openness is presence to Being. "Maximum openness," says Verhoeven, "gives maximum self-experience." (214, 37)

Primordial wonder is the emergence of man's openness to the whole of Being which makes him transcend the limits of his workaday and functional worlds. The philosophical "essence" (L. *esse*—to be) of a phenomenon is understood in the light of primordial wonder (Being). In this light it is understood that the essence of man is his *ex-sistence* in the etymological sense of the word (L. *ex* and *sistere*—to stand out, to emerge, to transcend). It is in this sense that the terms "existence" and "existential" are employed throughout the present volume, hyphenating these terms when drawing special attention to their etymology. In wonder, however, this understanding still remains implicit. It is not until one reflects upon wonder that the primary data of man's ex-sistence are disclosed as a unitary but differentiated phenomenon. Man finds himself Being-together-with-others-in-the-world. As a participant in the event of Being, man achieves his dynamic essence as a multidimensional openness to the totality of all that is. Here is an insight into the essence of man which far transcends the usual everyday and zoological definitions. Man is not essentially "an animal endowed with logic," but "a dynamic participant in the *logos.*" The logos is the differentiated self-manifestation of Being, or the meaningful structure of reality as a whole.

Since man's essence as Being-in-the-world is a unitary phenomenon, both the "Being-in" and the "world" must be seen not physically, but existentially. Man is not in the world the way a piece of candy is in a box. To be in a box is not essential for the candy; to be in the world is essential for man. The candy does not participate in the box, but box and candy remain side by side. Man participates in the world and is concerned with it (L. *interesse*—to be involved, to concern). This concernful "being-in" manifests itself in various ways: dwelling, loving, thinking, planning, cultivating, caring, building, etc. Therefore, the "world" is not the sum-total of all entities, but the referential totality of concernful involvements. Man can be in the world authentically or unauthentically: authentically, when he is concernfully involved in the all-encompassing process of Being, which is *the World (Welt)*; unauthentically, when he is concernfully involved in the tools, objects, and particular beings of his *surrounding world (Umwelt)*.

The foregoing elucidations have made possible a brief discussion of some other key terms of this book: "Self," "*ego*," "individual," "person," and "personality." Since these terms are used in a great many ways by a great many writers, it is important to define their meaning as they are used in the present volume. For instance, the terms "Self" and *"ego"* are often used interchangeably. Yet, their true meanings are literally worlds apart. For, as has been said above, man discovers his true Selfhood when he achieves his authentic ex-sistence, when he allows the event of Being to happen. In other words, the true Self is man's creative involvement in the World of Being, it is that which allows the World-forming Being-process to take place.

The true Self is spirit correctly understood. Some classical philosophers such as Aristotle and Aquinas hinted at the true nature of the human spirit by calling it "everything in a way" (all-encompassing). To them "the concepts 'spirit' and 'world' (in the sense of the whole of reality) are not only interrelated, their correspondence is complete." (172, 116) However, since "spirit" has been too often mistaken for a disembodied substance, an abstract world-reason, rationality, or mere cleverness, I prefer the more concrete sounding term "person." The true Self is the personal Self as the all-encompassing totality of concernful involvements. Only the person is truly universal in the sense of all-inclusive universality.

Things are essentially different, however, in the world of everyday surroundings. This workaday world is the place where man plans to build a house, where he is the president of the First National Bank, and where he washes himself every day. Yet, whatever he washes, it certainly is not his "true Self," his cosmic presence to Being. There is obviously a basic difference between the personal Self and the *ego* (L. *ego*—"I") of the surrounding world. Man perceives his everyday self-identity somehow as the sum total of his vital statistics held together by a permanent core which he refers to as "I." Yet, not a single one of these statistics, not even their sum total could identify him if it were not for the unity given to them by this enigmatic "I." In short, in man's workaday world, he experiences himself as an individual, i.e., as an integral and indivisible entity, set apart from all other entities in his surrounding world (L. *individuus*—indivisible).

As contrasted with the cosmic World of the person, the world of the individual comprises merely a particular segment of reality. This segment is outlined by the individual's dealings with the objects in his environment: the farmer dwells in his farm and cultivates his land; the mechanic's world is his workshop; the housewife takes care of her home; the student is concerned with school, etc. In the workaday world, primordial Being and the personal Self remain concealed. Only particular beings are encountered, and only from particular viewpoints. What, then, is the "I" (*ego*) which holds together the world of the individual, and underlies the multiplicity of his changing experiences? Within the confines of the workaday and functional worlds, the meaning of the *ego* remains "an awesome enigma" indeed (4, 110). For here the *ego* cannot be understood in terms of particular beings which it transcends, nor in terms of primordial Being which it does not reveal.

It is only in the light of primordial Being that the *ego* presents its essence and fundamental meaning. Here it is revealed that the *ego* is the true Self of authentic ex-sistence, but as concealed in the world of unauthentic ex-sistence. Or, as Heidegger puts it, "what expresses itself in the 'I' is that Self which, proximally and for the most part, I am *not* authentically." (88, 368) Just as the person is not a substance, but an authentic way of Being-in-the-world, so too the *ego* is not a substance, but an unauthentic way of being-in-a-world. Philosophers as diverse as Hume, Kant, and Sartre agree that one never experiences the *ego* as a substance or independent entity. One never experiences the "I" pure and simple, but only as "I think of something," "I love someone," "I am hungry," etc. "In saying 'I'," says Heidegger, "I have in view the entity which in each case I am as an 'I-am-in-a-world'." (88, 368)

Philosophically understood, the *ego* is the personal Self, but as concealed in the particularity of a surrounding world. This is why the *ego* holds together the world of the individual. Whereas the Self gathers all beings in their primordial unity of Being, the *ego* gathers all objects in the functional unity of the surrounding world. Whereas the personal Self lets beings present their essence in the presence of primordial Being, the *ego* lets beings take up a position "opposite to . . . ," it lets them be objects, i.e., appear-to-a-subject. The *ego* is a subject, for it "underlies" the multiplicity of changing objects in the "surrounding" world (L. *subjectum*—that which underlies). The *ego* as subject is not a passive subject-substance, but rather a "subject-process" (William James). Whereas the Self is a World-forming Being-process, the *ego* is a surrounding world-forming subject-process.

As I have said earlier, the World of Being and wonder transcends the workaday world. Yet, these worlds are not separate worlds. For it is within the usual workaday world that the unusual World of Being emerges as its own beyond. Man achieves authenticity only when he lives in both worlds at the same time. Man is an authentic personality insofar as he allows a living dialogue between the Being-process (Self) and the subject-process (*ego*) to take place in his ex-sistence. And this is precisely how I define the term "personality" as it is used in the present volume. The personality is the interplay of the personal and the individual ways of being-in-the-world, of freedom and determinism, of transcendency and immanency. The personality is an individualized person, an embodied Self, a spirit incarnate. It is important to realize that this definition is philosophical, and more fundamental than the usual definitions. Often "personality" means the visible aspects of one's character as it impresses others ("He lacks personality," "She has an attractive personality"). Allport's classic psychological definition of "personality" is "the dynamic organization within the individual of those psychophysical systems that determine his characteristic behavior and thought." (4, 28) Despite its merits within the classifying way of thinking, this definition practically equates "personality" with "character," and fails to think the essence of human ex-sistence.

And, finally, as an embodied Self, the personality is able to emphasize (not separate) either his personal Self, or his embodiment, or disengage himself from either emphasis. This ability differentiates the personality into three possible levels of emphasis. On the *personal level,* the personal Self (spirit) is emphasized. This level is characterized by Self-consciousness, all-encompassing openness, freedom, unity, uniqueness, wonder, and creative process. On the *bodily level,* the embodiment (matter) is emphasized. This level is characterized by opaqueness, side-by-sideness, determinism, multiplicity, homogeneity, exteriority, and passivity. And on the *functional level,* man disengages himself from his concrete involvement in both his Self and his embodiment. On this level man's abstractive way of being-in-the-world is emphasized. This level is characterized by impersonal observation, quantification, calculative thinking, controlling action, and systematization.

In order to facilitate this discussion of the mature personality, I want to schematically visualize these philosophical findings concerning the human personality in the following diagram:

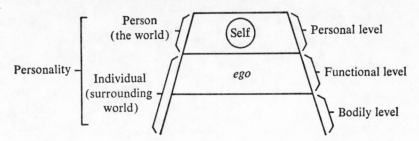

Man is not born mature. He has to pass through various stages to arrive at personal maturity. Yet he does not outgrow these stages, in the sense of leaving them behind, but successively integrates them into ever higher levels of maturity. The "genesis" of personal maturity belongs to its very "nature."

2

BIRTH AND
THE LIFE OF THE INFANT

A NEW PERSPECTIVE

Personal maturity is a *process* rather than a *state* of being. Personal maturity, as the creative participation in the Being-process is, fundamentally speaking, the continual birth of Being in man.

The various stages and crises on the road to personal maturity are as many stages and crises of the birth of the Being-process in man. In other words, the traditional topics of developmental psychology, such as birth, infancy, childhood, and adolescence, reveal their fundamental significance only if understood as progressive phases of the birth of primordial Being in man. They are philosophical, rather than merely biological or psychological phases and crises. What emerges in them is primordial Being, rather than merely biological or psychological functioning. These developmental stages and crises are existential rather than functional, for they involve man's whole ex-sistence, rather than merely topical functions such as emotion, perception, motivation, and motor behavior.

A new perspective for a genuine understanding of man as a developmental phenomenon is needed. The fundamental study of human development cannot simply be a branch of biological, sociological, or psychological sciences, for these functional sciences leave the essence of human development, the birth of the primordial process of Being, unthought. A fundamental understanding of both personal maturity and human development presupposes an explicit awareness of this primordial phenomenon. To grasp the fundamental meaning and unity of the data of developmental psychology, they must be viewed within the philosophical perspective of existential thinking.

The perspective within which one does a certain research is not itself among the data that emerge from this research. On the contrary, it is precisely the perspective that gives the data their specific meaning, and that determines the very nature and scope of the research. The perspective is decided upon even before the research gets started. When one is unsuccessful in finding the solution to a problem or in understanding the significance of a datum, often it is not because "more research has to be done," but because one is not working within the proper perspective. What is needed are not "more facts," but "new light" on the facts.

The original contribution of the present volume is not to do more research in developmental psychology, but to view the available material in a new perspective. By viewing the psychological data concerning the nature and genesis of the mature personality within the perspective of existential philosophy, one can supply the data "with the underlying philosophy which they now lack" (Maslow). By viewing the traditional data within this fundamental perspective, they appear in a new light, with new and fundamental significance. Even data which remained hitherto unnoticed begin to emerge.

The main purport of this book, therefore, is decidedly philosophical. This discussion of human development and personal maturity is not going to add another "Developmental Psychology" to the impressive list of studies on this subject already in existence. This does not mean, however, that the intent is to replace developmental psychology, to question its validity, or to minimize its importance. On the contrary, the findings of the developmental psychologist are not excluded or ignored, but importantly used.

Furthermore, this new perspective prescribes the plan of organization of this book. My main purpose is to arrive at a fundamental understanding of the mature personality. Personal maturity, as I have shown, is the continual birth-process of Being in man. Man, however, is not born a mature personality. He has to pass through various phases and crises of maturation that are, therefore, as many phases and crises of the birth of the birth-process of Being in man. In other words, man's entire life develops as a unified whole, his dynamism is one lifelong birth-process of Being, and what is commonly referred to as "birth" is but the first critical phase in this unending process of emergence. At the moment of birth the process of birth itself has not fully been born yet.

Ordinarily the unity of the course of man's life is interpreted in terms of "the span of time *between* birth and death." While within the context of the everyday world this interpretation is justified and adequate, it cannot provide a philosophical insight into the true nature of this unity. According to the ordinary conception, man finds himself somewhere between the moment of birth which has passed and is no longer actual, and the moment of death which is not yet real until it actually puts an end to his life. The beginning and the end are unconnected, and so are, strictly speaking, all the "nows" that fill up the stretch of life between these two boundaries. For only the experienced, present "now" is "real," the past "nows" have disappeared, and the future "nows" have not arrived yet. Man hops, so to speak, through this ever-changing succession of "nows" without any unity, except for his unexplainable "self" which somehow maintains a continuous selfsameness while it stretches along between birth and death.

Within the philosophical perspective, however, it is evident that the ordinary conception interprets the course of human life in terms of physical objects rather than in terms of primordial Being. It ascribes thinglike characteristics to the moments of time and even to the "self" traversing the span of time between the beginning and the end. It is only within the philosophical perspective that one understands that what constitutes the fundamental meaning and unity of man as a developmental phenomenon is the birth-process of primordial Being. Fundamentally speaking, therefore, human life does not stretch along "between" two unconnected thinglike boundaries: the closed fact of the moment of birth, and the closed fact of the moment of death as the mere "cessation" of the stretching-along of life.

On the contrary, what is commonly referred to as "birth" is but the first critical phase in the lifelong birth-process of Being in man. To-be-born is an essential characteristic of human nature. Man is a being in whom the process of birth never stops, and at no time during the course of his life can birth become "a thing of the past" for him. On the other hand, man's lifelong process of birth is fundamentally the birth of primordial Being in him. Primordial Being, therefore, is the lasting "end" of this lifelong process of birth. The word "end" is, of course, not to be taken here in the sense of "stoppage," but it means "aim" or rather "fulfillment." Being-towards-the-end is another essential characteristic of human nature. As born, man is already coming-towards-the-end, in the sense of fulfillment. There is no moment during man's lifelong process of birth in which the end is "not there yet." In fact, it is the "end" as the birth-process of Being which gives all "beginnings," all developmental phases of birth and rebirth their ultimate meaning and unity. Man does not move away from his beginning, he moves towards it. Man's life stretches itself along towards its own birth.

Philosophically speaking, therefore, the beginning (birth) at any stage of man's development is always and essentially connected with the end as the birth-process of Being. Man is a process of becoming; he is a self-developing being, a being that continually goes out into its past (birth) as a future possibility of Being (end as fulfillment). He begins by coming-to-the-end; he begins by being on the way towards his own beginning; he *is* the self-enriching ad-venture of the birth-process of Being.

THE MEANING OF BIRTH

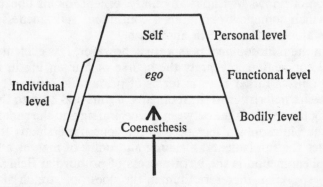

Birth, of course, is not really the beginning of human life, but rather its first critical turning point. Birth is the first existential crisis on the road to full humanness. Life begins at the moment of conception when the male sperm fertilizes the female ovum. The newborn baby at birth has already passed through several stages during the nine-month period of his prenatal development: he has successively been called a zygote, an embryo, and a fetus.

It is birth that terminates prenatal development, and constitutes the first critical turning point or existential crisis on the road to maturity. Birth begins the development of man as an independent being. Obviously, this independence should not be understood in the sense of mature independence, but rather in terms of "physical separateness." At the moment of birth, man begins life as a separate entity set aside physically from other entities out there in the world.

The newborn baby, however, is not merely a separate physical entity, an inanimate thing or object. He is at the same time an organic and experiential being that begins to depend on his own biological organism for respiration, digestion, and temperature control, and on his own budding awareness for contact with the world.

But, whereas the newborn baby after he has emerged from his mother's body is fully born as a separate physical entity, as a biological and psychological being, he is not fully born yet. In the first place, it takes between two weeks and a month for him to complete the transition from the fetal to the postnatal functioning of his biological organism. During this period, in which we call him a "neonate," he struggles for his biological existence and for adjustment to his newly won organic independence.

Furthermore, even when we begin to refer to him as an "infant," his organic independence has not yet fully emerged. He remains helpless and biologically dependent on his mother's constant care, without which he simply would not survive. "Even in the sense of biological development," says Erich Fromm, "birth has many steps. It begins with leaving the womb; then it means leaving mother's breast, mother's lap, mother's hands." (5, 53)

And finally, although the newborn baby has his own budding awareness, the awareness of himself as his own self has not emerged yet. Psychologically, he is still immersed in the primal "we-experience." He does not yet separate the "me" from the rest of the world.

Now, as I have shown in the preceding chapter, man is essentially a unitary but structured phenomenon. Man is not a physical thing plus a living organism plus a psychological entity plus a spiritual being. Man ex-sists. He is a spirit incarnate, an embodied person, a Being-in-the-world. Consequently, the human process of birth is all of one piece—from the physical separation from the womb and the birth of the biological organism to the birth of the psychological personality and the emergence of authentic ex-sistence. In other words, the entire process of human life is essentially a process of birth.

As a structural characteristic of man, the process of birth can never become an accomplished fact, nor can it ever be a mere fact in the sense of a static and closed thing or of a mere object for observation. The process of birth is fundamentally experiential and non-objectifiable; it is a process of unending emergence, a process which itself is never fully born, and which continues whether one's age be six, sixteen, or sixty.

What is commonly referred to as "birth" is but the first critical phase in the total existential process of the progressive birth of Being in man. If this first critical phase is regarded as final, if birth is understood exclusively in its isolation, apart from its total existential context, then one fails to grasp the very essence of the process of birth. The mysterious depth of its essential meaning is reduced to an observational datum for objectifying thinking, to the perfect finality of an accomplished fact. This is what happens when childbirth is understood exclusively in terms of a physical separation from the mother's womb. This, as I have shown, is also what happens when human life is understood in terms of the span of time between birth and death.

One agrees, of course, with the obstetrician about the importance of the physiological viewpoint for childbirth. During the actual process of childbirth it may even seem to be the all-important viewpoint. Yet, despite its practical usefulness and scientific significance, the physiological viewpoint remains unconcerned with fundamental meaning. And this is not a shortcoming of physiology. Within the pluralistic world of human thinking, physiological thinking is *functional,* whereas existential thinking is *fundamental,* for existential thinking grounds the phenomena in the primordial luminosity of Being.

Within the scope of the present book I am primarily interested in the fundamental meaning of the mature personality, and of the road towards personal maturity. In the present discussion of birth, therefore, the concern is with the fundamental rather than with a merely physiological understanding of this process.

In the light of primordial Being it is understood that birth is more than the physiological transition from fetal dependence to the postnatal functioning of an independent organism. For in the light of primordial Being, the fundamental meaning of birth reveals itself as the first existential crisis in the process of the birth of Being in man.

It is obvious that the fact of being born means a drastic upheaval and a dramatic change. The neonate is thrust from his passive, almost vegetable existence in the protective womb into a world in which he would perish if left to his own devices. It is also obvious that the whole dramatic event of this first existential crisis takes place exclusively on the material level, on the level of the concealment of Being.

Although during the entire prenatal period the child-to-be is a "distinct" organism, the symbiotic union with his mother prevents him from being an "independent" organism. It is precisely through the process of birth that his former existence of organic dependence disintegrates, and that he is thrown into a world where he can survive as an independent organism. It should be emphasized that his newly gained independence is not personal, but merely organic. It is the self-being on the level of materiality. And it is here that the philosophical significance of childbirth reveals itself: as the first existential crisis in the process of the birth of Being in man, it is the birth of independent being on the biological level, or the birth of an independent revelation of "the concealment of Being."

According to Heidegger the level of materiality is the "veil of Being." It is characterized by its concealment of man's Being-in-the-world, by its relative absence of self-consciousness, of unity, of structure, of originality, of self, of world and of Being. In other words, the world into which the child is born has its fundamental intelligibility in its predominance of material characteristics such as passivity, exteriority, homogeneity, opaqueness and automatic spontaneity.

It is precisely these characteristics which are in evidence where the psychologist describes how the infant behaves and perceives his world, especially during the early, neonatal period. The newborn baby acts with his whole body in a diffuse, unsynchronized fashion. In the homogeneity of this global mass-action, there is no coordination between the parts, no unity, no structure, no interaction, no functional organization. The homogeneity of his amorphous existence is equally visible in his reactions to distress and in his feelings of well-being. He expresses his distress with all-out crying accompanied by general movements of his whole body and an aimless twisting of his limbs. When he is undisturbed or experiences a feeling of well-being, he exists in a state of all-out tranquility, and usually sleeps or dozes most of the time.

The passivity of the neonate's existence reveals itself in many ways. He is thrown into a world not of his own choosing. He undergoes passively the cutting off of that first apron string, the umbilical cord. He cannot get out of the cradle on his own accord; for the most part he lies inert with his head turned to his favored side. His being is predominantly characterized by the negativity of what he cannot do: he cannot move his body, he cannot raise his head, he cannot grasp, hold or manipulate objects, he cannot smile, he cannot talk.

That he cannot talk is not so much because his organ of speech has not sufficiently developed yet, but rather because he is unable to know any objects or even his own self. Apart from his spontaneous crying because of discomfort or instinctual needs, he simply has nothing to talk about. It is precisely this negative feature which has given this period its name of "infancy" (L. *in* and *fari*—not speaking). If restricted to the merely physiological interpretation, one might wonder why "not speaking" has any priority over "not walking," "not smiling," or "not grasping." But within the perspective of this book, it becomes evident that this period is well-named. For the "not speaking" of the infant is concomitant to the concealment of his self and of the world of objects. He has nothing to talk about, because the essence of his existence is the concealment of his Being-in-the-world.

The passivity of the neonate's existence can also be seen in the way he responds to certain changes in the environment. In the beginning his reactions to external or internal stimuli are built-in and spontaneous in the sense of automatic. There is no mediating self between the stimuli and the infant's reactions. He passively undergoes his own reactions.

These reactions are unconditioned reflexes that have a distinct survival value.

But soon the infant is torn between his own reflexes and instinctual impulses on the one hand, and the behavior pattern of his parents on the other. This "being torn" is his first, and of course passive way, of coming into "ex-sistence." To be sure, he is not yet actively setting himself apart from the surrounding world. But he is somehow passively escaping the closed circuit of his own physiology by being torn between his own instinctual life and the objective order of his mother's schedule. Of course, for him the meaning of reality is not yet determined by its objectivity, but rather by the subjective way in which it satisfies his need for bodily and emotional well-being (the pleasure principle). For him the objective order of mother's schedule is merely the conditioned order of emotional sequences in which he has no free choice, but which awakens his anticipatory awareness and his conditioned reflexes that start in him the process of learning.

And, finally, the materiality of the neonate's world is characterized by the concealment of his Being-in-the-world. It is generally agreed upon that the young infant has no awareness of self, of world, and of Being. To be sure, one cannot observe infantile experience at first hand, nor is the infant able to speak about it in words. But his language of behavior is eloquent. And the inferences that can be made from it confirm the philosophical interpretation of his world as concealment.

Although the newborn infant is evidently conscious, he lacks "self "-consciousness completely. Fundamentally this is due not so much to the relatively undeveloped state of his sense organs, but rather to the fact that his Being-in-the-world is concealed. His consciousness is, in the words of William James, "one big, blooming, buzzing confusion." The world of the young infant is only a diffuse field of homogeneous awareness. It is a global and undifferentiated consciousness in which objects are coming and going without a frame of reference, without any objective significance, without being perceived as beings or even as "ob-jects" in the etymological sense of things "standing-over-against" him (G. *Gegenstand*).

For in this world of concealment there is no *him (ego)*, and, therefore, no ob-ject *(non-ego)*. The young infant is unaware of an environment or surrounding world. Nothing surrounds him since there is no *him*. His feet, his cradle, his body, his mother, and the light in his room are all one to him. When he is wet, the whole world is wet. From the objectifying viewpoint of the adult, he is a separate entity set apart from other entities in his surrounding world. But from his own experiential viewpoint, the neonate has no surrounding world. He merely has what the psychologists call a "coenesthesis" (Gr. *koinos* and *aisthesis*—common perception), an undifferentiated bodily sense, a global, organic awareness of his own physiology. In this coenesthesis no distinction is given between self and environment, between inner and outer world, between internal and external sensation. No differentiation is experienced between the whole body and its organic parts, between perceptual foreground and background, between the immediate sensations and a mediating self.

It goes without saying that within the context of this undifferentiated, self-less and amorphous "all," there cannot be any frame of reference. Consequently, the neonate experiences no differentiation between up and down, between past, present and future, between here and there, between reality and fantasy. He cannot distinguish between the presence or absence of anything, between people and things, or between animate and inanimate objects. The perceptional world in early infancy is a nebulous phenomenon like a London fog with objects coming and going without any meaning or frame of reference. Some rudimentary frame of reference develops as soon as the infant's experience begins to differentiate. This frame of reference, however, does not yet take on the stability of the surrounding world until a conscious *ego* has emerged as the center of a world of relations. This emergence is the basic event of "the crisis of autonomy," which will be discussed later.

THE LIFE OF THE INFANT

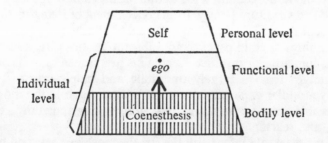

In the meantime, the period of infancy from the age of a few weeks until the crisis of autonomy is anything but static. In fact, infancy is also a continual process of birth, although no new existential crisis occurs during this period. The day-by-day development in infancy is a fascinating thing to watch, but it would be beyond the scope of this book to enter into any detail. It will suffice to give a brief sketch of the direction of this development.

Since this is a study of human development as the gradual birth of the Being-process in man, the concern here will be more with the development of the unitary phenomenon of man's "co-Being-in-the world" than with the development of merely isolated topical functions. In fact, a fundamental comprehension of the development of specific functions and particular phenomena is impossible without "comprehending" them in the etymological sense of "grasping them together" in the light of the birth-process of Being, without understanding them as structural characteristics of man's co-Being-in-the-world. In other words, man understands the way he feels, speaks, thinks, perceives, relates or behaves at any stage or crisis of his development out of the respective way in which he is in the world. After all, man really does pass through infancy, childhood, adolescence, and adulthood, but at no point is he ever pure emotion, pure intelligence, or pure behavior. These so-called functions are more basically ways of being-in-the-world at any given stage of development.

The direction of development in infancy is the same as that of man's entire life, namely from the concealment of the Being-process towards its gradual revealment. It goes without saying, however, that within the merely organic materiality of infancy a real awareness of individual being is not possible yet, much less an awareness of the authentic Being-process. In infancy, there is merely a rudimentary awakening of the direction. More specifically, this entails a gradual shift from passivity to activity and freedom, from undifferentiated homogeneity to differentiated and structured unity, from concealment of Being-in-the-world in the coenesthesis to a budding awareness of self, world, and others.

The findings of child psychology substantiate this direction of infantile development. For instance, during his first fifteen months or so, the baby changes from a largely immobile and helpless neonate to an aggressive toddler exploring the world within reach in the most active way possible, tasting, sucking, pushing, pulling, smelling, banging, kicking, and tearing.

The four-week-old infant still lies for the most part inert on his back; he still moves his body largely in the unsynchronized fashion of global mass-action. But this passivity gradually decreases when he begins to move his head, when he can be propped sitting for a short time enjoying holding up his wobbling head, when he begins to sit without support enjoying his broadening horizons. By nine months the baby will be able to raise himself on hands and knees and begins to crawl.

During the next three months he is under an irrepressible impulse to get onto his feet. By eleven months, he can pull himself to standing position with parental help. Once he has passed his first birthday he can pull himself to his feet unassisted. But he cannot walk without support yet; he cruises sideways while supporting himself on the playpen railing or on some other piece of furniture. Somewhere between twelve and fifteen months he takes his first steps alone, often at the invitation of mother's open arms.

Now he can walk alone. He gleefully propels his wobbling trunk with the staggering gait of his all-too-short legs in the direction of nowhere. It is at this point that we cease to refer to him as an "infant" and begin to call him a "toddler." From an existential viewpoint the toddler has reached an important milestone in his life. For his ability to walk into whole new worlds of objects, together with the emergence of his budding *ego* make a confrontation with his surrounding world unavoidable. The toddler walks straight into a new existential crisis, the crisis of autonomy.

Before discussing the meaning of this crisis, however, I want to illustrate the direction of the infant's development with yet another example: the infant's perception of his world. The newborn baby's perception reveals hardly anything; in fact, his coenesthesis is characterized by the materiality of the "veil of Being," and conceals rather than reveals his co-Being-in-the-world. His perception is passive, global, obscure, and undifferentiated. No distinction is given between the self and the surrounding world, between the whole and its parts, between perceptual foreground and background.

The neonate seems to perceive only considerable disruptions of his equilibrium such as hunger, pain, wetness, or sudden increases in the intensity of light or sound. Yet, he does not perceive these disruptions in isolated, specific, or localized perceptions. Whenever his equilibrium is disrupted, the whole world is in distress. On the other hand, when the neonate is in equilibrium, he seems to be in a twilight zone between sleeping and waking. The world is indifferent to him and normally he drifts into sleep.

After a few weeks, a new differentiation reveals itself. The baby becomes conscious of the gratification of his needs. Now the world can be either distressing, or neutral, or pleasurable. It is worth noting, however, that at this early stage "feeling" and "perception" are not yet differentiated, and that the world is perceived exclusively in terms of emotional meanings, and not in terms of object-ive meanings. It will still take a long time until real objects and their meanings become differentiated for the baby. In fact, this very differentiation marks the threshold between infancy and childhood.

It has been argued that the infant perceives real objects from the very beginning. When an object, for instance a rattle, is moved back and forth over the cradle, the infant will follow it with his eyes during the second month and also by moving his head during the third month. "Therefore" the infant must know and enjoy the rattle. This "therefore" sounds very much like the "psychologists' fallacy" (William James), the interpretation of the client's world in terms of that of the psychologist.

But the infant does not perceive objects at all. Consequently, he cannot perceive the rattle, nor does he even know that he himself is not a rattle. How, then, to account for the fact that he follows the rattle with his eyes, and seems to be enjoying it? The answer is: sense-pleasure play *(Funktionslust)*, the playful experimentation with the newly discovered sensory experience of seeing. This playful experimentation does not limit itself to infancy alone, but it continues throughout life.

Play is freedom in the process of freeing itself. Play, therefore, not only includes sheer delight in a newly discovered phenomenon, but also the seeking of ways of exploring, prolonging, and repeating it. This element of repetition in playful experimentation is sometimes called "the principle of repetitiveness" in developmental psychology. It goes without saying that in the sensory world of the infant, playful experimentation consists largely in a more or less automatic, homogeneous, and random repetition of the same act or experience. Whereas, in the multidimensional world of the mature personality, there is more leeway *(Spielraum)* for playful experimentation. Playfulness is a serious business for the growing child, and, as will be seen later on, a structural characteristic of mature seriousness.

To return to the perceptual development of the infant: the fact that the infant follows an object with his eyes does not mean that he perceives it as an object, as something standing-over-against him. This is why he does not realize that an object which has moved out of sight can be recaptured. "Out of sight, out of existence." This, at least, is how adults would put it. To the infant, however, the object was strictly speaking never "in sight," nor was it ever "in existence," for the simple reason that the object never was an object. What the adult perceives as an object appears within the perceptional world of the infant as an integral and hardly differentiated part of the immediacy of his bodily awareness (coenesthesis). On this level of mere sensory experience *"ego"* and "Being" are still fully concealed. Consequently, no awareness of subject or object (non-*ego*) or of their respective existence has emerged yet. The infant does not even perceive the immediacy of his own bodily awareness as his own, for he cannot contrast it with anyone else's.

After four or five months of age, the baby will begin to recognize the warm agglomeration of pleasurable sensations, visual patterns, and comfortable security that is called "mother." By about six months he will begin to count on this warm agglomeration to continue existing even when it is absent from the immediacy of his own bodily awareness. What all this indicates, is, of course, the beginning differentiation of his perceptual world. It is the first emergence of a budding *ego* and of a rudimentary frame of reference.

It is no surprise that his mother is among the first beings that become differentiated for the baby. For, obviously, it is the mother who has the greatest emotional significance for him. His fear of strangers, which begins to show itself during the sixth month, indicates that the other members of the family are also becoming differentiated. In the meantime, there is also a gradual differentiation of the objects in the infant's perceptional world.

To be sure, the infant does not perceive objects as things in themselves, but rather as emotional and behavioral meanings. During the first few months the infant perceives objects in terms of what they can do to him. They are "emotional meanings" that he discovers in playful experimentation, in sense-pleasure play. At the age of a few months, when the infant can grasp and manipulate the objects, he begins to perceive them in terms of what he can do with them. His playful experimentation with these "action-meanings" constitutes the beginning of a rudimentary skill play. This shift from a passive to an active relationship with reality suggests a major change in the nature of his perception, and clearly demonstrates again the direction of its development.

Another major change in the perceptional world of the infant takes place with the shift from the immediacy of his own bodily awareness to a rudimentary frame of reference. This change in terms of the infant's relationship with his mother has already been discussed. Now also the world of objects becomes differentiated. This means that various emotional and behavioral meanings become differentiated from one another and from an emotional or behavioral center that he does not yet know as his own. When the baby is six months or so, he will anticipate the reappearance of some object that has moved out of sight. He will even begin to show active resentment when something is taken away from him. All this clearly indicates that he begins to realize that objects can be recaptured, and, therefore, continue to exist even when they are absent from his perceptual world.

In other words, certain objects begin to take on some degree of permanence within a more and more reliable referential totality of perception. His coenesthesis differentiates into a growing stability of organization, into a rudimentary world. Philosophically speaking, this pristine articulation of the immediacy of the baby's bodily awareness is a rudimentary *logos,* an embryonic manifestation of the meaningful structure of reality. In the light of the *logos* it is also understood that the developmental "principle of differentiation" expresses the necessity for Being to emerge in a dialectical, articulated, or differentiated way. It goes without saying that the first differentiation of the baby's perceptional world takes place on the level of the concealment of his "Being-in-the-world" *(logos).* He finds a perceptional center (his own body) together with pleasurable agglomerations (his mother and family) in a growing field of emotional and behavioral meanings (the world of objects). Even by the time he has reached his first birthday, he has not yet set himself off from the environment by clear-cut boundaries. Because the *ego* is not yet clearly differentiated from the world, I employed the term "field" (total complex of interdependent phenomena) rather than "environment" ("surrounding" world). Nothing really "surrounds" him, for there is no *him.* One can truly begin to speak of "environment" as soon as a conscious *ego* emerges as the center of his field of relations. This emergence constitutes the essence of man's second existential crisis.

3

THE EMERGENCE OF
THE WORLD OF THE CHILD

THE CRISIS OF AUTONOMY

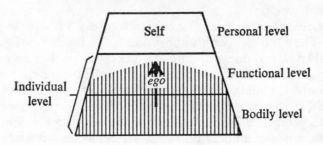

Although the first signs of the crisis of autonomy frequently appear by eighteen months of age, the critical stage does not start until the age of two. Suddenly, for no apparent reason and in the midst of his cheerful conformity, Johnny refuses to obey. He refuses to take orders, to eat his spinach, or to go to bed. For instance, when mother asks him to shake hands with a visiting aunt, he will put his hands on his back and answer with a flat "No!" Every parent knows the "symptoms" of this crisis only too well: stubborness, disobedience, negativism, resistance to parental demands and suggestions, and sometimes even temper tantrums. Equally well-known are the key words in his vocabulary: "No!" and "Mine!"

Unfortunately, the negativism of this resistant behavior often creates so many problems for his parents, that they fail to understand the positive meaning of this crisis. And, as a result, they also fail to understand the true educational situation. They will mistake the mere semblance of stubbornness and disobedience for real stubbornness and disobedience, and treat the child accordingly. Or they will interpret his

27

negativism in terms of pathology. They will see a psychiatrist about their problem child, and express their fears that his "maladjustment" indicates the first symptoms of "abnormalcy" or of "juvenile delin-quency." Even the psychological terms for this phase, "negativism" and *"Trotzalter"* (age of stubbornness), hardly suggest that one is dealing here with a crisis of birth.

Yet, a crisis of birth is precisely what this period of negativism is. Again, the fundamental significance of this crisis will be understood when, within the perspective of existential thinking, it is placed in the birth-process of Being in man. The central issue of this period, as the psychologists point out, is the emergence of the *ego.* This entails, as Erikson has emphasized, the birth of autonomy. (53, 251) For the child becomes aware of himself as a being set apart from other beings in his surrounding world. He develops a will of his own, and wants to do things for himself.

Philosophically, this means an existential crisis, a change in the level of being. The child escapes his imprisonment in the coenesthesis of the biological level, and opens up into the functional level of his existence. This second existential crisis on the road to full humanness is the crisis of autonomy. Its fundamental significance is the change from percep-tional field to surrounding world, from organic independence to indi-vidual independence, from the world of the infant to the world of the child. The crisis of autonomy, therefore, coincides with late infancy (1½–2½ years) and with early childhood (2½–5 years).

One is now prepared to com-prehend the different phenomena of the crisis of autonomy in their original togetherness as manifestations of the birth of individual being-in-the-world. The crisis of autonomy, as a phase of the birth-process of primordial Being in man, is a differentiated but *unitary* phenomenon. The individual phenomena of this crisis re-veal their full significance only as interdependent manifestations of the total configuration. For instance, the merely negative phenomena, such as stubbornness or disobedience remain mere appearances as long as they are seen apart from the referential totality of this existential crisis. They seem to be real stubbornness and disobedience, but their real meaning is essentially different.

It is necessary therefore, to relate the negative phenomena to the positive phenomena, such as the emergence of the child's *ego,* the discovery of his own autonomy, and of the coming into being of a surrounding world. It is also necessary to incorporate seemingly un-related phenomena, such as the child's "naming mania" and his fear in the dark, that are nevertheless, as the psychologists insist, typical of this period. And, finally, the educational problems typical of this crisis cannot be treated as a mere corollary either. On the contrary, both the child's resistant behavior and the parents' dilemma between authoritarianism and permissiveness are essential constituents of the existential crisis of autonomy.

As I have shown in the previous section, the one-year-old baby begins to discover a budding *ego* and a rudimentary environment, but he has not as yet clearly differentiated himself from the world. Even by the time he is eighteen months of age, he still has not fully set himself apart yet from others and from the world of objects. At this time, however, there is a radical change. By now he begins to show the first symptoms of intermittent negativism by various forms of "oppositional behavior" and by his repeated outcry "No! No!" But it is not until approximately his second birthday that his resistant behavior begins to take on dramatic proportions, and actually becomes a way of life. The emergence of his conscious *ego* has reached a critical stage during which he feels compelled to make the differentiation between himself and the surrounding world complete.

Philosophically speaking, the emergence of the child's conscious *ego* is the birth of an entirely new way of being-in-the-world. For with the emergence of his conscious *ego,* the child escapes the closed boundaries of his coenesthesis. His conscious *ego* adds a new level of being to his existence, namely the functional level, where he frees himself *from* his predominantly passive existence. He, thereby, frees himself *for* the possibility of actively encountering non-*egos,* or ob-jects in the etymological sense of placing them "before," or "over-against" himself. The emergence of his conscious and active *ego* (subject) is the condition for the possibility of discovering any *other-egos* and ob-jects. On the other hand, it is only by actively setting himself apart from or op-posing this surrounding world that he finds himself as an *ego,* as a separate individual. The emergence of the *ego* and the emergence of the environment are co-original, and constituted by their mutual op-position.

Now, the crisis of autonomy is fundamentally the child's discovery of his ego and his environment in their mutual opposition. And the oppositional behavior during this crisis is his playful experimentation with the discovery of this opposition.

By now it should be evident that the child's resistant behavior is not really "negativism" at all. On the contrary, during the crisis of autonomy the child is taking his second decisive step on the road towards his personal maturity by responding to the second turning point in the birth-process of Being in man. He transcends the infantile concealment of his being-in-the-world, and playfully establishes his autonomous *ego* as the unifying center of a surrounding world of ob-jects. He begins to com-prehend the meaningful structure of reality *(logos)*, but still in terms of particular beings rather than of Being. The crisis of autonomy is the emergence of the world of the child, or the birth of unauthentic being-in-the-world. The child discovers "beings" rather than Being, his individual *ego* rather than his personal Self, his surrounding world *(Umwelt)* rather than the authentic world *(Welt)* of Being. Yet the emergence of the world of the child marks an important milestone on the road to authenticity.

When during this crisis the child refuses to shake hands, to eat, or to go to bed, he is not really stubborn, but rather involved in the playful act of letting something take up a position opposite to him. His opposi-tional behavior is his way of being which allows something "which is opposed" (ob-ject) to manifest itself in op-position. This situation is interpreted here in terms of his "way of *being*" rather than merely in terms of a relation between subject and object. For the very possibility of encountering an ob-ject at all is based on the openness of the *ego* towards anything that manifests itself in op-position. It is based on the *ego,* not as individual subject, but as unauthentic ex-sistence in the etymological sense of "standing-out," of multidimensional openness towards ob-jects. The *ego* as unauthentic ex-sistence con-stitutes a horizon within which two beings can encounter one another and be-come subject and object.

Consequently, the oppositional behavior of the child should not pri-marily be interpreted in terms of a one-dimensional relationship be-tween a subject and an object. When the child resists *you,* he is not merely letting *you* take up a position opposite to him, he is building a multidimensional world. During the crisis of autonomy the child is fundamentally engaged in a playful experimentation with an act of orientation which constitutes a horizon of ob-jectivity in general. And it is this intentionality which underlies all his individual acts of resistant behavior. What is at stake in every single act of negativism is the establishment of his unauthentic ex-sistence, of a horizon of ob-jectivity in general. This fact is clearly illustrated by the case of a three-year-old boy, as related by Allport: "One boy, not yet three, made a daily visit to his grandmother's house across the street to announce (apropos of nothing), 'Grandma, I won't.' " (4, 118–19)

One is now able to understand the child's fear of the dark and his "naming mania" as integral manifestations of the crisis of autonomy. It is said that the child's fear of the dark is caused by his parents who tell him scary stories. Although, admittedly, this may intensify things, it certainly is not the cause of his fear of the dark. Why do all parents conspire to tell scary stories to this particular age group? Why do parents that do not tell such stories still have children that are afraid in the dark?

The answer is that the child's fear of the dark is not fear at all: it is his first existential anxiety. In fear, man is shrinking from an external threat. It is always a particular being or object in his surrounding world that he is afraid of, such as an unexpected noise, a dog, a snake, a dentist, a tornado, a burglar, or a fire. Now, the child's fear of the dark arises precisely in the *absence* of any and all objects. When mother turns off the light it becomes dark, all objects and the whole surrounding world disappear. As I have shown, during the crisis of autonomy the child finds himself as an *ego* only by actively setting himself apart from the objects, or by op-posing the surrounding world. The disappearance of the objects and the surrounding world creates the experience of the threat of the imminent non-being of his own *ego.* This phenomenon, in the language of existential phenomenology, is called "anxiety."

When the light goes out, and the surrounding world disappears, the child not only becomes helpless, but his very existence is at stake. When he is cut off from the world, he is cut off from himself. If asked what he is afraid of, his true answer would have to be "Nothing!" This, of course, does not mean "absolute nothingness," but rather the "no-thing-ness" of his world and the ensuing possibility of the non-being of his own existence. But since the child is incapable of reflection, he is more likely to project his fears which already reside in him into the darkness of his room. He will say that he heard a burglar in the closet, that he saw a spook behind the swaying curtains, or fears that a kidnapper is hiding under his bed. Although it is important to reassure the child that everything is safe, it is more important to leave a night light on in the child's bedroom during the night. For this will reassure him of the existence of his surrounding world, and thereby remove the threat of the imminent non-being of his own existence.

The child's "naming mania" can also be understood as an integral constituent of the crisis of autonomy. The child begins to perceive a world of objects and to set himself apart from this world. But he cannot perceive objects unless he can attach meaning to them, and differentiate them from one another. And this he cannot do without naming them. Naming objects, therefore, is an integral part of the child's playful experimentation with the discovery of his *ego* and his environment in their mutual op-position. This is why it is rightly said that "language helps put the child in touch with his environment and at the same time liberates him from it." (200, 118)

Language during this period or at any time in human life is not only a tool for communication, or a toy to play with, but more fundamentally a way of ex-sisting and a source of revelation. I will return to this later. But it should be clear by now that during the crisis of autonomy the naming of people and objects becomes the magic wand for the child that brings the environment into existence and fixes and stabilizes his own position in it. He ceases to be an in-fant, one who cannot speak. Indeed, his words are still highly concrete, they are still closely tied to the here and now. Names are not yet general terms that "stand for" objects, but they are still concretely imbedded in them.

During this period Johnny can be watched "at work" when, for instance, mother has set the table for dinner. Johnny will pick up a spoon and ask "Whadda?" Mother answers: "Spoon." Very satisfied, Johnny puts down the spoon, only in order to pick up the next one and repeat his question "Whadda?" This process may go on indefinitely. However, it is wrong to conclude from this that Johnny is a slow learner, because it takes him so long to find out what a spoon is. He probably knew it already the first time. He is merely engaged in naming things, in his playful experimentation with the discovery of his *ego* and the environment in their mutual opposition. Sometimes in the process he points to himself and asks "Whadda?" Mother says "Johnny." This only heightens the joyful sensation of op-position!

One is now prepared to face the educational situation, and to make some basic observations concerning the "typical" problems of negativism. Anxious parents find themselves suspended between authoritarianism and permissiveness. They may demand strict obedience, become authoritarian and block the child's psychological growth, inhibit his creative self-expression and repress his budding freedom. For they do not permit the oppositional behavior which the child needs to set himself apart from his surrounding world. Or else, many well-meaning parents, seeing the ill effects of authoritarianism, go to the opposite extreme of the *laissez-faire* method. They permit the child to do whatever he wants at any given moment without any limits or restrictions. They become overpermissive and turn the child into a disobedient, spoiled brat impossible to live with. Moreover they make him feel anxious, erratic, and insecure. For now the child is not given any opposition which he needs to set himself apart from his surrounding world.

It seems utterly difficult to sail between the Scylla of authoritarianism and the Charybdis of overpermissiveness. There seems to be no other choice. Either parents are disciplinarians and put the child on the road to maladjustment and psychopathology by blocking his psychological growth, or else they condone his disobedience and prepare him for a life of immorality. Any attempt to strike a healthy balance between the two horns of the dilemma will result, at best, in a compromise between two evils, and, at worst, in a self-contradiction.

However, the dilemma disappears as soon as one begins to understand the true meaning of the crisis of autonomy: the child's playful discovery of himself in opposition to his surrounding world. His seeming stubbornness and disobedience are not really stubbornness and disobedience at all. The negativity of his oppositional behavior is fundamentally very positive. By playfully allowing something which is opposed (ob-ject) to manifest itself in op-position, he sets himself apart from the environment and constitutes himself as the unifying center of his surrounding world. He begins to respond to his differentiated existence, and to listen to the voice of being in a multidimensional world. His dis-obedience (dis and obedire—to "listen" in "different directions") is not moral disobedience, but rather existential dis-obedience. It is his existential "listening in different directions" which is precisely the first step towards mature moral obedience.

By now it has become evident that both authoritarian and overpermissive parents fail to grasp the fundamental situation of the child in his crisis of autonomy. Both block the birth of his being-in-the-surrounding world by not permitting him to listen in different directions. The disciplinarian parent does not permit the child to listen to (obey) the voice of being in his own budding ego. The overpermissive parent does not permit the child to listen to (obey) the voice of his parental being. Both extreme positions fail to face the primary data of the child's existence, the multidimensional openness of his co-being-in-the-surrounding world. They reduce his very ex-sistence to an isolated entity, to a thing that can be "manipulated" or "left alone." Small wonder that the child's oppositional behavior is mistaken for stubbornness or disobedience.

Now, "educating" is not manipulating an object, or training an animal, but relating to a human being, a "co-being"-in-the-world. And it is because of this participation in the self-project of one another's Being that one evokes or draws forth the growth of Being in one another. It is only this fundamental meaning of education that does justice to Pestalozzi's well-known definition "Help to self-help," and to the etymology of the term "education" (from *educere*—to draw forth, to evoke). The genuine educational process is not coercive, but evocative; it is not manipulative, but cooperative; it is not a technical procedure, but a human relationship. The key factor in the educational process is not what we "say," nor even what we "do," but rather *"who we are"* (Guardini). In true education there are no technical devices that automatically lead to the desired results. "Ways of dealing with children are not merely procedures to be followed as in baking a cake: they involve human situations. . . ." (200, 69)

Both disciplinarian and overpermissive parents take the interpersonal relationship out of education. They misinterpret the meaning of authority and obedience by taking them out of context. "Obedience" for them is simply the blind submission to any and all commands, and "authority" the power to enforce such a submission.

For example, when Mother asks Johnny to come to dinner, to eat his food, or to go to bed chances are that she will get a flat "No!" for an answer. When this is the case, much depends on the existential quality of Mother's response. If she is overpermissive, she will let the child have completely his own way, afraid to inhibit his spontaneous impulses of self-expression. But, in fact, this is precisely what she does. For she inhibits the budding need of the child to listen (obey) in different directions, and coagulates his budding authority into the autocratic will of a dictator. Johnny becomes insecure, erratic, and manages in no time to tyrannize the entire family.

If, on the other hand, Mother is authoritarian and domineering, it is she who will tend to tyrannize her Johnny. Her commands call for instant obedience; she doesn't take "No!" for an answer, and often intimidates the child with veiled threats ("Listen, or else. . ."). Mother's authoritarian control of Johnny takes the listening out of his obedience, literally "petrifies" the child and makes him insecure, neurotic, and submissive. Overpowered by a superior force, Johnny becomes fearful and subdued. His submissiveness is not obedience at all. On the contrary, it is merely a mechanical and crippling conformism which forces the child to repress his need to do his own creative listening (obedience) and which makes him surrender his own budding authority.

The only healthy way to deal with Johnny's negativism is within the context of the educational process as a human relationship. When Mother realizes that Johnny is neither disobedient nor pathological, but is getting a will of his own, she can, despite the inconvenience, remain unperturbed and friendly, and even enjoy his oppositional behavior with a sense of humor and pride. At least she will understand and tolerate it without feeling offended or outraged. For instance, when Johnny is pleasantly settled with a toy, Mother's call, "Johnny, put away your toys, dinner is ready," may come like adult brutality and evoke a sudden outburst of negativism. Mother can prevent this outburst by giving advanced notice that dinner will be ready in about ten minutes. This gives Johnny time to get used to the idea that he has to terminate his play and enter the world of culinary adventures. Yet, the dinner table is another notorious source of trouble during this period. Especially when Mother is generally overprotective and domineering, the child often resorts to the dinner table as his only chance to play his game of opposition. "Eat your spinach!" "No!" When Mother becomes anxious and tries to force the food down his throat, she may create a real feeding problem where none existed and none should be. Only when she relaxes her general attitude towards the child, and gives him his food leaving the rest to his own initiative will the problem vanish. He does not "have to" eat; he *may* eat! Another crucial situation often arises at bedtime. "Johnny, it is time to go to bed!" Answer, "No!" At the earlier stage a simple rephrasing of the command may do the trick: "We are going to bed now!" Mother makes Johnny regress to the "we-feeling" of his infantile coenesthesis where no opposition is experienced. When this no longer works, she may make a game of what she wants him to do. "Let's see who can get up the stairs first." This enables Johnny to assert himself in playful opposition . . . on his way to bed. Thus Mother manages to let Johnny both listen to himself, and, by diverting his attention from the original object, listen to her also. A similar purpose is served by the "multiple choice." "When you go to bed you may take your teddy bear along, or you may undress yourself, or I will read you a story." "I want the story!" Again, Johnny asserts himself, but . . . to go to bed or not to go to bed, that is *not* the question.

This is not to say that the parents should not impose some discipline and limits on the child's behavior. On the contrary, the educational process demands it. The child needs both internal and external discipline. The parent-child relationship, as I have shown, is characterized by the mutuality of their creative listening (obedience). It is precisely this creative listening which constitutes the essence of internal or self-discipline (L. *discere*—to learn, to listen). On the other hand, the interpersonal relationship between parent and child "incorporates" the physical and social determinisms of the surrounding world. Consequently, the creative listening of internal discipline has also to listen to physical limitations, social structures, moral rules and regulations, and other determinations imposed upon it by the external world. And this is what constitutes the essence of external discipline. Genuine discipline is essentially a dialogue between internal and external discipline.

Of course, during the development from infancy to maturity a gradual shift of emphasis should take place from external to internal discipline, or from help to self-help. But at no time should the one be used without the other. To the extent that the child has only an embryonic self-discipline, and cannot yet find the limits and structures for himself, the parents have to come to his assistance. They have to set some limits and provide him with some structures that are guidelines for his budding self-direction rather than restrictions of his freedom. External discipline, therefore, should be consistent in the existential rather than in the mechanical sense of the term. Mechanical consistency turns external discipline into a rigid system of external controls which enforces mechanical submission on the part of the child, and becomes coercive and arbitrary rather than growth-provoking. The child who perfectly adjusts in submissive conformity to all parental commands will not give his parents any trouble, but is himself headed for serious trouble.

Only when external discipline is consistent in the existential sense is it growth-provoking. External discipline does not limit, but rather channels the child's behavior when it is put at the service of internal discipline, when it is consistent (*con-sistere*—to stand together) with the loving service of the parent and the budding self-direction of the child. External discipline, therefore, is growth-provoking only when it is consistent with the principle of emancipation, when it gradually decreases with the increase of the child's self-discipline. Parental guidance and control have to stop whenever a child can do something for himself. Parents should not continue their help wherever a child is maturationally ready for self-help.

Once the child has successfully passed the crisis of autonomy, he has

THE WORLD OF THE CHILD

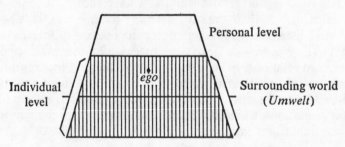

Personal level

Individual
level

ego

Surrounding world
(*Umwelt*)

made himself quite at home in the surrounding world. He has now reached the developmental phase of childhood proper, which extends from the end of the crisis of autonomy to the onset of pubescence, or from the age of five to the age of ten or eleven. Again, the primary purpose of the present section is not to discuss child psychology, but rather to reveal the world of the child in its fundamental significance as a dynamic phase of the birth-process of Being in man. For, although the world of the child does not encounter any existential crisis, it is anything but static.

By viewing some basic developmental data of the world of the child within their philosophical perspective, it will be discovered that it is a world in process, a world of "not yet" exemplified by the child's desire to grow up. Here one must remember that man's being-in-the-world is not like the being of candy in a box. Earlier I have refuted this physical-istic type of philosophy which interprets the individual man as an "I-thing" inside a "body-thing" inside a "world-thing." Man's essence is being-in-the-world, and his "being-in" is multidimensional presence, creative participation, existential involvement. Likewise, the world of the child cannot be studied apart from the child, and vice versa. The child *is* his being-in-the-world-of-the-child. The individuality of the child *is* the unifying and world-forming subject-process which progres-sively constitutes and discloses the world of his surroundings. It is precisely on the direction of this world-forming process that the discus-sion will now center.

By the time the child has passed the crisis of autonomy, he has constituted the world of the child as a horizon of environmental ob-jectivity. By now the impression may have been created that I endow the child with an adult understanding of objectivity. But nothing is further from the truth. The road to objectivity is a slow and laborious process of development. And at the age of three the child finds himself only at the beginning of this process. This begin-ning objectivity established during the early phase of childhood (3–6 years) could be called animistic objectivity which gradually evolves into realistic objectivity during late childhood (6–12 years), whereas the possibility of truly abstractive objectivity does not arise until pu-berty (11–14 years).

The fact that during the crisis of autonomy the child sets himself apart from the surrounding world does not imply that he recognizes immediately any definite limits between the self and the external world. On the contrary, in the early stage of this development the psychical and the physical are still far from being completely differentiated. For him the inner world of his own thoughts and feelings and the outer world of inert things are not yet two separate realms. He still lives within the things he perceives, and these in turn affect and color the entire mood of his experiential life. He still lives in a world of diffusive participation which makes him ascribe to the outer world what takes place in the inner world and vice versa. Consequently, "his own feelings and thoughts and wishes flow out into and influence the objective world, animating and coloring and shaping it so that his world includes much that is quite surprising to adults." (200, 156) In short, in this early stage the worldview of the child is animistic. For instance, when the child falls off the sofa, he might say, "Naughty sofa!" He may feel that it is the trees which by waving their branches make the wind blow. He might be found involved in a lively conversation with his teddy bear. He is amazed that the moon "wants to follow him" wherever he walks. Or he is frightened by a clap of thunder because "the clouds are angry."

From what has been said, it follows that one cannot agree with the usual definition of "animism" in the child, or for that matter in the primitive, as "the tendency to endow inanimate objects or phenomena of nature with 'minds,' 'souls' or 'spirits.' " For the phenomenon of animism arises precisely from man's inability to make any such distinctions. "Animism" is rather the first, primitive perception of objective reality where the distinctions between life and inanimate matter, between person and thing, between inner and outer world still remain largely embedded in perceptual participation.

The world of the early child is a predominantly animistic world which gradually begins to fluctuate between animism and realism, and then evolves into the predominantly realistic world of childhood proper. It is precisely these animistic and realistic worldviews that provide a basic insight into the respective worlds of early and late childhood. I will elucidate this by making some basic observations concerning a few structural features of the child's world.

The animism of the early child affects his entire being-in-the-world. Its immediate counterpart in this world is magic. As I have shown, the relation between the early child and his world is one of diffuse participation. Now, this relationship is called "animism" to the extent that reality affects the child, and "magic" insofar as the child affects reality. Animism is the child's primitive perception of reality, whereas magic is his primitive action upon reality. Jean Piaget illustrates this relationship with his example of children who believe that the sun follows them. "When the emphasis is on the spontaneity of the sun's action, it is a case of animism. When they believe it is they who make the sun move it is a question of . . . magic." (169, 133) Magic, therefore, is a mode of human behavior which through its diffuse participation in an all-pervasive, transcending, and mysterious power attempts to directly and concretely influence or control a thing or event in accordance with the wishes of the agent. Both animism and magic are rooted in the diffuse participation which characterizes the early child's being-in-the-world. Or, as Piaget puts it, "it is just at the time when feelings of participation arise from the differentiation of the self and the external world [the crisis of autonomy], that the self assumes magical powers and that in return, beings are endowed with consciousness and life." (169, 133)

As discussed earlier, the individual *ego* is not a static, independent entity, but rather a world-forming subject-process that frees objects for their discoverability in the surrounding world. Animism and magic in childhood are precisely the inchoative phase of this world-forming process. They are the child's primitive ways of grasping his world in the twofold sense of respectively understanding and mastering it. Animism and magic are rudimentary forms of rational thinking and scientific control which do not fully emerge until puberty.

This magico-animistic discovery of the world is both fascinating and frightening for the child. Both animism and magic arise, as I have said, from a differentiation of the world within an intimate sense of participation. Now, on the one hand, the world of the early child is no longer wrapped up in the closed-circuit of his undifferentiated bodily sense (coenesthesis). His *ego* emerges, and with it a strange new world of objects. To the extent that he is involved in the wonders of this new world, he is thoroughly interested and fascinated. On the other hand, the world-forming *ego*-process transcends not only the infantile coenesthesis, but also any merely bodily experience or activity, and even any particular being. To the extent that the young child transcends the familiar, he is confronted with the unknown, with the all-pervasive threat of uncontrollable and mysterious powers. He is thoroughly frightened. He has his first experience of the uncanny, of a rudimentary existential anxiety. The young child lives in a world which is both enchanting and spooky, both fascinating and horrifying. It is easy to see here the analogy between this experience of the child and the mature experience of the horrifying and fascinating mystery of Being. Indeed, philosophically speaking, the fairy magic of the child's world is the first, primitive, and unauthentic manifestation of the primordial world of wonder. The idea that the world of the young child is an enchantingly beautiful fairyland, a paradise without any basic fears or anxieties, is a mere fiction in the minds of "perfectly adjusted" adults. Small wonder that truly mature and authentic persons have an infinitely better under-standing of the child than the realist who has "outgrown" any trace of magic and mystery.

The child's earliest conception of the world is a magico-animistic one. He believes that his actions and his thoughts can bring about events, and that mysterious powers are latent in all things. Soon he extends this view and finds human attributes in all these phenomena, and begins to explain his world in terms of interactions between these anthropomorphic creatures. His world becomes populated not only with elves, fairies, and other benign beings that fascinate him, but also with sinister creatures: goblins, dragons, ogres, witches, spooks, and kobolds that haunt him day and night. He feels helpless before these malignant monsters against whom he must constantly defend himself. The world in which he is actually involved by now is the world as fairy tale. This is why he is so immensely "inter-ested" in fairy tales. He loves to hear them, even when they are frightening. Only unwise parents try to avoid any and all scary situations. For they ignore the fact that it is the child's developmental task at this age to create a magico-animistic world with all its fascinating and frightening aspects. The child will have to use his own playful and magical resources to handle his own existential anxieties. By repeatedly listening to fairy tales, by playfully pretending that he himself is a witch, by casting a spell on the spooks, by shooting the dragons, and by ritualistic games he scares these sinister creatures (his own anxiety) into submission. Here are found the magic beginnings of self-control. The meaning of magic cannot be restricted to primitive science alone. The earliest discovery of being-in-the-world is magico-animistic. The fairy tale world is a primitive *logos*. His inter-est in fairy tales is not merely a characteristic of the early child, it is his very being-in-the-world. By constituting his primitive world as a fairy tale, he arrives at a primitive understanding, articulation, and mastery of himself and his world. The fairy tale is rudimentary ethics, rudimentary religion, rudimentary philosophy, rudimentary art, in short, rudimentary authenticity.

From the foregoing it follows that the world of the early child cannot be regarded as the mere product of his imagination. For this view presupposes a sharp boundary between his world of facts and his world of fancy and dreams, a boundary which does not exist yet at this animistic stage of development. For instance, when a child has had a nightmare, he will receive little comfort from his mother's assurance that "it was only a dream." (Much comfort, however, from the reassur-ing value of her loving presence.)

To adults, the young child seems to play fast and loose with the truth. He deceives adults and becomes an outright liar in order to get things his way. Yet, what is really deceiving is the appearance of willful deception. For, again, it is the magico-animistic inability of the child to distinguish between thought and reality that accounts for the appearance of untruthfulness. If by "truth" is meant the agreement between thought or statement and reality, then the very notion of truth, and, therefore, of untruth is inconceivable to the child. Truth is what is true (agree-able) to him here and now. And when events are disagreeable to him, he can magically change them in accordance with his own wishes merely by thinking or saying them differently. This is magic, not lying. Let me illustrate this with an example. Johnny points proudly to the floor, and shouts, "Puddle!" Mother's angry reaction is, "Did *you* do that?" Johnny remains unperturbed and says, "No, Granny did." Mother's anger, now compounded by his "lying," makes her retort, "You dirty liar! What did you promise me?" Yet, it is Mother who makes a compounded mistake. She does not realize, first, that Johnny is "proud" of his new discovery that he *has* wet himself, and that this, according to Gesell, is the first of the three stages of bladder control (the others being his awareness that he *is* wetting, and that he is *about* to wet) (200, 131); second, that one cannot "manipulate" an autogenous activity (spontaneously emerging upon completion of the physiological underpinnings); third, that the very notion of "promise" is meaningless to a child who can neither control his bladder nor himself; fourth, that oppositional behavior is evoked by making this issue the main feature of his existence; fifth, that Johnny sees a magical rather than a causal connection between himself and the puddle; and sixth, that it takes just another act of magic (the magic use of the word "Granny") to change an unpleasant truth into an agreeable one.

It goes without saying that the earliest use of language is also a magical one. The toddler's magico-animistic participation in his world does not allow him to use words as names that stand for objects. This clear dichotomy between words and things would contradict his animistic worldview. The toddler's words still remain concretely embedded in things, they do not re-present things, but rather make them magically present. The name of a thing is for him a part of the thing or even the thing itself. He can bring about things and events simply by uttering their names. For instance, by being able to use the word "Mamma," he can give permanence and stability to his awareness of mother, and can recreate her whenever he needs her. When the omnipotent magician, seated in his high chair, bangs his spoon on the tabletop and shouts, "Eat!" he is not merely expressing his desire to eat, but he is also using the magic word that brings about the desired event. He is like the primitive priest who tries to make it rain by repeatedly shouting the magic word, "Rain, rain, thou must come," or like the sorcerer who conjures ghosts by calling their names.

Interpreting the child's earliest use of language in terms of his magico-animistic being-in-the-world provides a more philosophical insight into his "naming mania," which earlier in this chapter was found to be an integral constituent of the crisis of the autonomy. It is precisely with the magic wand of the word that the child conjures up his animistic world and begins his developmental task of establishing a horizon of environmental ob-jectivity. He merely has to name the object to establish it as an ob-ject. It is literally by magic that the child's *ego* and his surrounding world come into ex-sistence. It is through word magic that he first transcends the merely emotional and behavioral meanings of things in the here and now of his infantile immediacy, and that he begins to establish the permanency of a world of ob-ject meanings. And it is through word magic that he begins to order, to master and to comprehend his animistic world, and to fix and stabilize his own position and involvement in it.

All this, of course, takes place in a continuous, but very gradual process of differentiation and revelation. For instance, "words" are already heard in late infancy when the baby uses his "expressive jargon" (Gesell), i.e., words mixed in with mere emotional utterances. These so called "words," however, are not really words yet. They are merely word sounds, merely emotional and behavioral utterances without the object-meaning of magic words. Yet, the word-sounds of late infancy and the magic words of toddlerhood have in common that they originate from spontaneous imitation on the part of the child. Imitation, here, is of course not to be understood in the adult sense of a deliberate copying of the behavior of self-contained objects or persons. On the contrary, imitation in the young child results precisely from the absence of this distinction between the internal and the external. According to Piaget, this imitation "is due to a sort of confusion between the self and others." (169, 128)

The young child is not taught to imitate; he does so by virtue of the undifferentiated co-being of respectively his "we-feeling" in infancy and his animistic participation in toddlerhood. When Mother says "bye-bye," Johnny says "bye-bye." When Mother is cleaning the house, Johnny wants to clean the house. And, even, when another child cries, Johnny may begin to cry himself. The earliest form of sympathy results "less from a feeling of compassion than from an inability to distinguish the other child's emotions from his own." (200, 144)

Gradually during early childhood the toddler frees his perception and his language from his merely emotional and magical involvement, and begins to fluctuate between an animistic and a realistic view of the world. Yet, his first factual perception is still a far cry from the adult's clear-cut perception of objects as self-contained beings. For instance, seated on the carpet Johnny is stroking a kitty, and asks Mother, "Whadda?" Mother says, "That is a kitty." Five minutes later Mother finds Johnny stroking the carpet saying "kitty, kitty." "You fool," says Mother, "that is a carpet, not a kitty." Unconvinced Johnny continues his love affair with the carpet. For when Mother said "kitty," he did not have the visual perception of a youthful member of the cat family, but rather the tactile perception of fluffiness and furriness. And this is "exactly" what he is perceiving again. It is, therefore, perfectly logical —to him—to call the carpet "kitty." His logic is still a feeling-thinking, a rudimentary *logos,* a primitive revelation of factual reality. At this stage of development the budding ob-ject meaning is still very much embedded in the emotional aspects of the child's perception. He certainly perceives the ob-ject, but as a bearer of salient perceptual features rather than as a definite, independent being or self-contained thing. In his one-word sentences, just as in his world of perception, the being of the ob-jects still remains implicit. It is not until childhood proper that he begins to free the ob-jects of his surrounding world for their discoverability as independent beings.

Roughly between the ages of five and ten or eleven, the child moves away from animism, and becomes progressively a realist. The fundamental significance of this developmental stage is that it first reveals the world of environmental beings as a necessary phase in the birth-process of Being. From this it should not be construed, however, that by now the child and his world begin to exist side by side. The child is not a subject that discovers his surrounding world as an object out there in space. The child does not relate to his world by just looking at a mere collection of independent things or neutral objects in the three dimensionality of an empty space.

On the contrary, as discussed earlier, the individual is not a subject-thing surrounded by the world as an object-thing, but rather a subject-process concernfully involved in the task of establishing a horizon of environmental ob-jectivity. The child is not a realist because he knows things as independent of himself, but rather by letting them be as they really are in his surrounding world. And he lets them be as they really are precisely by letting them be involved as concrete objects in the experiential totality of his world. He is interested in objects insofar as they affect his immediate emotional, cognitive, and behavioral needs. He still perceives the object-meaning of an object in terms of its concrete emotional meaning and behavioral possibilities (percept), rather than in terms of its abstract and universal definition (concept). Although his ability to deal with the abstract gradually increases during childhood, the process is a slow one, and he never fully acquires this ability until puberty.

Even the acquisition of the child's percepts has a slow beginning. As I have shown, his earliest percepts are merely crude percepts that delineate a poorly differentiated area of experience. For instance, when Johnny watched a horse being removed from a buggy he remarked, "Cow broke." Given the inability of his diffuse perception to transcend the concrete immediacy of the here-and-now, to differentiate between living and inert beings (both moved) and between the perceptual characteristics of similar but different kinds of objects, he was logical. Or, to use another example, Johnny's earliest use of the word "Daddy" is practically as a proper name. The word designates exclusively his own concrete father here-and-now. Said Jimmy, "Daddy bought a car." Retorted Johnny, "*You* don't have a Daddy. *I* have a Daddy!"

A crude concept begins to emerge out of the percept when Johnny greets any adult male as "Daddy." This crude concept becomes less crude and more differentiated when Johnny, as Church and Stone put it, begins "to distinguish between Daddy (large *D*), who lives at his house, and daddies (small *d*), who live at other children's houses." (200, 125) In other words, although the child's ability to differentiate and to conceptualize increases throughout childhood, the concrete perceptual world of his home will continue to be his primary frame of reference and his source of security until the onset of puberty. His world, therefore, remains for several years to come a here-and-now world: *his* mother and father, *his* bedroom and *his* place at the dinner table, *his* backyard and *his* playmates. The concreteness of his home also remains his perceptual and emotional anchorage when he gradually begins to incorporate such far away places as the corner drugstore, the school, and the church, and such distant times as "yesterday" and "next week."

The child at the age of five is no longer wrapped up in the instantaneous here-and-now of the infantile coenesthesis, but finds himself in the highly dynamic and differentiated here-and-now of his surrounding world. He has outgrown the magico-animistic indeterminateness of his fairy tale world where things happened "once upon a time, in a faraway land. ...." But he is still totally unable to determine his position in space and time with mathematical accuracy or in terms of abstract spatial and temporal concepts.

The child does not understand the "here" and the "there," the "now" and the "then" in terms of an abstract coordinate system. He experiences them as concrete places for anchoring his unifying and world-forming subject-process through which he places objects and events in the familiar closeness of his environment. The child progressively forms his surrounding world by making room for the things and events he is interested in within the world of his immediate desires, needs, and activities. In other words, he does not find his world "in space," but he finds space "in his world" insofar as his being-in-the-world discloses itself as a spatializing process. Orientating things and bringing them nearer to the referential context of everyday familiarity is constitutive for the world of the child. This nearness is not ascertained by measuring distances, but rather in terms of its relevance to the world of concernful involvements. That which is closest to the child is not what is at the shortest distance from him. Closeness for the child is determined by his familiar activities and positions which articulate his world according to his particular needs and interests. Space and time for him are respectively "a place for" and "a time for," such as "a place to swim," "a time for eating," "a time for playing," etc. If asked, "What is time?" he may answer "Time to get out of bed," or "Time to be ready for school." (65, 440) Gradually he develops the ability to read maps and to use clocks. The perception of map-space and clock-time constitutes a semi-abstraction. The red dot on the map "stands for" the corner drugstore, and eight o'clock "stands for" bedtime. The possibility of a purely abstract conception of space and time does not emerge until puberty.

Before bringing this chapter to a close, however, I want to show how the child's thinking and playing as structural characteristics of the same world-forming process follow the same pattern of development. It has been argued that the thinking of the child does not develop through essentially different stages, but that his increasing ability to think is merely due to the increase in factual knowledge and experience. Knowing a greater number of facts enables him to make generalizations and to handle problems of greater variety and complexity. However, this superficial and quantitative interpretation of the child's growing ability to think overlooks some of the basic data. As I have shown elsewhere, authentic thinking is the creative process of man's articulated or dialectical self-disclosure as Being-in-the-world. (19, 54–64) Thinking cannot be defined in opposition to being. It is essentially an integral constituent of our being-in-the-world. And just as man has to pass through various existential levels to arrive at authenticity, so also his thinking has to pass through the very same levels of existential development.

Despite the continuity of these levels as phases of one and the same birth-process of authentic thinking, there is also a basic discontinuity between them. For man passes through essentially different ways of thinking corresponding to the essentially different ways of being-in-the-world. And a different way of being-in-the-world entails a different intentionality. Since the intentionality of the world of the subject co-determines the kind of objectivity and the meaning of a perceived phenomenon, "the *same* fact becomes a different fact in a different world." (19, 77) "In other words," say Stone and Church, "to shift from one level of analysis to another does not mean merely to look at the same phenomena from a greater or lesser distance; it means to look in a different way at a different set of phenomena." (200, 30) And here are found the philosophical foundations for the psychological principle of emergence: "the new and emergent phenomena at each level must be accounted for in terms of new, emergent principles." (200, 31) Entering a higher level of thinking results from the original emergence of a new way of being-in-the-world, and, consequently, cannot be explained in terms of a lower level, or reduced to a previous way of existence.

The child is a world-forming subject-process which successively discloses an animistic, a realistic, and an abstractive world of environmental objectivity. And as the articulation of this progressive disclosure, the child's thinking too is successively animistic, realistic, and abstractive. These philosophical insights are corroborated by the findings of psychology. It goes without saying that the unarticulated immediacy of the infantile coenesthesis cannot properly be called "thinking" yet. The first articulation emerges when the child discovers his primitive world of magico-animistic objectivity, and begins to explain this world in terms of interactions between animate creatures. This primitive, animistic thinking is a rudimentary *logos*. With the beginning of childhood proper, the world of realistic objectivity emerges, and after some fluctuating between an animistic and a realistic view of the world, the child's thinking becomes predominantly realistic.

During childhood proper, the child is experientially involved in the differentiated process of dis-covering the concrete immediacy of his surrounding world. His thinking, therefore, is concrete and realistic, and involves his mind, his heart and his hands. He thinks with his entire being. "When the child builds a block tower, caresses a seashell, asks a question, or strikes out at a playmate, he is thinking. That is, he is in the process of formulating a concept of reality, fitting new experiences into the framework of his established reality, rearranging his reality to accommodate new experiences, trying out his notions to see how they work; he is constantly solving problems and learning." (200, 190) He cannot disengage his thinking from his behavioral involvement, and, consequently, he cannot preplan his actions. The adult advice, "Think before you act," remains quite meaningless to this age group. Approximately at the age of seven or eight years, the child begins to develop the ability to make some generalizations and to think in a semi-abstract way. But it is not until puberty that the ability of truly abstractive thinking emerges. For it is not until this time that he is able to live on the functional level, to disengage himself from his concrete involvements, and to discover the merely quantitative face of things. Again, the direction of the development is evident.

This chapter on childhood cannot be concluded without having at least touched upon the phenomenon of play. For play has always been looked upon as a distinctive feature of the world of the child. In fact, the "perfectly adjusted" adult regards it as *the* distinctive feature. For him the world of the child is the world of make-believe, the world of the playroom, whereas the world of the adult is the real world, the world of serious work. Yet, as I will show later on, this perfectly adjusted adult has abdicated his own creative freedom in favor of mechanical functioning. And this results in what Sartre calls "the spirit of seriousness." The static and fixated world of the perfectly adjusted adult is immature and "deadly" serious. Interpreting both the seriousness of personal maturity and the play activities of the child in terms of his categorizing thinking, he dichotomizes and distorts the nature both of play and of seriousness.

Play is freedom in the process of freeing itself. Now, the most fundamental and serious task of the mature personality is the self-actualization of his authentic co-Being-in-the-world. The freedom of this self-actualization is not absolute, but essentially limited. For it is a freedom-in-the-world, a freedom incarnate. The freedom of the mature personality is essentially involved in a creative conflict with the unfree determinisms of his incarnation: character, subconscious and instinctual life, cultural institutions, etc. In other words, the most serious activity of the mature adult is his freedom in the process of freeing himself. This is the playful seriousness of self-actualization. The truly mature person is not deadly serious, but his seriousness is essentially play-ful.

A child's play, on the other hand, is essentially serious. It is as serious as mature seriousness is playful. And this is not unexpected. For the fundamental significance of infancy, childhood, and adolescence as developmental stages is existential and not merely functional. They are successive phases in the birth-process of man's authentic co-Being-in-the-world. The seriousness of the child's play, therefore, is the playful seriousness of personal maturity *in statu nascendi*. The child's play is the performance of his developmental task as world-forming subject-process. It is essentially through play that the child frees himself for the emergence and progressive revelation of his entire ex-sistence. No wonder that the child becomes irritated when adults don't take his play seriously. For this literally means that adults don't take *him* seriously, and, therefore, that they reject his very existence. Play is not only the work, but even the very ex-sistence of the child.

From the foregoing it follows that play is a structural characteristic of man's co-Being-in-the-world, of the emergence of man's ex-sistence in its entirety. This fundamental insight has some important implications for the understanding of play in childhood. In the first place, play like any structural characteristic of man's ex-sistence, has no particular purpose outside itself, but is engaged in for its own sake. Play is not a function, but a way of being-in-the-world.

Secondly, any "nothing but" theory of play that tries to explain this phenomenon exclusively in terms of a particular aim or function fails to understand its very essence. Let me illustrate this with a few examples. It is said that "the child plays only to work off his surplus energy." Yet, he does not stop playing when he has worked off this energy, but he keeps playing until he is exhausted. In fact, it is precisely through his play as a structural characteristic of his emerging ex-sistence that he increases his energy, his ability to act as a world-forming subject-process. Another theory of play teaches that "it is the release of the child's emotional tensions." This would mean that the child without emotional tensions would find it difficult to play, whereas the opposite is known to be the case. The tacit assumption of this functionalism is that the total reduction of all tensions is what constitutes maturity. Nevertheless, I have found that maturity is essentially "playful," and, therefore, essentially a creative con-flict or an existential tension between man's freedom and determinism. A child's play does not only prepare for real life, but it is real life in an embryonic way. A similar form of functionalism suggests that "the child plays in order to practice his skills to be used in real life." Of course, the child practices his skills and exercises his growing abilities in play. But this does not reduce play to a function of his skills. The child does not play "in order to." He plays because it is sufficient and rewarding in itself. He plays for the sake of playing rather than as a means for something else. He plays because it is his way of being-in-the-world. It is precisely through play that he learns not to put his play at the service of his functions, but to subordinate his functions to the very playfulness of his emerging existence.

Still another theory claims that "a child's play is his recreation." The term "recreation" here is always taken in the functional sense of either "pastime" or "recuperation." Yet it is quite meaningless to apply these adult conceptions of recreation to the play activities of a child. The child does not need a "pastime," for he has no "spare time" and therefore, no time to be killed. He either sleeps or plays. This theory, moreover, hardly accounts for the spontaneity, the enthusiasm, and the total involvement on the part of the playing child. The "recuperation" theory is equally meaningless. Recuperation from what? From fatigue or exhaustion? The child solves this problem by sleeping. And whenever he does not sleep, he plays. Does he recuperate from playing by playing? This sounds like casting out the devil by Beelzebub. To be sure, play is essentially recreational and therapeutic in the fundamental and non-functional sense. It is through the very playfulness of his ex-sistence that man frees himself for his progressive participation in the creative birth-process of Being. It is through his playfulness that he transcends himself and is re-born everyday. According to the usual interpretation, man uses play as recreation in order to recover from his serious work. But the un-usual and fundamental meaning of play reveals that man is "re-creation," creating himself anew through the playful seriousness of his emerging ex-sistence.

It is through playful re-creation that man accomplishes what I have called earlier his unifying and world-forming Being-process. Man constantly integrates his past structures, functions, and data into new, emergent phases of being and revelation. His being-in-the-world becomes more differentiated, but also organized into a more and more inclusive unity. His existential playfulness as the creative "interplay" of freedom and determinism gives increase to his emergent participation in the *logos* which sets all things apart in their primordial unity of Being. Through this continual integration and re-integration, man re-creates himself and becomes more and more whole. Existential play is essentially "therapeutic" (Gr. *therapeuoo*—healing). For it gives increase to man's wholeness, his full humanness or mental health. And it restores this health by re-integrating it wherever it has become disintegrated. Here one has found the philosophical foundation of still another psychological principle of development, namely, the principle of "hierarchic integration," or, as Stone and Church call it, of "functional subordination." This principle states that "differentiated structures and functions become organized into new, more inclusive patterns." (200, 33) A discussion of the developmental pattern of the child's play activities will provide an opportunity to illustrate this principle with a few examples.

Already the infant, as we have seen, has a rudimentary way of playing. This rudimentary form of play is what I have called sense-pleasure play. The infant cannot play with toys yet, since he does not know objects, and toys are objects to play with. His sense-pleasure play takes great delight in feeling, exploring, prolonging, and repeating the visual, tactile, and motor sensations of his coenesthesis. This play is, as I have shown, predominantly passive. He playfully experiments with what things can do to him, i.e., the emotional meaning or pleasure value they can have for the sensory awareness of his coenesthesis. It is sense-pleasure play which he is engaged in when he kicks his legs or plays with his fingers, when he coos and chuckles, when he stares at his own hand or sucks his thumb. Gradually, however, the infant shifts to a more active relationship with reality, and begins his playful experimentations with what he can do with things. In addition to their emotional meanings, he now becomes interested in their action-meanings, and sense-pleasure play branches out into a rudimentary form of *skill play*. He playfully explores reality by way of tasting, sucking, pushing, pulling, smelling, kicking, banging, and tearing.

Somewhere in the middle of infancy, the baby will begin to show active resentment when an object is taken away from him. This indicates his budding awareness of the fact that things can reappear, and, therefore, continue to exist independent of his immediate perception of them. His playful experimentation with the new discovery of his embryonic world is *peek-a-boo*. From now on he begins to enjoy the game in which his mother covers her face and hides herself, and then suddenly uncovers her face and reappears, calling "peek-a-boo!" The alternating realization of mother's frightening absence (boo!) and her reassuring presence (peek) is clearly an embryonic form of the delightful terror of "hide-and-seek," and ultimately of the horrifying and fascinating mystery of Being.

Toddlerhood is the halfway mark between the infantile coenesthesis and the child's world of concrete objectivity. Strictly speaking, he does not yet play with toys (objects to play with), but rather with raw materials such as water, mud, pebbles, etc. He gets a delightful mixture of emotional and behavioral experience out of making mud pies, filling empty containers with sand and pouring it out again, throwing pebbles, playing with water and similar activities. Moreover, real skill-play emerges. He likes to open doors with a bang and slam them shut, to pound his pegboard, to climb the furniture and the staircase, to lift heavy objects, to push things around, to load his wagon with blocks and unload it again, etc. These skill-play activities are engaged in for their own sake, they are satisfying in their own right. Yet, these early activities are still impulsive, unplanned, and unorganized. The action value of the objects is so inviting that he can scarcely resist. Staircases "have" to be climbed, heavy stones "have" to be lifted and doors "have" to be opened. The toddler's skill-play still lacks initiative, continuity, and integration.

But in the meantime, one may not overlook the social aspect of play. For play, as a structural characteristic of man's *co-being*-in-the-world is essentially social and socializing. Human beings play together because they *are* together. Their "playing together," therefore, passes through the same existential stages as their "being together." Now, during early infancy this social togetherness is not yet differentiated. In terms of sociability, his narcissistic sense-pleasure play is solitary play. An embryonic sociability emerges with the first smile, and through games such as peek-a-boo and patty-cake. The way in which toddlers play together is a curious phenomenon known as "parallel play." They do their own thing side by side. "There is no overt interchange, but there is every evidence of taking satisfaction in the other's nearness." (200, 110) In such activities as making mud pies, Johnny is not playing *with* Jerry, but *beside* him. And it is precisely this togetherness which gives a new (social) dimension to the fun of his play. However, side-by-sideness is a structural characteristic of the togetherness of material things. It is the way pieces of candy are together in a box. Consequently, the awareness of this kind of togetherness in parallel play constitutes a most primitive form of sociability.

A slight advance is made in associative play when the children begin to play in clusters. In this form of play, the children experience their sociability not only in their side-by-sideness, but also in their play interests. When they see one child telephoning, it becomes contagious. The urge to do the same tends, due to a lack of differentiation, to spread from child to child. Church and Stone give a graphic account of this phenomenon. "There may be an epidemic of telephoning, each child speaking into his own instrument, sharing the fun of phoning, but not conversing like older children." (200, 146) Whereas in parallel play, they do their own thing side by side, in associative play they do the same thing side by side. But neither in parallel play nor in associative play are they able yet to do a common thing together. This form of sociability is known as cooperative play in which the children work together for a common purpose and share an integrated play project. Of course, this cooperative play presupposes on the part of the children a greater ability to organize and integrate their world than toddlers are capable of.

It is precisely during the crisis of autonomy that the child arrives at such an organization and integration of his concrete world of environmental objectivity. It is therefore during the later part of this crisis and during the first half of childhood proper, or roughly between the age of three or four and the age of eight, that cooperative play is predominant. Yet, the crisis of autonomy is a slow, gradual, and laborious process of development.

The child still lives in a world of diffuse participation. This is why, as I have shown, his earliest conception of the world is a magico-animistic one. He discovers and establishes his germinal world as a fascinating and frightening interplay between the anthropomorphic creatures of his fairy tale world in which he is totally involved. The magico-animistic process by which he forms his fairy tale world is his play, for it is the way in which he frees himself for a primitive understanding, articulation, and mastery of himself and his world.

With the developmental shift from animistic objectivity to realistic objectivity, the child's magico-animistic play begins to evolve into imitative or dramatic play. The child begins to imitate or re-enact themes or scenes from his everyday surroundings. During the early beginnings of dramatic play, the child becomes sufficiently differentiated from his environment to have a somewhat realistic perception of it, but not enough to fully escape his diffuse participation. His early dramatic play, therefore, results from a spontaneous imitation, or the inability to distinguish between the internal and the external. He is not taught to imitate, nor is his imitation a deliberate copying of his everyday surroundings. His early dramatic play is still impulsive, unstructured, solitary, and restricted to simple themes, such as: telephoning, shaving, feeding his teddy bear, dressing up, etc.

Whereas sense-pleasure play and skill-play are still predominantly restricted to the bodily level, magico-animistic play and dramatic play can be seen as the inchoative stages of the emergence of the child's individual *ego* in his surrounding world. This emergence of the child's individuality is the crisis of autonomy, the second existential crisis in the birth-process of Being in man. It can now be understood that this crisis itself is a form of play which functionally subordinates the forementioned forms of play to higher, more structured and integrated ways of playing. As I have shown earlier in this chapter, the child's negativism or oppositional behavior during this crisis is a playful experimentation with the experience of setting himself apart from his environment. Fundamentally speaking, his negativism is playful self-assertion.

Already during the crisis of autonomy, the child begins to weave the simple themes of his dramatic play into more complicated patterns. And socially, he gradually shifts from solitary and parallel play to a simple form of cooperative play. Moreover, his impulsive and disconnected skill-play activities become subordinated to the more structured and integrated play projects of construction play. A few examples will illustrate these developmental transformations.

During the crisis of autonomy the simple, solitary, and spontaneous re-enactments of everyday life, such as telephoning, shaving, or dressing up, become gradually subordinated to more complicated themes of dramatic play. The children will play house, store, school, or train together. These more complicated imitations of their concrete here-and-now world require at least some simple form of cooperative play. The children no longer play side by side, but integrate the various roles they assume into a structured pattern. They begin to interact and truly play together. They begin to relate to one another as playmates, which is their characteristic form of sociability. This developmental period is, of course, the later part of the crisis of autonomy and early childhood proper, or roughly the child between the ages of three and eight years. During the earlier part of this period, cooperative play spontaneously emerges as a loosely organized play group. For instance, when children "play house," i.e., re-enact the roles of the different members of the family, their play is hardly preplanned and organized, and they easily change their roles as they get bored with their parts. "Now let's pretend *you* are the baby!" Their "let's pretend" indicates that they know the difference between reality and fantasy. On the other hand, in their actual playing they are *not* pretending, they are *not* making believe, but they fully identify themselves with the roles they assume. It is not until the school years that their cooperative play becomes more preplanned and better organized, and that they begin to insist on the realism of their various play activities.

It is also during the crisis of autonomy that the toddler's impulsive and unorganized skill-play activities become functionally subordinated to the more and more complicated structures of the child's construction play. The toddler, for instance, may enjoy manipulating blocks just for the sake of lifting them or loading them on his wagon. But the five-year-old can build highly integrated structures. The same functional subordination can be observed in the child's use of other materials. The young toddler likes to pour water and sand and to make simple mud pies; the three-year-old makes roads and tunnels with wet sand; the five-year-old builds sand castles; and the seven-year-old may even try his hand at an Indian village.

It is difficult to overestimate the importance of the principle of functional subordination for this study of the mature personality. For man does not develop into personal maturity by growing in a merely additive way, or by outgrowing his earlier phases and stages. Man does not develop like a butterfly by shedding his cocoon, nor like an onion by the mere addition of successive layers. Man develops by playfully re-creating his entire ex-sistence, by continually re-integrating all his former structures, functions, and values into the unitary whole of his emerging personality.

As we have seen, it is approximately at the age of seven or eight years that the child becomes able to relate to reality in a semi-abstract manner. His thinking, his language, his perception of the world, and his awareness of space and time begin to partially disengage themselves from the concreteness of his involvement. He becomes able to deal with reality in a semi-abstract way. He becomes interested in the facts that things are structured, that somehow they are "put together" (L. *struere* —to put together). His new, semi-abstractive way of being-in-the-world makes him discover the "structuredness" of things, and engage in a playful experimentation with this discovery. Gradually he becomes interested in rules and structures for their own sake, regardless of their concrete applications or contents.

By the time the child is ten years of age, he seems to have fulfilled his developmental task of childhood proper. He is happy, busy, well-balanced and well-adjusted. This is why the philosopher Rousseau calls him *"l'enfant fait,"* the complete or perfect child. "Ten, like five," says Gesell, "is a model age. Both ages bring to partial fulfillment the trends of immediately preceding development." (65, 212) Yet the developmental calmness of this age is really the stillness before the storm: the existential crisis of adolescence.

4

THE FIVE WORLDS
OF ADOLESCENCE: 1

Adolescence is not only the most challenging and adventurous, but also the longest and most troublesome crisis in human life. Since the publication of Stanley Hall's *Adolescence* in 1904, scores of comprehensive studies on the subject have been written. One might expect, therefore, that by now the problem of adolescence has been solved. By now it should be known what constitutes adolescence, how to cope with its problems, and how to prevent them from arising.

Yet, the problems of adolescence remain, and so does parental perplexity. And it is not only the practical problems of adolescence that have not been solved, but also the numerous theories that have been advanced to explain adolescence have themselves resulted in "disagreement on basic assumptions as to what actually constitutes adolescence." (161, 3–4)

But does not proposing still another theory add to the confusion? The answer is that instead of adding still another particular theory, the present study is providing all particular theories with the underlying philosophy which they now lack. Viewing the psychological research within the philosophical perspective does not replace the psychological theories of adolescence or minimize their importance, but rather uses their findings importantly. Indeed, the usual findings of adolescent psychology gain in significance and integration when viewed within the unusual perspective of existential thinking.

It is within this perspective that one understands what fundamentally constitutes adolescence: the emergence of primordial Being in man. This emergence takes place in five different stages that, philosophically speaking, are five different ways of being-in-the-world. These stages are literally "worlds apart."

Before engaging in a discussion of adolescence, it may be helpful to present its stages schematically in the light of the existential levels of human ex-sistence. (1) The world of pubescence is basically still the environmental world of the late child. But drastic changes are taking place on the bodily level. This puts the child in an awkward position. This also reinforces the already existing movement towards the functional level. (2) The world of puberty is the horizon of abstractive objectivity, which constitutes the world on the functional level. (3) When the adolescent moves away from the functional level, but is as yet unable to discover the world of the person, he finds himself "nowhere." The world of the negative stage is the world of no-thing-ness. (4) The adolescent overcomes this painful period with the awakening of his personal Self. The world of early adolescence proper is the emerging World of the personal level. (5) But the adolescent has not completed his developmental task until he has achieved a hierarchical unity of all levels. He accomplishes this task in the world of late adolescence proper where he integrates the newly discovered personal Self into the whole of the adult personality. The following visual schematization of the adolescent worlds gives the average ages for men (women's being one to two years earlier):

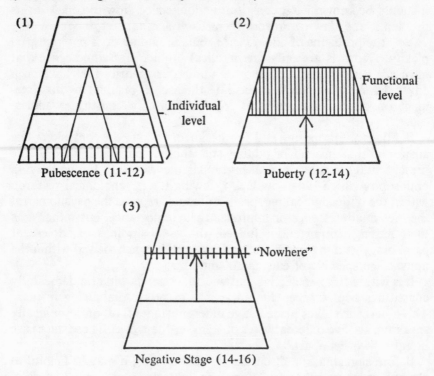

(1)

Individual level

Pubescence (11-12)

(2)

Functional level

Puberty (12-14)

(3)

"Nowhere"

Negative Stage (14-16)

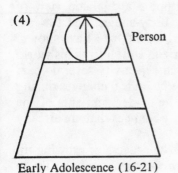

Early Adolescence (16-21)

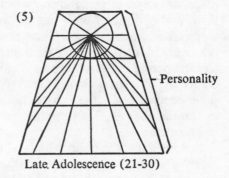

Late Adolescence (21-30)

PUBESCENCE OR THE AWKWARD AGE

The ten-year-old is normally happy, busy, relaxed, and well-adjusted. He lives in the world of late childhood proper, the world of semi-abstractive involvements in environmental objectivity. The basic features of this world continue into the period of pubescence. Fundamentally speaking, during this first period of adolescence the child, although imperceptibly shifting in the direction of abstractive objectivity, still remains a child. Those who call this period "late childhood" are, therefore, fully justified. However, I prefer the term "pubescence" because this period is characterized by its dramatic growth into bodily and reproductive maturity (*pubes*—genitals) which sets it apart from the child's world. Its beginning is marked by a spurt in bodily growth, and it continues with various changes in body proportions and with the maturation of the primary and secondary sex characteristics.

Yet, these biological changes, important as they are, mainly concern those who study the human body from an *objectifying* viewpoint. The biologist, the physiologist, and the physician study the human body as body-object. But the human body is more fundamentally a body-subject (Merleau-Ponty), a lived body, an embodiment of the *ego* or of the Self. Man is *present* to his body. He not only *has* his body, but also *is* his body as the lived immediacy of his surroundings, as his way of ex-sisting in the world (Marcel). Within the existential perspective of this study, I am, of course, mainly interested in the changes of the body as body-subject. The significance of these changes is that the adolescent finds himself in a different way in his world. Both the biological and the existential viewpoints have their own respective validity, but they are by no means interchangeable. Nor can the biological changes be regarded as the sole cause of the existential changes. For, in the first place, this causal explanation would presuppose a dualistic view of man, and contradict both the nature of the body-subject and the primary data of human ex-sistence. Secondly, the child, as I have shown, is already in the process of expanding his horizon and shifting his world from concrete objectivity towards abstractive objectivity several years before the biological changes take place. The biological changes during pubescence are not the causes, but rather the co-determinants of the existential changes. They reinforce and modify changes that are already in progress.

For instance, the child who is already in the process of growing up receives a sudden impetus from the spurt in physical growth. To be small is to be like a child, to be tall and big is to be like an adult. When the child begins to grow taller, he somehow feels that he is a child no longer. He can meet the adults on equal footing and comes to expect to share their privileges and respect. The enormous increase in size and physical energy greatly expands his action radius and his ability to explore the world. Yet, psychologically and philosophically, he is still more a child than an adolescent. During pubescence the adolescent finds himself in the awkward position of being neither child nor adult.

Although the bodily changes during pubescence are important from a biological viewpoint, their significance for this study lies mainly in their psychological and existential implications. Endocrinologists have discovered that the key to all these changes is found in the pituitary gland, an endocrine gland located at the base of the brain. It is this master gland which stimulates the thyroid, the adrenals, and the gonads (sex glands: the testes in males and the ovaries in females), and through them brings about the bodily changes characteristic of pubescence. Yet, the age of the onset of pubescence varies considerably with sex, race, climate, heredity, locality, socio-economic status, intelligence, and physical health.

The main features of the bodily growth and development during this period are well-known. In both sexes there is a spurt of growth in height and weight; the rapid growth of arms and legs accounts for the long-legged, awkward appearance so characteristic of this age. Moreover, the body does not only increase in size, but it also changes its proportions. In all this it follows the principle of asynchronous growth (various parts of the body grow at various rates at different times). For instance, the growth in height precedes the growth in width; the growth of the nose precedes that of the rest of the face. During pubescence the teen-ager is outgrowing the typically rounded and harmonious features of the child's face, but has not yet developed the rather oval contours of the adult profile. He is forced to live with a somewhat distorted, bird-like facial mask.

Some other features or criteria of pubescence in boys and girls are the appearance of pubic hair and of axillary hair, the eruption of the second molars, and the ossification of the cartilage particularly in the hands. In fact, X-ray pictures taken of the hand and wrist provide us with the most accurate single criterion of pubescence (skeletal age). In girls, there is a marked widening of the hips (caused by the enlargement of the pelvic bone and the development of subcutaneous fat), a beginning development of the breasts, and, during puberty, the menarche (beginning of menstruation). In boys, there is a marked widening of the shoulders, the appearance of a beard, the lowering of the voice, and, during puberty, the beginning of nocturnal emissions ("wet dreams"). It is during puberty that the reproductive changes of pubescence reach a climax. And these changes are immense. Before pubescence the adolescent *is* a child, shortly after puberty he can *have* a child.

It goes without saying that these drastic bodily changes put the child in an awkward position physically, psychologically, and existentially. No wonder that the period of pubescence is called the "awkward age." Physically, his body no longer "fits" in his environment. It becomes a problem to be solved. Psychologically, he feels stigmatized and socially unacceptable. Existentially, he does not know where he stands and worries about his self-identity.

For instance, due to the rapid growth of his arms and legs, the boy may find cars too small, beds too short, ceilings too low, and distances too short. When invited to a party, he wants to shake hands with the hostess, but hits her in the stomach instead; trying to apologize, his voice insists on squeaking at just the wrong time. He blushes and wishes he could hide. Impossible. On the contrary, his rapid increase in size has made him taller, and thereby so much more visible. Both boys and girls have lost their coordination and motor balance of childhood. Moreover, they don't know where they are heading and what their ultimate profile will be.

Obviously, during pubescence the body ceases to be the spontaneous and unreflected incarnation and unfailing instrument it used to be during late childhood. The security of a familiar body is lost. The body is no longer perfectly tuned in to the world, to the self, and to others. The body now becomes a problem to be solved. The child becomes very self-conscious about his bodily appearance and begins to reflect on it. His body-image, his mental picture of his bodily self, particularly insofar as it is accepted or acceptable by important others, becomes precarious. Consequently his self-identity becomes precarious. He cannot find himself, and a new identity crisis has begun. He wonders if he is normal, if he is socially acceptable.

He feels, to use the language of Goffman, that he is "stigmatized" and begins to use techniques of "information control" and "tension management." He tries to pass for normal by trying to correct or improve his figure and to regain his lost coordination by swimming, playing tennis, or by engaging in other sports or exercises. He will try to use "information control" by de-emphasizing or concealing his discreditable features. For instance, the boy may use deodorants, Clearasil, and shoulderpads. He also will seek support from those who share his stigma by joining people of "his own kind" in clubs and gangs, and by withdrawing from social interaction with the "normals," i.e., children and adults. (70, 1–104)

Most important, however, is the existential implication of the bodily changes during pubescence. The body is no longer in tune with the world; it no longer provides the child with the security of his familiar surroundings. On the contrary, it has become an obstacle that stands in the way of his being-with-others-in-the-world. The child's body that has been his most intimate and unfailing instrument for dealing with the problems of his world, is "out of order," and has itself become a "pro-blem" to be solved. Heidegger's phenomenological description of tools or instruments that are "out of order" reveals the fundamental meaning of the bodily changes during pubescence.

According to Heidegger, the meaning of a tool *(Zuhandenheit)* and man's perception of it are only given within the experiential totality of his environmental involvements, within his concernful dealings with the integral workshop of his workaday world. A tool never has a meaning in itself; it is always related to a referential totality. Its basic feature is its referential character, its "being-*for*-something." For instance, a hammer has no meaning or definition when taken by itself. A hammer is only understood in the act of hammering, and can only be defined in its referential nature as a tool *for* pounding metals or driving nails. Only when a tool or instrument is "out of order," is damaged or otherwise unsuitable, does it become "conspicuous," and is it perceived "out of context" as an "ob-ject" or a thing-in-itself *(Vorhandenheit)*. When the hammer fails to function properly and becomes unsuitable, it loses its referential character of instrumentality. Man stops hammering and takes the hammer "out of context" by "looking at" it as a thing-in-itself *(Gegenstand)*, as a "pro-blem" to be solved. He disengages himself from his experiential involvement and reduces the hammer to a mere "ob-ject" and no more. Moreover, in the process, the totality of the workshop becomes visible, the world begins to announce itself *as* world. (88, 102–7)

During pubescence, the child's body becomes an unsuitable instrument. As a result, the pubescent body becomes conspicuous. It becomes a thing to be concerned with, an object to be looked at, a problem to be solved. The spontaneous, integral, and unreflected embodiment of the child begins to disintegrate, and with it the world of the child. Whereas the child's body-subject was a happy incarnation, the pubescent body is experienced as an awkward body-object standing in the way of this incarnation. It is here that one discovers the philosophical meaning of the bodily changes in pubescence. The problems created by these changes are not only physical and psychological, but first and foremost existential. For by objectifying his lived embodiment, the adolescent reduces his very being-in-the-world to a "pro-blem," to something standing over against him. He thereby disengages himself from his experiential and emotional involvement in his world. Pubescence withdraws from the concrete incarnation on the bodily level into the abstractive and functional level which constitutes the world of puberty. Philosophically speaking, pubescence differs from late childhood in the fact that the shift from concrete objectivity to abstract objectivity which is already in progress becomes reinforced and co-determined by the existential changes of the embodiment.

One is now prepared to comprehend the developmental features of pubescence in their original unity of meaning. These features are manifestations of a phase in the birth-process of Being. It is the phase where man moves away from his concrete embodiment (individual level) towards the abstractive way of being-in-the-world (functional level). This functional level is the level of "calculative thinking" and "controlling actions" (Heidegger); it is the level of "objectification" which characterizes man's scientific or "primary" reflection (Marcel). "Primary reflection," says Marcel, "is forced to break the fragile link between me and my body that is constituted here by the word 'mine'. The body that I call my body is in fact only one body among many others. . . . It is not enough to say that this is objectively true, it is the precondition of any sort of objectivity whatsoever, it is the foundation of all scientific knowledge." (146, 113) It is easy to see that this distancing of oneself from concrete involvements results in a dualism of body and *ego*.

Although pubescence is, of course, an indivisible process, one can distinguish the features that predominantly indicate a disengagement from concrete embodiment, and those that reveal the discovery of a semi-abstract world. As I have shown in the previous chapter, the child's own home remains the primary frame of reference throughout childhood. This begins to change when, in pubescence, the child moves away from his concrete embodiment. The child no longer feels at home with his own home. He looks for a (still concrete) "home away from home" in the form of a cave, a den, a hut, or a treehouse. Within his home he complains, "Can't a guy have any privacy around here?" He asks for his "*own* room," and puts a sign on the door: "Keep out," or "Genius at work." His explorations of his widening world take him further and further from home, both in body and spirit, until home becomes something like a runway where he takes off for his explorations and lands again for refueling (he calls it eating and sleeping).

It goes without saying that his withdrawal from the bodily level and from any participation in his home life entails a withdrawal from his emotional involvements and from the intimacy of his familial ties as well. There is a gradual diminution of warmth, affection, and intimacy in his relationship with his parents and his brothers and sisters. He feels that he is "rejected" by his parents. This is evidenced by characteristic utterances during this period: "The way that my parents treat me, they must have adopted me." "Everybody is always picking on me." Or, as Mark Twain describes the feelings of Tom Sawyer, "He was a forsaken, friendless boy; nobody loved him; when they found out what they had driven him to, perhaps they would be sorry." The emotional and affectionate intimacy of his younger siblings becomes a threat and annoys him. "Why don't you get lost?" "Leave me alone." "Cut it out." "Get off my back." "Why don't you grow up?" "You're a pain in the neck." "You're impossible." "Why don't you go live somewhere else?"

He begins to realize that he and his parents are "worlds apart," that his parents' unchanging attitudes are "behind the times," and that, as a result, he is no longer understood. "Let's face it Dad, we live in different worlds!" "Mother, you don't u-n-d-e-r-s-t-a-n-d!" "Did you ever see my parents?—Middle Ages!" "You're the meanest Mother in the block, and all the kids know it." No wonder that, as Gesell says, "great scenes can occur: stamping feet, yelling, talking back, calling names—'dope,' 'stinker,' 'liar,' 'old meanie.' " (66, 391)

Unfortunately, many parents blame either themselves or their teenager for their deteriorating relationship. However, nobody is to be blamed for the simple reason that nothing is wrong. The decrease in affection and the increase in conflict are neither abnormal nor immoral.

They are painful but healthy concomitants of the process of emancipation. As Ginott puts it: "As parents our need is to be needed; as teenagers their need is not to need us. This conflict is real; we experience it daily as we help those we love become independent of us." (68, 11)

Since the child is attempting to free himself from the emotional intimacy of his familial ties, he *wants* to be at odds with his family. Gottlieb illustrates this fact with the example of Sally. "We've just got to get a new dining room set," she says. "This one is hopelessly old-fashioned." Useless to counter that the set is new and that everyone likes it. "I wish you could see the dining room at Rosalind's house," Sally says. "Everything there is so lovely." "This," says Gottlieb, "is the crux of the matter. Everything somewhere that isn't home is 'lovely', not because it actually is nicer but because the time has come for Sally to turn her eyes from home, to focus her interests and affections on someone outside of the family." (74, 75) It is this same phenomenon which causes the increase in rudeness in pubescent boys. His withdrawal from his body-subject reduces the delicacy of his emotional perception. There is a decrease in sensitivity for the feelings of others and in compassion ("fellowship of feeling"). Both his behavior and his language become rude and rough as is evidenced by the increase in quarrelsome behavior and by the frequent use of swearing and slang.

Thus far I have reflected on the reverse side of the fabric of pubescence: the withdrawal from concrete embodiment; I now want to discuss some positive features as manifestations of the discovery of a semi-abstract world. As I have shown, the late child is able to deal with reality in a semi-abstract way. He is fascinated with the fact that things are structured, that somehow they are "put together" (L. *struere*—to put together). His playful experimentation with the "structuredness" of things not only continues into pubescence, but becomes its basic way of life due to the added impetus it receives from the withdrawal from the bodily level. The developmental data characteristic of this period, nicknames, ritual clubs, "taking things apart," collections, hobbies, and ritual games, find their unity of meaning in this playful experimentation with the structuredness of things.

For instance, it is not by accident that children of this age call one another by nicknames. Nicknames are characteristically stereotypes by which children identify one another during pubescence. For stereotypes constitute the typical way of knowing and perceiving in a semi-abstract world. The child has moved away from the concrete percept of childhood proper, and has not yet arrived at the abstract concept of puberty. This stereotype is his in-between form of perception, one which is structured, stylized, skeletal, and standardized. If, in addition, one remembers that at this age the awkward body-object has become his existential "pro-blem," that he feels self-conscious and "ex-posed," that he feels that his body is on display and that everyone is talking about his appearance, one has understood both the fact and the content of his nicknames. He is quick to seize on any idiosyncracy of bodily appearance, of manner and skill. The following sampling of adolescent nicknames is given by Luella Cole: "Shrimp, Skeeter, Beanpole, Bug, Spider, Butch, Fatty, Big Boy, Shorty, Baldy, Whitey, Spike, Whale, Swede, Machine Gun, Blubber, Foxy, Squeaky, Piggy, Barrel, Dopey, Slinky, Bull, Cotton, Slim, or Tiny." (39, 29) Since nicknames express his way of understanding reality, having a nickname, even a derogatory one, gives him a feeling of being understood and a sense of belonging.

The emergence of the ritual club constitutes another example of the child's playful concern with the structuredness of reality. By age eight or nine, a marked change appears in the child's patterns of affiliation and loyalty. When he begins to feel rejected by his parents, he drops his identification with adult society and establishes a growing identification with a group of his peers. The gang and the club become a joyful association of the stigmatized. He forms a separate subculture with traditions, values, rules, and loyalties of its own. This subculture shows a great similarity with primitive cultures. "It is handed down by word of mouth, it includes many rituals whose original meaning has been lost, it is hidebound and resistant to alien—in this case, adult—influences." (200, 206)

Of course, there is a gradual progression in the structuredness of the children's group experiences. During middle childhood, loose clusters of children are seen playing together in the playground or the street. Then, in late childhood, as sociograms show, one finds "hierarchies" of chums. It is during this same period, and continuing into pubescence, that the children begin to form loosely organized gangs and more tightly organized, though usually short-lived clubs. The possibility of organizing or structuring sociability is a new discovery for this age. This is why the gangs and particularly the ritual clubs of pubescence are engaged in for their own sake. They are, fundamentally speaking, playful experimentations with the structuredness of social reality. It is not until puberty (twelve to fourteen) when the children withdraw into the functional level, that this structuredness becomes functionally subordinated to particular aims.

The ritual club is characteristic of the period of pubescence. This phenomenon clearly demonstrates the children's playful experimentation with the structuredness of their social reality. Here I want briefly to discuss the meaning of the ritual club, reserving some further reflections on the gang for the section on puberty. The ritual club is, of course, a secret club, meeting in secret places or hide-outs, establishing codified rules, and using secret passwords and secret language (cryptology). The issue is not that they want to keep this or that particular secret, but that they enjoy their peer-group solidarity only by leaving out their parents, by *being* a secret from the adult world. These "stigmatized" reassure and support one another by means of collective information control. They are interested in secrecy as a style of life, as a form of being-in-the-world. Again, it is the form, the structure, the style they are concerned with, rather than the content of any particular secret. Their secret club is a playful experimentation with the tribal excitement of a membership in a secret society to be enjoyed for its own sake.

They spend weeks or months organizing and structuring their club. They elect officers; they assign roles and functions to the grass-roots membership; they make rules, laws, and bylaws; they establish initiations, ritual ceremonies, secret passwords, and solemn oaths. And when, after weeks or months, the organization of the club is finished, then the club, too, is finished—it falls apart. What to many adults has been an abortive attempt to organize a club, was in fact a successful attempt to discover the possibility of social organization. Again, it was a playful experimentation with the structuredness of social reality for its own sake.

Moreover, the ritualism which characterizes not only the secret club of pubescence, but the entire phase between eight and twelve is yet another way of revealing the structuredness of the world. The ritualism of the secret club with its iron-clad rules, its formal initiations, its solemn oaths and mysterious codes of behavior is well-known. But ritualism also pervades the child's everyday relationships in this period. This, according to Church and Stone, is clearly demonstrated when, for instance, "two children, catching themselves saying the same thing at the same time, instantly fall into the ritual of locking their little fingers together, making a silent wish, and then exchanging the prescribed phrases before they break the hold with a ceremonial flourish and remain mute until a third person speaks to one of them and breaks the spell—if they speak without this release, the wish is lost." (200, 210) Even the child's solitary existence is filled with ritualism. On his way to school, he avoids stepping on the cracks in the sidewalk, lest the teacher call on him. When he looses a tooth, he puts it under his pillow and makes a silent wish. He knocks on wood after mentioning his good fortune. Or he may feel a secret compulsion to touch every single lamppost, or to count every passing Volkswagen.

In order to understand the meaning of ritualism in pubescence, it is important to grasp the true meaning of authentic rituals. Rituals are prescribed or customary procedures or codes of behavior providing formal structures for religious or other solemn celebrations. Since man is a *person incarnate,* the celebration of his ultimate concern takes place within his embodiment in physical, social, and historical structures. This is why authentic rituals as the embodiments of celebration in procedural structures are not instruments of celebration, but rather integral constituents of its very manifestation. They cannot be justified by any means-to-end type of explanation. Rituals are what in my *Existential Thinking* I have called "fundamental sym-bols." (19, 120-7) In fundamental "sym-bols," two meanings are thrown together (*sun—*together; *balloo—*to throw): a literal meaning and a cosmic or primordial meaning. For instance, the ritual of purification with water does not "re-present" spiritual purification, but it "presents" what it symbolizes, it brings it about. In other words, in authentic rituals the element of procedural structure and the element of celebration are not given separately. They are not independent constituents signifying in their own right, but they form a simple organic composition. This entails, of course, that in authentic rituals the element of procedural structures cannot be objectified or formalized, or dealt with apart from the element of celebration without corroding the very nature of their symbolism. This theme will be enlarged upon later.

But the foregoing elucidation should suffice to demonstrate that the ritualism of pubescence is objectified ritual, ritual reduced to magic, ritual taken out of context, unauthentic ritual. Once again, it is evident that pubescence is concerned with the structuredness of reality. Its ritualism is to be understood as a playful experimentation with rituals as procedural structures for their own sake regardless of their symbolic value. It should be evident, however, that this ritualism of pubescence has nothing to do with the stifling effect of pathological compulsion or with the ineffectiveness of "mere magic."

On the contrary, the child has reached a point in his development where his unifying and world-forming subject-process discloses an ever-widening horizon of semi-abstractive objectivity. Disengaging himself from the here-and-now of concrete percepts, but as yet unable to arrive at universal concepts, he structures his world, as I have shown, in terms of classes, categories, or stereotypes. This not only explains his use of nicknames, but also his interest in "the insignia and ranks of army and navy officers, the distinctions between types of airplanes, the flags of the United Nations, etc." (65, 190) But, what is more, he can no longer unify his world by incorporating things into the concrete intimacy of his immediate concerns. The unification of his world which he begins to perceive in terms of classes becomes one of "classification." According to Gesell, from the age of eight on he increasingly "likes to classify, to arrange and to organize." (65, 180) Small wonder that he is so fascinated with ritualism. As a unifying process, it holds his world together, it gives him security and a magic domination over reality. As a playful experimentation with the possibility of structuring and organizing reality it frees him for the ever-widening horizon of his semi-abstractive world. And as the ritualistic interplay with his peers, it assures him of his co-being in the world, and helps him overcome the threat of loneliness and insecurity.

For the anxiety of loneliness and insecurity is becoming a real threat at this age. Although fascination with ritualism is still predominant, it is not the whole picture. As I have shown earlier, the child's disengagement from his lived involvements results in a dualism between a body-object and an outside world on the one hand, and an unknown, insecure *ego*-subject on the other. There emerges a sense of loneliness in a vast and largely impersonal world. Two vaguely distinct problems begin to announce themselves on the basis of this budding dualism. One of the problems is, "How can I master and control the distant world and overcome my feelings of separation?" This is the predominant problem during pubescence. It is through ritualism that the child finds the solution. His ritualistic play with the rules and structures of reality provides a magical domination over the world. And his ritualistic interplay in the gang or the club provides a magical identification with his peers. All this, of course, is fascinating and adventurous. The child feels reassured, and full of cheer and enthusiasm.

But the child needs his ritualism and his peer-group affiliation to reassure him of his place in the order of things and to compensate for the growing uncertainty about his self-identity. For the second basic problem he has to cope with during this phase is to find an answer to the question, "Just who am I?" By placing the world at a distance, he experiences a sense of isolation and a loss of identity. Although this problem is only vaguely felt at first and does not come to a head until the negative stage, it causes him much anxiety, especially when alone. Both literary and professional authors have noticed the ambivalence of the child's existence: he seems fascinated with the spirit of adventure when with his peers, but anxious and somewhat homesick when alone. Twain, for instance, writes about the normally cheerful Tom Sawyer: "He wandered far away from the accustomed haunts of boys, and sought desolate places that were in harmony with his spirit." Blair and Burton, mentioning the possibility of obtaining two rather distinct impressions of this age, state that "group studies revealed them to be carefree, buoyant and cheerful; studies of individuals showed a good deal of strain and conflict." (16, 217–18)

This mysterious *ego* is the all-pervasive and transcending world-forming process which through ritualistic behavior attempts to structure and control the world of the pubescent child. Here are all the ingredients of magic as defined in the previous chapter. It is obvious that this magic ritualism is not "mere magic" in the sense of ineffectual behavior. For it effectively discloses the world of semi-abstractive objectivity as a necessary phase in the emergence of personal maturity. Nor is this magic, as has been alleged, a simple leftover of the toddler's magic. For whereas the toddler's magic emerges from the infantile coenesthesis, is animistic and affects the world through anthropomorphic creatures, the magic of pubescence emerges from the world of the child, is ritualistic, and affects the world through impersonal rules and structures. The toddler's magic is the magic of the fairy tale; the magic of pubescence is the magic of alchemy and ritualism. Both forms of magic represent different existential levels of human development.

This section will conclude with some brief observations concerning a few other characteristic features of pubescence. In the light of the foregoing elucidations, they have become self-explanatory. Parents are sometimes worried about the destructiveness of this age, because "they take everything apart." Yet, when a little child delights in demolishing a tower of blocks before he is able to rebuild it, he is not destructive, but rather engaged in sense-pleasure play. When, in puberty, he takes the clock, the radio, or even the car apart, he is not destructive, but engaged in the playful discovery of the structuredness of things. How does he know how a thing is put together unless he takes it apart, unless he disassembles it? "His so-called destructiveness," says Gesell, "may well be a form of constructiveness in reverse." (65, 365) He is not destructive, but analytic. And it is for the same existential reasons that he even begins to take his parents apart. He begins to see them objectively and to subject them to his criticism. They are no longer omniscient and omnipotent, but finite human beings with undesirable traits and qualities.

Yet another characteristic way of playfully discovering the structuredness of things that emerges during puberty is the making of collections. Of course, the younger child already collects almost anything he finds, and hides it away in his pockets or his chest of drawers. Yet these rudimentary collections are merely miscellaneous and unorganized aggregations. Even a single search of the pockets of a nine-year-old boy may produce two pencils, a "precious" stone, a rubber band, a sea shell, some coins, bottletops, a match box, a whistle, a piece of chalk, a nail, a postcard, and a live frog. It is not until pubescence that the collections become more specialized, organized, classified, and orderly displayed. Collections of stamps, coins, postcards, dolls, or nature specimens are most common in this period. Once again collections are a ritual play of structuring and controlling reality. Or, as Church and Stone aptly put it, "his collections provide a magical domination over reality," and "can be seen as the world reduced to a scale where he can possess and manage and order it." (200, 213)

And, finally, the nature of pubescence as the playful discovery of the world of semi-abstractive objectivity is clearly revealed in the major forms of play interests of this phase: ritual games and hobbies. Play with toys is popular until the eighth year; after this stage games become all-important. And this is to be expected. For a game is a competitive form of play structured according to a set of rules involving skill, chance, or endurance on the part of two or more persons. Games are different from toys and earlier forms of play: they are highly structured and determined by strict rules to which the players have to conform. It is self-evident that games, anything from card and table games to football and baseball games, satisfy the play interests of pubescence. The only kind of toys that they are interested in are those that fulfill the same requirements, such as erector sets, puzzles, magic tricks, and chemistry sets. Whereas in late childhood, the ritual games such as London Bridge or Farmer in the Dell are predominant, in pubescence there is an increasing emphasis on competitive games based on teamwork and resulting in a score.

Although both games and hobbies reveal the pubescent world of semi-abstractive objectivity, they do not do so in the same manner. Games, as I have shown, playfully reveal the corporate structuredness of this world. But hobbies, as I will demonstrate, help the individual child to free himself for yet another feature of his semi-abstractive world, namely the possibility of specialization. For "abstraction" means withdrawal, separation, diversion of attention (ab—from; tra-here—to draw). And objectification is abstraction. For, by placing the object over against himself, man withdraws from both his own unique involvement and the experiential quality of the object. He separates a partial aspect from the original, total phenomenon. He directs his attention exclusively to the kind of object he is faced with, to the aspect it has in common with a group or *class* of objects (L. *species*—class, kind). In short, abstraction entails classification and specialization. This explains why children form rudimentary collections, miscellaneous aggregations, and that the collections become more specialized, organized, and classified during pubescence. It also explains the appearance of hobbies as a typical form of play interest during pubescence. Their hobbies can be seen as a playful experimentation with the discovery of the possibility of specialization for its own sake. Typical hobbies include stamp-collecting, woodcarving, keeping bees or pets, photography, building models, etc. Yet classification or specialization is not yet generalization or truly abstract thinking.

THE WIDENING HORIZONS OF PUBERTY

Although pubescence and puberty overlap and shade into each other, they are nevertheless distinct phases of adolescence. Their fundamental difference is, of course, rooted in the difference of their respective degrees of abstraction. While pubescence discloses a world of semi-abstractive objectivity, it is the prerogative of puberty to deal with the world in a truly abstractive way. Pubescence withdraws from the concrete, individual world of the child, and moves towards the abstractive existence of the functional level. But it is not until puberty that the ability to exist on the functional level and to disclose a truly abstractive world emerges. How the child perceives his world depends on how he forms his world. And this, again, depends on the existential stage of his development.

The world of puberty is the world of the functional level of human existence. This functional level is a truly abstractive way of being-in-the-world. Man withdraws from both his lived involvements and the experiential concreteness of reality in such a manner that the outer world reveals its merely quantitative face. Reality becomes accessible to exact observation, mathematical calculation, and experimental verification. By translating external reality into an abstract system or network of mathematical and functional relationships, man arrives at the possibility of a scientific understanding of and a technological mastery over the material world. The functional level is the level of calculative thinking and controlling action. Man can only control reality when he can predict the effect of a cause. And he can only predict the effect of a cause when the cause exhaustively explains the effect. This presupposes determinism, or the mechanistic, billiard ball kind of causality. The characteristic way of thinking on the functional level is the abstractive, impersonal, mechanical, and unreflective thinking of logical reasoning and causal explanation. Elsewhere I have shown how the dialectics of logic is indeed an unauthentic manifestation of the dialectics of the *logos* or the articulated birth of Being in man. (19, 85–110)

Developmental psychologists generally agree that by about the age of twelve or thirteen, when the child enters the functional level of puberty, the ability for truly abstract thinking, logical reasoning, and causal explanation emerges. This scientific attitude administers, of course, the deathblow to any remainder of magic or ritualism. But it signals also the beginning of a new play interest. As is well-known, children of this age love to debate, to discuss or argue just for its own sake, regardless of the content. Here, again, one is dealing with the playful experimentation with a new discovery, namely the possibility of abstract and logical reasoning. Their debate has little in common with an authentic dialogue in which the participants are striving together for a shared insight or truth (L. *cum* and *petere*—to strive together). On the contrary, their debate is a competitive contest with a score. Their only aim is to show that they are right, to defeat their opponents and to come out victoriously, enjoying themselves in the process.

The increased ability for abstraction and logical reasoning greatly expands the horizon of puberty. The child, as we know, is still immersed in the concrete here-and-now of his immediate concerns. During pubescence, he becomes a discoverer and adventurer. He expands his interest into distant people and faraway places; he explores his ever-widening world, and is fascinated by the unknown; he wants to know what is on top of the mountain, what is over beyond the hill, what peoples and places look like beyond the borders of his country. When John puts on his jacket to leave the house, and Father asks "Where are you going?" his answer is, "Out!" This seemingly impolite answer is nevertheless extremely expressive and accurate. For it says, "Away from home!" "None of your business!" and "Destination: the unknown!" His very ex-sistence as a world-forming process is a transcending of limits, an exploring expedition.

With the beginning of puberty, a major shift in the way the child widens his world takes place. For, as I have shown, by about the age of twelve there is a remarkable increase in the child's ability for true abstraction. This allows him to expand his world in a manner which up to now was impossible. He moves away not only from the concrete here-and-now towards absent and distant reality, but even from all reality by translating it into an abstract system of quantitative symbols. He moves away from mere classification by including several classes or species in a wider class, "a class of species" *(genus)*. This enables him not only to classify, but also to generalize, to arrive at concepts and to define reality in terms of proximate genus and specific difference. And this, in turn, allows him to find security not so much in the concrete structuredness of reality, as in the logical coherency of an abstract system of mathematical and functional relationships. And, finally, he no longer attempts to organize and control his world through the magic of his ritualism, but rather through the understanding and application of the universal laws of nature.

It has been explained how the love for debate during puberty has its meaning in the child's playful experimentation with his newly discovered ability for logical reasoning. Other structural phenomena of this phase point in the same direction. For instance, his hobbies assume a more technical and scientific character. "At thirteen," says Gesell, "individual hobbies take shape in the arts and sciences. The hobbies are often foreshadowed in a previous year by an exploratory interest in photography, chemistry, microscopy, electricity, carpentry, and building of models." (66,425)

Yet another indication of the child's arrival at the functional level in puberty can be seen in the shift from the ritualistic club to the legalistic spirit of the gang. The puberty gang shows clearly the characteristics of the functional level. The abstractive co-being-in-the-world affects, of course, the nature of the peer society. The total disengagement from his individual involvement reduces his we-feeling to a submission to the impersonal "they," and his object-relation to the univocal sameness of general concepts, or the mathematical exactitude of objective norms and natural laws.

In the gang the adolescent drops his identification with his parents and with adult society, and becomes totally obedient to the omnipotent "they" of the gang. He wants to dress the way "they" dress, to see the movies "they" are seeing, and to stay up late because "they" are. He refuses to wear overshoes because "they" don't wear them, he thinks about parents and adults exactly the way "they" do, and has the same opinions about everything as "they" have. Here we recognize, of course, Heidegger's description of the "they" *(das Man)* as the impersonal subject of man's unauthentic being-with-one-another. Since the impersonal "they" is neither any particular subject nor the sum total of all subjects, it is the "nobody" to whom every human being has already surrendered himself in his unauthentic being-among-one-another *(Untereinandersein)*. (88, 166) Heidegger uses significantly the expression "among"-one-another rather than his usual "with"-one-another *(mit)*. For on this unauthentic level, man's co-being, far from sharing the intimacy of Being, stands in subjection to the dictatorship of the "they," which entails the greatest possible existential distance of co-being. As a result, the "they" absorbs the particular subject and deprives it of its individual responsibility. Everything is reduced to unquestioning self-evidence, averageness, and self-less uniformity.

Not only does the child in puberty obey the authority of the "they" rather than that of his parents, he also strives for the self-less uniformity of sameness. He wants the same age, the same dress, the same size, the same code of behavior, and even the same sex. Anything and anybody deviating from the same averageness is mercilessly rejected as an intolerable exception. Anyone who is too tall or too fat, who wants to dress or to think differently, or who is simply of a different sex is automatically excluded. As Church and Stone put it, "At least when in the presence of their gangs, boys and girls elaborately shun each other and speak with ringing contempt of the opposite sex." (200, 218) When the boy begins to complain "Girls drive me nuts!" and the girl begins to find all boys "disgusting," the period of sex aversion has started. This period signals the discovery of the existential difference between the sexes at a stage where exact sameness is required and no difference tolerated.

It goes without saying that the morality of the gang consists in loyalty to the "they," or team spirit. This is not a morality which they are taught, but one which arises as a structural characteristic of their co-being as gang members on the functional level. This is why this morality is impersonal, functional, and legalistic. Its main virtues are fair play, "the strict conformity to the unwritten rules and regulations" of the code of the gang, and honesty which adds the connotation of "the absence of cheating." Without this, the gang simply cannot function, cannot *be* a gang. "This loyalty," says Hadfield, "extends to each and every member of the gang, not for personal reasons, and quite irrespective of any personal qualities, but simply because they are members of the gang." (76, 210)

This impersonal "fair play" morality of puberty has, of course, the structural characteristics of the functional level. They judge the moral value by the externals of an act, with little regard for personal motives and extenuating circumstances. Not the spirit but the letter of the law reigns. They have a mathematical rather than proportional conception of justice. For instance, when a teacher punishes two boys differently for the same offense because he takes personal circumstances into account, the whole class will react with "That is not fair!" This, of course, is a clear example of legalism which is more concerned with the letter than with the spirit of a rule. It should be obvious by now that both the thinking and the morality of puberty are abstractive. Its kind of thinking is that of conformity with the abstract rules of logical reasoning, and its kind of morality is that of conformity to an abstract set of static rules, norms, and general principles.

The change from adult-code to peer-code is not an easy process, but a period full of conflict and painful uncertainty. This confusion is reinforced by another conflict of this period that arises from the dualism between body-subject and body-object. For, on the one hand, the child objectifies his concrete embodiment and reduces his life-world to a body-object. On the other hand, he achieves reproductive maturity which creates feelings, desires, and urges in his body-subject that resist any possible objectification. These powerful genital drives of his body-subject have no place in his abstractive scheme of things. To be sure, the time will come when he will incorporate these genital drives into the integral process of heterosexual maturity. But, for the moment, personal maturity has not yet emerged. Personal love and personal thinking are still impossible. This is why he has nothing to integrate his genital desires in, nor is he able to understand the meaning of his own developmental predicament. He is forced to live in a period of what Jersild calls "sexual unemployment," and this both frightens and puzzles him. The overwhelming strength of his body-subject's instinctual urges leaves his objectifying *ego* defenseless. He feels helpless, restless, and does not know where all this is leading him. It is obvious that during this period conditions are ripe for the occurrence of masturbation. During puberty, masturbation is practiced as a reduction of the physiological tensions of the genital urges and of the psychological tensions of loneliness and anxiety, and also as a playful experimentation with newly discovered experiences. The findings of the Kinsey report confirm that it is indeed during this period that the highest frequencies of masturbation occur. (126, 238)

And, finally, there is the conflict which arises from the dualism between the external world on the one hand, and the internal *ego* on the other. This dualism, as I have shown earlier, began to make itself felt during pubescence as a result of the child's abstractive being-in-the-world. His budding dualism gave rise to two questions: "How can I master and understand the external world?" and "Just who am I?" During puberty, his growing ability for abstract thinking allows him more and more to deal with the first question. For his characteristic way of thinking is that of the natural sciences and of their applications in technique. But when, by about the age of 14, he reaches the perfection of his abstractive abilities, he also arrives at a total subject-object dichotomy. Now he experiences his internal *ego* as completely separated from the external world, which results not only in a feeling of loneliness and anxiety, but also in a desperate search for his lost identity. The answer to the question "Who am I?" eludes him altogether. Much of the noise he makes during this period is merely overcompensation for his insecurity, a whistling-in-the-dark. When Junior plays his records, the house trembles.

Philosophically speaking, his *ego* at this stage is the empty, *a priori* principle of the possibility of any abstractive objectivity. This philosophical insight, however, is no comfort to the adolescent. When he approaches the question "Who am I?" with his typical abstractive thinking, he experiences a radical limitation, but does not know why. He does not know that he is confronted with "non-objectifiable" reality. He only knows that there is no place for him in his vast universe of functional and mathematical relationships. To know this universe is one thing, but to live in it is something altogether different. He despairs over the meaning of life, and wonders if his life is not ultimately "a tale told by an idiot." When this happens, he has entered the next phase of his development, the negative stage of adolescence. Little does he realize that his loss of identity signals the advent of his true Self-discovery.

5

THE FIVE WORLDS
OF ADOLESCENCE: 2

THE NEGATIVE STAGE OF ADOLESCENCE

At first glance, it looks as if the negative stage of adolescence is not a distinct phase at all, but rather an intensified continuation of what had started already in pubescence. Roughly between the ages of fourteen and sixteen in boys, and between thirteen and fourteen in girls, the adolescent has deep feelings of insecurity, defies adult authority, is secretive, rebellious, and difficult to deal with. But haven't these features been discussed as developmental phenomena of pubescence and of puberty? Indeed, they have. And to this extent the negative stage certainly is a continuation of the preceding phases. But it is a continuation that comes to a head, that reaches a critical turning point, and indicates a radical discontinuity in the continuity. An accurate description of the structural phenomena of the negative stage will reveal both the fact and the meaning of this discontinuity. By contrasting its syndrome with the features of the preceding stages, it will be seen that, indeed, a new world has been entered. And this new world is intelligible only as an integral constituent of the person, namely as an affirmation of the no-thing-ness of its Being. In other words, it is the negative stage that constitutes the actual beginning of man's growth into maturity (*adolescere*—to grow into maturity). It brings about the transition from preadolescence (pubescence and puberty) to the period of adolescence proper.

While the preadolescent child was still bursting with vitality, was enthusiastic, adventurous, and a loyal member of his gang, with the beginning of the negative stage all this comes to a sudden end. For no apparent reason, he withdraws from his peer group, and becomes bored, indifferent, and utterly lonesome. He loses interest in his adventures, his hobbies, his collections, and even his friends. He moves around the house in an aimless fashion, with nothing to look forward to. He becomes moody and irritable, and does not know what to do with himself. Almost overnight, he becomes listless, restless, and refuses to listen to reason. Suddenly, and for no apparent reason, the enthusiastic discoverer of the world turns into "a rebel without a cause."

In contrast with the preadolescent urge to explore, to compete, and to perform, the negative stage is characterized by a radical disinclination to work, to be involved, or to achieve anything at all. Nothing makes sense, nothing matters. Whereas the preadolescent is outgoing, extroverted, and only lonesome when away from the gang, brooding, introversion, and loneliness become a way of life during the negative stage. Unlike the preadolescent who could be bored with a book, a class, or a particular game, the adolescent in the negative stage experiences existential boredom. His whole world is boring; he is interested in nothing. While the preadolescent finds his security in the logical structuredness of reality and in the codes of the gang, in the negative stage there is no security at all. He finds himself trapped in a dark room with no exit. The preadolescent could explain things with the help of his reason, but in the negative stage he experiences the impotence of the same reason when it comes to the crucial question "Who am I?" He cannot explain himself, and wonders if he has gone "crazy." He wonders if it is not absurd to exist.

From the foregoing, it should be obvious that one is dealing here with a truly distinct phase of adolescence. It was Charlotte Bühler who first recognized this fact and gave the name "negative stage" to this period of adolescence. However, before attempting to understand the phenomena of this negative stage in their proper perspective, it might be interesting to hear the adolescents express themselves. For instance, their frequent use of the word "hell" is noteworthy. They tell you to "go to hell"; they do things "just for the hell of it"; they warn their parents, "Hell, I am no baby any more"; they complain that they feel "depressed as hell," etc. The following statements are all familiar: "Nothing ever happens around here" (existential boredom); "Let me alone," "Nobody loves me," "Shut up," "Drop dead" (social withdrawal); and "I don't care!" (existential indifference). J. D. Salinger's excellent novel about the negative stage, *The Catcher in the Rye,* has become a classic. Its hero, Holden Caulfield, introduces himself to the reader: "You'll probably want to know where I was born, and what my lousy childhood was like . . . and all that David Copperfield kind of crap." Later on the reader is informed of Holden's private feelings: "I felt lonesome, all of a sudden; I almost wished I were dead," and "I don't get hardly anything out of anything. I'm in bad shape. I'm in lousy shape." And, speaking about the world around him, he feels that "Mothers are all slightly insane," that "All those Ivy League bastards look alike," and that "The whole damn world is phony." (186)

It goes without saying that the negative stage can be excruciatingly difficult for both the adolescent and his exasperated parents. They complain that "a complete change has come over him," that they "can't get through" to him, that they "don't understand him" any more, and that he "doesn't listen to reason." They wish they could help him, but even their slightest attempt to make him feel comfortable and "at home" meets with sharp resistance and is potentially explosive. Neither the adolescent himself, nor his well-meaning parents are able to make any positive sense of this incorrigibly absurd world. Nor, for that matter, are conventional education and conventional society, impregnated as they are with the spirit of abstraction. The calculating and objectifying attitude of the technocratic culture investigates reality, and nothing else. It wants to have nothing to do with nothing. To take "nothingness" seriously is "counterproductive." The negative stage is at best a passing unwillingness to grow up, and at worst a temporary insanity.

Small wonder that the negative stage is the most misunderstood period of human development. In fact, it doesn't even seem that there is anything to be understood at all. There is nothing positive, nothing to get hold of, nothing that makes any sense—at least as long as the negative stage is approached from the everyday or functional levels of existence. However, a philosophical reflection on the negative stage demonstrates that this stage does not reveal its true meaning as a biological or psychological, but only as a philosophical phenomenon. This means that the phenomenon of the negative stage receives its meaning directly from the primordial luminosity of Being.

For, as I have said, primordial Being is not a particular being, object, or thing, but the mysterious presence of an all-encompassing process. Primordial Being is no-thing. Now, in the negative stage, primordial Being begins to announce itself, without as yet revealing itself. The adolescence discovers the no-thing-ness of primordial Being without discovering primordial Being itself. He discovers, so to speak, the reverse side of the fabric of Being. This is why he cannot understand the fundamental meaning of his own predicament in the light of Being. This is why he mistakes his experience of no-thing-ness for that of nothingness.

In the negative stage, the adolescent experiences what, in *Existential*

Thinking, I have called a "limit-situation." (19, 30–31) In a limit-situation, man loses his foothold in the world of particular beings or things, becomes suddenly aware of the fundamental limitations of his existence, and discovers the radical contingency of all beings encountered. In a limit-situation, man's familiar world loses its solidity and its obviousness, and begins to disintegrate as the ultimate anchorage of his existence. A limit-situation reveals the fundamental limits of any and all particular things and situations. It points within these situations to a possible transcendency, indicating thereby that there is something more fundamental, without revealing what that something more fundamental really is. It goes without saying that the negative stage of adolescence is such a limit-situation.

As an existential limit-situation, the negative stage transcends the everyday world of the child and the functional world of puberty. For man experiences limits only when he transcends that which he experiences as limited. This means that the negative stage transcends the levels of all particular beings, things, and standpoints, and somehow reveals what-is in totality, albeit in a negative way. The negative stage transcends the functional level of physics, and is a truly meta-physical phenomenon. From all this it follows that, fundamentally speaking, the negative stage is a distinct phase of adolescence, and a significant step forward in the development of personal maturity.

The negative stage, therefore, is basically not negative. This initial transcendence is at once also the initial turning point in the crisis of adolescence. For it reverses the flight towards the anonymity of abstractive thinking and of the "they" of the gang. Instead of being turned away from his *ego,* the adolescent takes his first step towards personal maturity by moving in the direction of his *ego.* This happens, as I have shown earlier, at the end of puberty when the objectifying process comes to a head and reaches a critical turning point. The subject-object dichotomy is complete, and although the adolescent still looks for particular reasons to explain the why of his predicament, he finds that no-thing can solve the awesome enigma of his *ego.* To be sure, particular things and logical reasoning retain their validity within their restricted levels, but in relation to the question "Who am I?" they reveal their ultimate impotence. Now the *ego* is compelled to solve the enigma of its own identity in complete isolation. But here it finds no-thing at all. In the negative stage, "nothing makes sense." The adolescent is as yet incapable of grasping his negative experience in the all-encompassing light of primordial Being. For, the *ego* is not a particular being or thing, but primordial Being as covered up in unauthentic ex-sistence.

Consequently, the adolescent fails to grasp the positive meaning of the experiential nothingness of his *ego*. He finds himself in a completely unintelligible predicament. He cannot understand that his negative stage has a positive meaning, that it is essentially the concealed discovery of the no-thing-ness of primordial Being. He cannot understand how his negative experience that "nothing makes sense" contains a positive message which announces that "no-thing-ness makes sense" (for it reveals what-is in totality), and that "no thing makes any ultimate sense" (for it lacks the comprehensive universality of personal Being).

The essential meaning, then, of the negative stage is that it constitutes the concealed discovery of the No-thing-ness of primordial Being. When understood in this light, its structural phenomena will reveal their true meaning and original unity. In the first place, the negative stage begins suddenly and unexpectedly and for no apparent reason. Here I may repeat what I have said elsewhere about authentic inspiration, which is "sudden and unexpected by reason of the nature of that which manifested itself in it, namely . . . the *all-encompassing* experience of Being." (19, 157) Although, in the negative stage, only the no-thing-ness of this phenomenon is discovered, it still constitutes a transcendence of any and all particular beings, things, or reasons. Consequently, the negative stage arises as a unitary phenomenon and an indivisible experience. In other words, the negative stage cannot arrive in a succession of separate parts, or be explained in terms of particular reasons. Its sudden and unexpected emergence reveals the unmotivated upsurge of what-is in totality. As is to be expected, those who do not accept "the principle of emergence," and insist on merely causal explanations run into unsolvable antinomies. For instance, the bio-social approach in psychology explains that this stage is both "caused" by society, since it emerges after the peak of the bodily changes has passed, and that it is "caused" by the body, since society does not change overnight.

The world-forming subject-process of the negative stage reaches, as I have shown, the point of complete abstractive objectification. Existentially, this entails the total withdrawal from any and all particular involvements. The adolescent "loses interest" (L. *interesse*—to be "involved") in his former hobbies, work, and even friends. He simply "doesn't care." He reduces his social contacts to nothing; he feels out of touch and utterly lonesome. There is absolutely nothing that can interest him anymore. He is not simply bored with a book, a class, or a game, but with everything. His boredom is more fundamental. I call it "existential boredom," which is a limit-situation and announces the advent of transcending meaning. "This profound boredom," says Heidegger, "drifting hither and thither in the abysses of existence like a mute fog, draws all things, all men and oneself with them, together in a queer kind of indifference. This boredom reveals what-is in totality." (85, 364) For in this boredom, the no-thing-ness of primordial Being announces itself in the *ego,* without as yet revealing itself in the person.

Since the adolescence feels that no-thing happens and no-thing makes sense, all he can do is wander around the house in an aimless fashion with no-thing to look forward to. He is bored to death. His life has no meaning, no structure, no unity whatsoever. The chaos or anarchy of his world is perfectly incarnated in his unkept appearance, and in the mess which he calls his room. He calls the meaning of his very existence into question, and wonders "why there is anything at all and not rather nothing." This Leibnizian question, to be sure, is a metaphysical question, but not yet the primordial question of Being about which he is still completely in the dark. The passage from the limit-situation of the negative stage to the primordial situation of early adolescence still requires the emergence of a new world, a world which he can either accept or reject.

Small wonder, moreover, that at this stage he does not "listen to reason." For the logical or impersonal reason deals only with particular beings or classes of beings, but never with what-is in totality. This is why he discovers the impotence of this reason with regard to questions such as "Who am I?" or "Why is there anything at all, and not rather nothing?" On the other hand, his ability to think in accordance with the *logos,* or his personal reason, has not emerged yet. Consequently, he simply has no reason to listen to. This somehow puts him in a dilemma. For it seems to him that reason is only good for things that don't matter. But, then, how is he ever going to answer his most urgent question, "Who am I?" He may feel that he is going crazy. He really doesn't see any "reason" to live; it is meaningless to be compelled to live in an absurd world.

All this, of course, also puts many parents in a dilemma. They are completely at a loss for an answer to the question "What to do now?" What is to be done when the adolescent suddenly refuses to "listen to reason," defies authority, and becomes moody and rebellious without any apparent reason? Whatever the parents do, it seems to make matters worse, and not doing anything makes them feel guilty as parents. Yet the parents could feel more relaxed and avoid at least more serious mistakes if they could understand the true meaning of the negative stage as it has been explained it in the present section. They would realize that the negative phenomena of this phase signify a positive step forward towards maturity. The adolescent may be mixed up, but he is not psychologically ill. His behavior may look irrational, but he is not insane. He may not "listen to reason," but his disobedience is not immorality. He may be in a dark night of boredom, despair, anxiety, and loneliness, but this prepares the dawn of the primordial light of Self-discovery.

In the negative stage, the adolescence experiences nothingness which is fundamentally the no-thing-ness of his *ego*. This experience is not a passive state of being, but a highly dynamic phase in the birth-process of Being, or in the progressive dis-covery of his authentic Self. The adolescent is setting himself apart from anything and anybody. He radically rejects the unauthentic levels as having any ultimate value. He actively "nihilates" (Sartre: *néantisation*) any and all objects, beings, and things. It is through no-thing-ness that his *ego* comes into the world. He defies any external authority, refuses any outside help, and radically breaks away from any form of childlike dependency. This is why any attempt on the part of the parents to influence the adolescent, not only through the use of force or reason, but even by means of affection and compassion, meets on the part of the adolescent with an attempt to reinforce his nihilating activity. For any outside influence reestablishes precisely the very things and values he is trying to break away from.

Let me illustrate this with an example. Carol was sitting at the dinner table when Mother asked her to pass the salt. When by accident she dropped it, Mother told her to be more careful. This caused Carol to tell her Mother to shut up. Mother showed her hurt feelings by starting to cry, telling Carol how inconsiderate and ungrateful she was, and how much she was disgracing the family. "I hate you!" retorted Carol. Then Mother tried to patch up the argument by throwing her arms around Carol and sobbing, "My poor baby, I know you didn't mean it." With this emotional display of affection and compassion, Mother tried to reestablish the emotional ties with her daughter. The result was devastating. An undescribable explosion followed, through which Carol withdrew even farther from her Mother's affection in her attempt to sever all childlike ties with her.

If Mother had merely said something like "Okay! Okay! That is enough" (to show her objective disapproval), and then had turned her attention to somebody else at the table, Carol would still have simmered for a while, but that would have been the end of the incident. Rather than showing compassion or forcing help on the adolescent in the negative stage, parents should use the following approach: be *available* when wanted, and *don't interfere* when not wanted. Parents may try to help the adolescent on the functional level, but this *no longer* makes any sense to him. Or else, they may try to assist him on the personal level, but this does *not* make any sense to him *as yet*. Any help is experienced as interference, as a threat to his independence, and is met with opposition, defiance, and rebellion.

The adolescent rejects any external help, but is not ready yet for genuine self-help. This makes both the adolescent and his parents seem helpless. It seems that there is nothing the adolescent can do about the incomprehensible nothingness of his world and his unexplainable urge to defy authority. And it seems that there is nothing the parents can do to help the adolescent out of his predicament, except for being available if asked for help.

At first glance the situation seems hopeless. Nothing can be done about it. It seems that both the adolescent and his parents are compelled to wait passively for the problems to solve themselves. Hurlock quotes Gardner as saying "My main therapeutic approach to the parents of adolescents [is] 'It will pass. It will pass.' " (97, 10) There simply are no educational techniques, methods, or devices to help the adolescent out of his negative stage. On the contrary, even the slightest attempt to be helpful meets with resistance and rebellion, and makes matters worse. For whatever parents do or say is external help coming from the very levels the adolescent is breaking away from. The transition from loved protector to suspected foe is often one of the bitter experiences of parenthood, for it appears as though the role as a helping parent has ended—and failed.

Too many parents, indeed, regard the situation as hopeless, and themselves as a failure. If they could understand the true meaning of the negative stage and of their own educational position with regard to this stage, they would see that there is little real cause for concern. On the contrary, they would welcome the negative stage as a positive, normal, and healthy phase in the process of maturation. And they would not mistake their own noninterference and availability for forced permissiveness or mere passivity and indifference.

In the first place, as I have said, the negative stage is anything but a passive state of being. It is a highly dynamic phase in the development of the person. The adolescent's nihilating activities and his defiance of authority may be viewed as the breaking of the umbilical cord of emotional and intellectual dependency, and as the discovery of the no-thing-ness of his personal Self. Rather than reproaching him for the negativity of his existence, he should be admired for his courageous willingness to let go of all former certainties in the face of nothingness. He should be admired for his listening to the dreadful call of nothingness, which constitutes his truly ethical obedience to the developmental task of this period. The dread he experiences here is neither the fear of a threatening object, nor the paralyzed world of neurotic anxiety. It is the "cosmic dizziness" created by the existential limit-situation of the negative stage. It is existential *anxiety* (Danish—*angest*) in the Kierkegaardian sense of the revelation of freedom as possibility. "Dread," says Kierkegaard, "is giddiness in the face of nothingness, that is, in the face of what is not, but which might be, by the action of a freedom which does not yet know itself; just as physical giddiness is simultaneously the fear and the attraction of emptiness." (111, 158) The no-thingness of the adolescent's *ego* is simultaneously the freedom from everything and the haunting abyss of nothingness. This is the freedom which Sartre calls "a horrible yoke." By letting himself be overwhelmed by this existential anxiety, the adolescent prepares himself for another overwhelming experience which is no longer merely dreadful, but also blissful in its awe-fulness: primordial wonder. When this emerges, a new phase in adolescence has been reached: the world of early adolescence proper.

EARLY ADOLESCENCE PROPER: THE AWAKENING OF THE PERSONAL SELF

The world of the negative stage and the world of early adolescence proper are direct opposites. The negative stage, as we have seen, is characterized by anxiety, loneliness, boredom, and meaninglessness. The adolescent lives in a vacuum, in no man's land. In contrast, early adolescence proper opens up a wonder-ful world of unexpected meaning and fulfillment. The adolescent emerges as a profound Self-presence to the whole of reality, and his future appears as a promised land of infinite possibilities. His world takes on an added dimension of mystery, depth, and cosmic intimacy.

Since the actual discovery of the personal Self constitutes the beginning of authentic ex-sistence, early adolescence proper achieves the positive beginning of personal maturity (L. *adolescere*—to grow into maturity). This means that from here on the questions raised in the first chapter with regard to the problem of mature adulthood will begin to answer themselves. This also means that the discussion of early adolescence will meet with the same difficulties as the attempt to answer the question of maturity. For instance, it seems that there is no single objective criterion for the attainment of early adolescence in evidence. The paucity of material on early and late adolescence is well-known. As compared to the earlier phases of adolescence, little research has been done in its final stages. There is a common complaint that only few observable data can be detected, and that the issue of adolescence proper is a question of value judgments rather than of scientific research. As the actual transition to adulthood, adolescence proper is regarded as an adjustment to adult values. And what these values consist in is determined by a given culture or society. Adulthood is what society says it is. And adolescence proper is a "cultural invention."

That these difficulties stem from a lack of philosophical penetration has already been my conclusion from earlier discussions, and will become more and more evident in the pages that follow. But some brief observations about the misconception of adolescence proper as a "cultural invention" are in place here. Underlying this misconception is the dualistic philosophy of the radical dichotomy between subject and object. "The term 'culture,' " says Rollo May, "is generally in common parlance set over against the individual, e.g., 'the influence of the culture on the individual.' This usage is probably an unavoidable result of the dichotomy between subject and object in which the concepts of 'individual' and 'culture' emerged. It, of course, omits the very significant fact that the individual is at every moment also forming his culture." (153,60)

It is man's nature to be cultural, i.e., to transform the physical world into a human dwelling place. In other words, man builds an ensemble of economic, scientific, technological, social, political, artistic, and moral creations to assist him in the progressive liberation and actualization of his authentic Self. This view of culture brings man into the realm of what Hegel called the "world of objectivized spirit." Yet as soon as this objectivized spirit is divorced from man's personal spirit, culture becomes fixated and hinders rather than helps his personal growth and the humanization of the world. The relationship between man and culture is one of mutual giving and receiving. Man liberates himself through his culture, and his culture impels him to free himself still further. Culture is alive only when it is continually nourished by and directed towards the human spirit in a veritable dialogue in which man should have the first and the last word. Consequently, the process of maturation is essentially more than mere "acculturation."

The view that adolescence proper is a cultural invention presupposes cultural determinism, which not only contradicts the very nature of culture, but also refuses to face the characteristic phenomena of adolescence proper. In fact, it is one of the basic characteristics of adolescence that the young person differentiates himself from whatever culture he has grown up in. He can only achieve his Self-discovery by not taking anything for granted in his culture, by examining it critically, and by living in a creative conflict with it. In other words, the very phenomenon of adolescence is a living refutation of cultural determinism. To accept adolescence is to reject cultural determinism; to accept cultural determinism is to reject adolescence.

Unfortunately, cultural determinism is an integral part of our *Weltanschauung*, which equates the "normalcy" and "maturity" of a person with his conformity to the social expectations of a given culture. It goes without saying that in such a view there is no room for the adolescent. For his developmental task is precisely to call the status quo of his society into question, to re-evaluate all values and to assume a personal stance in the whole of reality. Instead of assisting the adolescent in this task, society attempts to manipulate him into succumbing to social domestication. It becomes increasingly more difficult for the adolescent to discover himself in creative conflict with society, to grow into healthy maturity and to *be* an adolescent. The technocratic society turns the creative conflict of adolescence into a destructive generation gap. The very phenomenon of adolescence has to be destroyed because of its subversive nature.

Today, therefore, one is confronted with the phenomenon of "the vanishing adolescent" (Friedenberg), a phenomenon which brings to mind Huxley's *Brave New World,* in which everything is under perfect control, but nothing makes any sense, and in which "normalcy" is equated with "statistical average." Generally speaking, man cannot actualize his full humanness or achieve his authentic Self in the absence of an opportunity for creative conflict between himself and his society. "Consequently," says Rolf Muus, "adolescence is less of a distinct, social phenomenon in lower social classes (this might explain the fact that Spranger, Remplein, and Gesell are mainly concerned with middle class youth) or in primitive society (as Mead demonstrated in Samoa)." (161, 158)

From all this it should be clear that this study of normal adolescence, and *a fortiori* of normal maturity is not based on statistical average, but on man's living in accordance with the essence of his dynamic existence. In other words, normalcy here is not measured in terms of static conformity, but in terms of personality growth. Adolescence comes to pass only in those who continue to develop beyond the stage of puberty. Adolescence is normal, even though it occurs only in a statistical minority. In speaking of adolescence, Robert Nixon states that "No one knows, with any precision, how many young people actually do undertake the work of growth, but my own guess is that the average would fall somewhere between 10 and 15 per cent of contemporary American youth." And then he adds, "I believe the percentage is increasing, and that it is higher than it has ever been before." (162, xxv)

All this has been a long preliminary to what I now propose to do: to examine in outline the basic features of early adolescence proper to see how they organize themselves into interdependent characteristics of the actual discovery of the personal Self. Now, as I have said, the personal Self is man's participation in the process of Being, and, therefore, it is first discovered in the primordial phenomenon of wonder. Consequently, when viewed as a phase in the birth-process of Being, early adolescence is essentially the discovery of primordial wonder.

It is the primordial phenomenon of wonder that offers a fundamental insight into the true meaning and original unity of the characteristic features of early adolescence proper. Once again, I want to emphasize that from here on I will be discussing the nature, the structure, and the dynamism of personal maturity. For adolescence proper constitutes the actual growing into maturity and the emergence of authentic ex-sist-ence. "This momentous emergence," says Robert Nixon, "seems to occur most commonly at around fifteen or sixteen." (162, 4) The emergence of personal maturity precedes the attainment of adulthood by several years. Yet the "reflective awareness" of the emergence of the authentic Self develops only gradually.

Our philosophical reflections have already shown that early adolescence proper is essentially the emergence of the primordial phenomenon of wonder. This fact has an implication of the greatest importance for this study. Namely, it is primordial wonder that constitutes the single, overall criterion for the attainment of adolescence proper as the beginning of personal maturity. This basic insight will gradually be verified and elaborated upon throughout the remainder of the present volume. Another important implication is that early adolescence is fundamentally a personal phenomenon, and that its structural features show their true meaning and unity as integral constituents of primordial wonder. In the following discussion of the structural features of early adolescence, one will see something else, namely, how remarkably these features correspond with Maslow's description of peak-experiences in "self-actualizing people" (149, ch. 12) and of cognition of Being in peak-experiences (150, 67–96).

But is this not giving too much credit to early adolescence by ascribing to it experiences that seem to be the prerogative of especially talented people of mature age? The answer is that there is no such prerogative. Primordial wonder is not the prerogative of a special talent, but of *man as man,* and remains the lasting source and immanent origin of authentic ex-sistence. Maslow himself says that peak-experiences are not "a kind of all-or-none pantheon into which some rare people enter at the age of 60," but that "in theory, they can come at any time in life to any person." (150, 91)

Nevertheless, it should be noted that Maslow's accurate phenomenological descriptions of the peak-experiences remain without a sufficiently rigorous philosophical grounding. An understanding of the fundamental rootedness and interconnectedness of the peak-experiences is missing. Maslow fails to show how the peak-experiences reveal their fundamental meaning and interrelatedness as manifestations of the primordial phenomenon of wonder. The challenge here is to discuss the characteristics of early adolescence (roughly between 15 and 20) in such a way that they reveal their fundamental meaning and interdependence as manifestations of the emerging world of wonder (Being).

Among the first indications that the negative stage has come to an end is the fact that the adolescent no longer feels lonesome, even when he is alone. In fact, he even begins to enjoy being by himself as a new, unique, and wonder-ful experience. He delights in being all by himself in his room listening to music; he loves to be alone on the beach watching the sun set over the ocean, or to lie in the grass gazing at that great expanse, the sky, all the while listening to and pondering the riches of his own new experiences. It is easy to see that it is the emergence of primordial wonder which constitutes the change from the painful "loneliness" of the negative stage to the wonder-ful solitude of early adolescence. For wonder reveals both the all-encompassing presence and the uniqueness of the personal spirit.

This is why the adolescent, after surviving the loneliness of the negative stage, suddenly discovers the mysterious and lush oasis of meaningful Selfhood in what seemed to be the endless dessert of life. Now he wants to be by himself to savor the new experience of life, to take a creative pause to ponder his inspirational world, and to halt in amazement. Now he needs "solitude" and cherishes its blessings. "The need of solitude," says Kierkegaard, "is a sign that there is spirit in a man after all." (125, 102) Loneliness is negative, solitude positive. It is in the solitude of primordial wonder that the dual gift of primordial "openness" and "unique Selfhood" is first bestowed on the adolescent. And it is in the silence of this solitude that he begins to listen to the essence of things and first discovers his as yet undifferentiated intimacy with the totality of all that is.

It goes without saying that this emergence of primordial wonder signals a radically new beginning in the life of the adolescent. In the lifelong birth-process of Being, it constitutes the first actual revelation of this all-encompassing phenomenon. And with this revelation the adolescent has arrived at the end of "the road *to* maturity" (childhood), and at the beginning of "the road *of* maturity" (personal maturity as a process). It is precisely the developmental task of early adolescence to take the first step on this road of maturity.

I now want to sketch some of the characteristic phenomena of early adolescence as interdependent manifestations of the primordial luminosity of wonder. In the first place, the early adolescent loves and needs solitude. When wonder emerges, the adolescent discovers his true Self as his unique but as yet undifferentiated presence to the all-encompassing phenomenon of Being. No longer does his sense of identity merely depend on other people to tell him what he is and where he stands, as was the case in childhood and puberty. His newly emerging Self-identity is the unique, mysterious, and experiential awareness of his intimate Self-presence to the totality of all that is. This intimate experiential involvement in the whole of Being puts an end to his loneliness and boredom. His aloneness no longer means separation, but rather closeness. His re-vived interest in himself and in the cosmic meanings and values of reality creates an exuberance of primordial enthusiasm. He is overwhelmed by what is happening to him (O. Da. *happe*—to occur without prevision), and profoundly inspired by the new promise of life. It is obvious, here, that the characteristics of the world of early adolescence coincide with those of primordial wonder.

Again, it is within the primordial luminosity of wonder that the main concerns of the early adolescent become intelligible. The early adolescent is not primarily concerned with any particular being, function, or meaning. What he is fundamentally interested in is the new openness of his very ex-sistence, which reveals to him an entirely new world of freedom, responsibility, and meaning. This openness is not the physical openness of a box, but rather the experiential openness of presence, involvement, and participation. Wonder, as the principle of openness, places man in the presence of the all-pervasive mystery of Being. And it is this very act of transcendence that man becomes most intimately present to himself and discovers his authentic Selfhood.

It is the same act of transcendence, the same experience of wonder, that breaks the chain of causality, that frees man *from* the mechanical determinisms of physical and social forces, by freeing him *for* his capacity to let his authentic Self "happen" in the creative presence of primordial Being. Wonder is our principle of authentic freedom. The freedom of the early adolescent is no longer the mere freedom of choice of childhood, but rather his creative Self-determination as participant in the all-encompassing event of Being, his freedom to be.

It is also primordial wonder, therefore, that opens up the adolescent's personal responsibility. This new responsibility is authentic response-ability. It is the ability and willingness to be the author of one's own responses to Being. Responsibility has no significance for the early adolescent unless and until he gives it the test of his own experience of meaning and value. Personal freedom and authentic responsibility are not mutually exclusive phenomena. On the contrary, "Freedom and responsibility," says Rollo May, "go together: if one is not free, one is an automaton and there is obviously no such thing as responsibility." (151, 148) It is precisely the emergence of personal freedom in the early adolescent that enables him to creatively respond to the whole of reality.

This emergence of primordial wonder in adolescence constitutes the beginning of personal maturity. It is only the beginning, but it is a great beginning. For it is the beginning of true greatness. Greatness consists in man's being *capax universi,* in his capacity to encompass the all-encompassing phenomenon of Being. Greatness, therefore, is not to be confused with material wealth, fame, or popularity. True greatness is spiritual immensity, existential catholicity, personal unlimitedness. This is why true greatness is not the prerogative of a handful of celebrated people, but rather a structural characteristic of every adolescent and every mature personality.

Yet, whereas the mature personality is explicitly aware of the limitations of his greatness, the early adolescent is not, and that is his limitation. In the mature personality, the greatness of wonder is explicated and differentiated: on the one hand integrated in the workday world, on the other explicitly received as a gift. In early adolescence, however, the emergence of primordial wonder is a global, undifferentiated, pre-reflective manifestation of the phenomenon of Being in his life-world *(Lebenswelt).* No differentiation is given yet between his Selfhood and the all-encompassing universality of primordial wonder. It is precisely this fact which accounts for some of the most misunderstood features of the early adolescent: his radicalism and absolutism, his idealism, his over-exaggeration, and his uncompromising stance in the face of reality.

Because the early adolescent experiences himself in an undifferentiated unity with the totality of all that is, his own world is perceived by him "as if it were for the moment the whole world" (Maslow), and his own uniqueness "as if he were the sole member of his class" (Maslow). In other words, he perceives his new Self and its basic features as absolute and unlimited. His openness, his freedom, his responsibility, his uniqueness, his enthusiasm are all unlimited. He experiences the inexhaustible potentialities of his cosmic openness as if they were fulfilled already. "He wants," according to Stone and Church, "to enjoy his new powers in total freedom, uncontaminated by the practical demands of life." (200, 316) Similarly, his unlimited feeling of responsibility for the entire world is more visionary than practical.

Even his unlimited sense of uniqueness is so unique to him that it is absolutely unparalleled. He thinks that he stands absolutely alone in his cosmic discovery of Being, and does not realize yet that others too can make this discovery. Whatever or whoever preceded him is not unique, and, therefore, is regarded as spiritually insignificant or even as prehistorical. For history, he feels, begins with him. Interesting enough, there is some truth in this. For one speaks of history in the authentic sense only where man's awareness breaks the chain of merely mechanical causation. And it is precisely primordial wonder in early adolescence that opens up this historical perspective. History does make a new beginning with the awakening of authentic consciousness in every human Being. What the adolescent does not yet realize, however, is that history begins and began in others too, and that the mere potentiality of historicity is not yet its full actualization. This happens when primordial wonder differentiates into the world-forming Being-process of the mature personality. "This world-building," says Heidegger, "is history in the authentic sense." (89, 62)

It is for the same reasons that the early adolescent rejects the Establishment, resists enculturation, and severly criticizes the institutional Church, moral and educational systems, societal expectations, and political organizations. He seems possessed with a Messianic mission to revolutionize the world, to make a radically new beginning with man's philosophy of life, and to bring about a "re-evaluation of all values" (Nietzsche). This Messiah complex, together with its unbounded enthusiasm, have always been a constant source of irritation for the "normally adjusted" adults. And, to make matters worse, the undifferentiated discovery of the totality of all that is (Being) causes the adolescent to think that he knows it all. "True enough," says Schwarz, "this exuberant sense of godlike omniscience and almightiness is the main feature of the adolescent—and makes him so trying to live with." (192, 37)

From all this it follows on the one hand that the adolescent is genuine in his pursuit of excellence and in his search for an ideal and perfect world. And this is what constitutes the essence of idealism (not to be confused with "philosophical" idealism). Within the pre-reflective context of wonder, he tries to be true to the discovery of his unadulterated Selfhood and to the authentic meanings and values of life which he is still in a tentative process of feeling out rather than thinking through. The ensuing wonder-ful creative flashes and firefly insights explain his characteristic fondness for aphorisms, slogans, and proverbs.

On the other hand, however, it is evident that adolescent idealism shows the characteristics of his respective phase of development. This means that the idealism of the early adolescent resembles that of a radical, unpractical, and visionary enthusiast. Stone and Church give the following accurate description of the early adolescent's idealism:

Very little that he sees around him matches the glory he senses in his new powers. By comparison, the world of everyday adult activities, the world of political machinations that he reads about in the papers, looks tainted and shopworn. The young adolescent, viewing himself largely from the inside, experiences himself as pure spirit, and the only worthy external counterparts of this experience are to be found in the majesties and austerities of religion, in the beauties of nature, in certain idealized public or fictional personalities, in poetry or music, in political abstractions—in short, in reality seen from a great distance. (200, 316)

Yet, it is with their interpretation of this idealism that one must take issue. "A great part of the adolescent's idealism," they say, "probably stems from his resistance to growing up." (200, 316) Here they mistake the inability to differentiate for the refusal to grow up. They fail to distinguish between the adolescent's healthy and courageous response to his cosmic dynamism, and the pathology of a cosmic stagnation in the hippie, the rebel, or the eccentric. They do not recognize that the exuberance of the adolescent's idealism is really his inability to differentiate, disguised as an exaggerated affirmation of sovereignty. They do not realize that his inability to feel at home in the established world of "normal" adults is the healthy beginning of personal maturity, that it is an achievement and not a disease.

What constitutes the world of the early adolescent is his discovery of primordial wonder as the mysterious and undifferentiated Self-presence to the totality of all that is. In this creative process of Self-disclosure, the adolescent transcends the particular world of his childhood, and enters the universal World of the person. Wonder reveals to him that the world of work and functions, the world of particular beings and objects, is not his entire world, and not even his most significant world. He no longer perceives himself as a "subject"-entity within an external world of "object"-entities, but rather as a creative participant in the primordial World of Being. He escapes for the first time the closed world of his *ego* as the environment-forming subject-process, and arrives at the cosmic openness of his true Self as the World-forming Being-process.

This means that the adolescent has to engage in a "re-evaluation of all values." He has to break away from his familiar acceptance of notions such as truth, reality, certainty, goodness, honor, etc. They do not reveal their fundamental meaning within the subject-object dichotomy of the surrounding world, but rather within the all-encompassing context of concernful personal involvements. The adolescent no longer understands these notions exclusively in terms of their relatedness to the external world, but rather in the light of his Self-presence to the totality of all that is. "Truth" no longer means "that which corresponds to external reality," as the boy thought at the age of ten. "Goodness" is not merely "that which corresponds to external rules or dictates, or serves an external purpose." "Honor" no longer refers exclusively to the regard in which one is held by "outsiders."

The truth that emerges in early adolescence transcends the mere truth of correspondence between subject and object. It is the truth of revelation which dis-closes a new and all-encompassing reality that is more real than the merely external reality of things. This fundamental truth of revelation is, as Heidegger rightly says, the truth as *a-letheia,* the truth as the *un-veiling* process of the primordial World of Being. (88, 256) Early adolescence as the dis-covery of the true Self is the wonder-ful event by which the adolescent emerges into the primordial truth of Being. This gives him at least an implicit awareness of the fact that the truth of the primordial "phenomenon" of wonder (Gr. *phaines-thai*—to come to light) is neither the truth of correspondence (for wonder is all-encompassing), nor the truth of coherency (for wonder is undifferentiated), but rather the trustworthiness of its original revelation (truth: O.E. *treowth*—reliability, trustworthiness).

This original revelation of the adolescent's new Self in a new World of unlimited horizons takes him completely by surprise, both literally and figuratively. It catches him unprepared and fills him with astonishment. Its causes are unknown, and its significance is overwhelming. It requires his willingness to let go of the ultimacy of causal explanations, rational motives, and proven certainties. And it demands his courage to accept the radically mysterious and "unmotivated upsurge of the World" (Merleau-Ponty) as a significant and truthworthy phenomenon. Primordial wonder is an all-encompassing phenomenon, and cannot be explained on the basis of any particular beings, causes, reasons, or motives. Wonder is self-originating and self-justifying, and cannot be perceived, understood, or validated in terms of anything other than wonder itself.

Consequently, there is nothing in the pre-adolescent stages of development that automatically prepares the early adolescent for his developmental task: his Self-discovery in wonder. The transition from childhood to early adolescence is a transition for which he is never prepared, a transition for which there are no guidelines, a transition which he has to make all alone in the uniqueness of his creative solitude. Small wonder, therefore, that the adolescent is sometimes frightened and bewildered, and temporarily regresses to an earlier stage. This is not harmful unless it becomes an unconscious and permanent defense mechanism that blocks the revelation of wonder and fixates him on an immature level of existence.

But when the adolescent does accept the significance and trustworthiness of wonder, his perception of reality changes radically. It is no longer the child's self-evident sense-perception of a surrounding world, or the critical but impersonal objectifying ob-servation in the abstractive world of puberty. The all-encompassing phenomenon of wonder transcends any such subject-object dichotomy, and is not perceived by any particular human faculty, but rather by the experiential openness of the person in its entirety. The early adolescent does not achieve his perception of wonder through ordinary sense-perception or in an act of merely intellectual knowledge, but in a creative act of "original perception." This original perception, as I have shown elsewhere (19, 132–36) is "the lived experience of his mysterious Self-presence to the whole of Being." The experience of an original perception is completely new to him. Never before did he have a perception that comes neither from without (for wonder is all-encompassing), nor from within (for wonder transcends the subject-object dichotomy), but that arises out of his "wonder in the face of the world," and comes to light "in its own right." Early adolescence *is* original perception, or the birth of the natural light *(lumen naturale)* of the phenomenon of Being in man (*phainesthai*— to come to light).

It is often said that this original perception of early adolescence is a "merely subjective" experience. This, however, is a serious and damaging misunderstanding of the situation. Indeed, the early adolescent is personally involved in his perception of wonder or the experiential question of Being. But this personal involvement does not make his original perception merely subjective. On the contrary, it makes it clear that the "mere subject" cannot perceive wonder, and that "person" and "subject" are by no means synonymous. They are even on different existential levels. The subject *(ego)* relates to the external world only, whereas the person relates to the whole of Being. Or, as Rollo May puts it, "The ego is the *subject* in the subject-object relationship; the sense of being occurs on a level prior to this dichotomy." (153, 46) In other words, the all-inclusive reality of the person transcends the subject-object dichotomy, and, consequently, the very possibility of subjectivism.

This holds true even for the affective condition in which the early adolescent finds himself. The phenomenon of wonder does not leave him cold or indifferent, but it involves him personally, and affects him to the core of his Being. He is deeply touched and moved by what is happening to him. The primordial revelation of the all-encompassing mystery of Being both fascinates him and fills him with awe; it places him in his primordial dis-position both in the sense of "mood" and of "openness" (*dis*—apart; *ponere*—to place). Wonder *is* the primordial mood of the adolescent, which places him in the unconcealment or truth of primordial Being. Here one finds, strangely enough, a "mood" that opens up the "truth" of Being, and cannot be merely subjective.

I say, "strangely enough," for the adolescent is surprised, and so are the philosophers and psychologists who think exclusively within the contexts of the subject-object dichotomy. It is customary to reduce all feelings, moods, and emotions to third class phenomena in the make-up of the human personality, to regard them as mere "epiphenomena," as "merely subjective experiences." The "primordial mood," however, opening up the truth of Being, is philosophical rather than merely psychological; is an act of the "person" rather than an experience of the "subject." When Plato called wonder the *pathos,* the "basic mood" of the philosopher, and the *arche,* the "beginning" and "guiding principle" of philosophy, he was certainly not thinking of a merely subjective experience. Heidegger discusses "primordial mood" as one of the structural characteristics of the "openness" of Being. (88, 169–182) He employs the German term *Befindlichkeit,* which implies the primordial "disposition" of being "attuned to" the whole of Being; Self-discovery;

being "placed" or "thrown" into this experiential Self-discovery. This "thrownness" is given in existential *anxiety,* and existential anxiety is always "pervaded by a peculiar kind of peace." (85, 366) Genuine "happiness" and "existential anxiety" are interdependent and mutually inclusive phenomena. This, again, expresses the primordial mood of wonder that reveals to the adolescent his Self-presence to the fascinating and awe-inspiring mystery of Being.

It is through primordial wonder that the early adolescent transcends the world of "pro-blems" (questioned ob-jects), enters the realm of the "meta-problematical" (Marcel), and finds himself in the presence of the mystery of Being. When wonder breaks into his consciousness with an overwhelming suddenness, he is astonished at the radical mysteriousness of all that is insofar as it is. At first he may become frightened, bewildered or even panicky. For, as Pieper remarks, "Wonder acts upon a man like a shock, he is 'moved' and 'shaken,' and in the dislocation that succeeds all that he had taken for granted as being natural or self-evident loses its compact solidity and obviousness; he is literally dislocated and no longer knows where he is." (172, 133) The adolescent is lost in an "oceanic feeling" without finding any anchorage, without finding even the slightest trace of familiarity. Wonder has disrupted the system of certainties that secured the identity of his *ego.* Wonder has deprived him of the unquestioning self-evidences of childhood, and replaced them with the new but uncanny certainty that nothing is self-evident or self-explanatory *as being,* that everything is groundless, unsettled, questionable, and mysterious *insofar as it is.*

Such is the dis-position in which the early adolescent finds himself. Nothing in his previous existence, nothing of what he has learned so far can explain the significance or ascertain the validity of his original perception of wonder. This perception requires a leap into a radically new world. And this leap remains a leap in the dark, a leap which he doesn't know he is qualified to make, until he actually makes it. He does not learn to wonder; he begins to wonder. This in fact, holds true for every real beginning. As I said in *Existential Thinking,* "We do not learn a beginning, we begin a beginning." (19, 9) At the heart of educational activities is always something nonteachable. One learns to swim only by swimming. It is not until the adolescent swims in the mysterious ocean of Being ("oceanic feeling") that he perceives the significance and validity of primordial wonder. It is not until the adolescent takes his "oceanic feeling" seriously, and opens up to the primordial unconcealment of Being, that he perceives, although still in an undifferentiated way, the truth and reliability of this primordial experience.

In short, it is precisely through his Self-presence to the unconcealment of Being that the adolescent perceives the reliability of its self-manifestation. Or, to put it differently, it is through his personal trust as a participant in the trustworthiness of Being that he ascertains the significance and validity of this primordial self-evidence. This radically new certainty which emerges in adolescence is cosmic and mysterious, personal and experiential *(aufweisen)*, and is no longer based on the unquestioning certainties of childhood, or the proven certainties of puberty *(beweisen)*. It is for the first time that the adolescent discovers the radical questionability of all his obvious and unquestioning self-evidences.

The emergence of primordial wonder accounts for yet another characteristic feature of early adolescence: the emergence of the phenomenon of beauty. In fact, it seems that this feature epitomizes all other characteristics of this period. Aesthetic values permeate their whole existence. Not only do the adolescents show a profound interest in the beauty of nature and the beauty of art in its various manifestations, but they also begin to beautify their rooms, their appearance, and their social conduct; they become seriously interested in decorum and etiquette. Their diary is beautiful, their love is beautiful, their world is beautiful, and even they themselves are beautiful.

All I have said thus far about early adolescence could have been said in terms of the "aesthetic phenomenon." For the discovery of primordial wonder *is* the discovery of the aesthetic phenomenon. When I said that the early adolescent transcends childhood and puberty, or the usual, everyday world of work and functions, it was not meant to imply that he withdraws from this world altogether. On the contrary, the all-encompassing experience of wonder cannot be a separate world hovering over the usual world of everyday existence. The adolescent does not withdraw from his usual world, but merely from its usual meaning by perceiving it in the un-usual depth of a primordial perspective.

In other words, in early adolescence, the usual workaday world and the unusual world of wonder are not given and do not signify separately, but the usual world opens up into the unusual world as "its own beyond." In *Existential Thinking,* I have shown that this is what constitutes the essence of the "aesthetic phenomenon" or the nature of genuine beauty. (19, 181–82) And since early adolescence *is* the emergence of primordial wonder, or the unconcealment of the truth of Being in

the ordinary world of workaday existence, the world of early adolescence is essentially a world of beauty.

This world is a fundamental sym-bol, a world in which the usual
world of work and function and the unusual world of wonder are
"thrown together" (Gr. *sun, balloo*— to throw together). A fundamental symbol transcends merely functional and utilitarian values and
referential or semantic symbols that refer to a meaning or reality other
than themselves. A fundamental symbol does not re-present, but it
presents and originates what it symbolizes. A fundamental symbol does
not serve a purpose outside itself; it is non-utilitarian and must be
attended to for its own sake. Man does not wonder "in order to." And
a question such as "What is it good for?" offends the dignity of the
aesthetic phenomenon. Dignity is that which is to be respected for its
own sake. According to the famous saying of Kant, "All things have
a price, man alone has dignity." The aesthetic world of early adolescence is a world that has to be lived, respected, and enjoyed for its own
sake. The adolescent discovers for the first time reality that is an end
in itself, rather than a means to an end; or, in the terminology of
Maslow, he discovers reality that has "Being-value" rather than "defi-
ciency-value."

When the early adolescent begins to perceive the usual world aes-
thetically, he begins to perceive it in its very Being for the first time.
He no longer perceives things as concrete or abstract objects standing
over against a subject, but he begins to listen to the essence of things.
And he perceives their essences when he perceives them in their transparent presence to the primordial luminosity of Being. This fundamental sym-bolism of his "aesthetic" perception, therefore, coincides with
what has earlier been called his "original" perception. When the adolescent perceives his world as both beauti-ful and wonder-ful, he perceives
his world in truth. This perception, as I have said, cannot be subjective,
unless, of course, these terms are taken in their inflated sense of titillat-
ing the senses, exciting, or sensational. Genuine aesthetic perception is
original perception. In this connection, it is worth noting that the word
"aesthetic" is derived from the Greek *"aisthanesthai,"* which means
"to perceive," and that its original pre-Socratic and its present existential meaning is not dichotomized into sense perception and intellectual
perception, but indicates a perception by the whole of man's ex-sistence.

The adolescent's aesthetic perception of his world also dis-locates his
usual perception of the common patterns of space and time. They are
no longer perceived in their ordinary, functional sense, or in terms of
"space . . . for" and "time . . . for." Elsewhere I have shown that in

the aesthetic perception, "space becomes something ethereal and time turns into a reposeful now in which everything is simultaneous." (19, 118) This, of course, is due to the non-utilitarian and all-encompassing awareness of oceanic feeling in wonder, or the cosmic sympathy in the phenomenon of beauty. It is precisely the emergence of this oceanic feeling that dis-locates the ordinary patterns of space and time in early adolescence. In *Existential Thinking,* I attempted a description of this dizzying, cosmic, and wondrous phenomenon, which also depicts the adolescent's original perception of space and time. "The comprehensive universality is given and the comprehensive universality is in suspense. Consciousness steps out of the narrow bounds of the *ego* and a transcendent intuition is awakened in which limitless horizons open up and foundations disintegrate, in which everything becomes at the same time infinitely remote and intimately close, and in which one's being is reduced to a drop in the infinite ocean while at the same time the infinite ocean seems to be contained in the drop. Things can no longer be localized in time and space, but seem to be freely floating while they are drawn into a whirlpool of a kind of mysterious omnipresence." (19, 46)

Wonder dis-closes original spatiality as the cosmic, all-inclusive expanse of the openness of Being. Maslow refers to this original spatiality when he states that in peak-experiences "the whole of the world is seen as a unity, as a single rich entity," or that, particularly in love and beauty, "one small part of the world is perceived as if it were for the moment all of the world." And he rightly attributes this phenomenon to man's cognition of "the whole of Being" in such experiences. (150, 83)

Similarly, wonder dis-closes original temporality, which transcends the usual experiences of time as clock-time, as a flux of moments, or as time . . . for. In the cosmic and all-inclusive world of wonder, the "here" and the "there," the "now" and the "then," the "close" and the "far" merge. Primordial wonder as the mystery of Being is a question which encroaches upon its own data. Primordial wonder dis-closes the primordial presence of Being *(present)* by coming towards *(future)* its own data *(past).* Primordial wonder, therefore, is not in time, but it is temporalizing. Original temporality is a creative and circular process of self-disclosure. In early adolescence, the unique moment (*momentum*—movement) of wonder ingathers the three dimensions of original temporality in their original and still undifferentiated togetherness. Wonder, here, is still an ar-rested moment of disclosure, a resting movement, a reposeful now in which everything is simultaneous.

It is often said that the early adolescent's activities are a waste of time. For he enjoys a life of leisure, spends a great deal of time in dreaming, musing, and idling, and engages in endless bull sessions with the crowd. At first glance, this certainly looks like a waste of time. However, the foregoing elucidations present the positive and fundamental meaning of all this. In the first place, the adolescent is in the process of discovering authentic temporality, which is an end in itself and no longer "time . . . for." Now, time that cannot be used cannot be wasted either. Moreover, in the context of original temporality, the adolescent is in the process of discovering the authentic values and meanings of life that are to be appreciated for their own sake, and not as something to be used; that are "end" experiences, rather than "means" experiences. And, as I have shown at other stages of development, the new discoveries become the object of playful experimentation. Far from being a useless waste of time, the adolescent's enjoyment of leisure, his dreaming and musing, his spontaneous group discussions are playful ways of discovering the supreme significance of non-utilitarian values.

The often dream-like consciousness of the adolescent is fundamentally his getting ready for the basic inspiration of life: primordial wonder. In *Existential Thinking* I have shown how this dream-like consciousness is a structural characteristic of the creative process. (19, 159–61) "It is our fundamental willingness to surrender to the 'oceanic feeling' of wonder, to inhibit all our individual urgencies, and to disengage from any theoretical or practical concerns that hold us down on the level of our unauthentic existence." (19, 160) The adolescent's dream-like consciousness transcends his everyday activities and any preoccupation with particulars, and presents him with the chiaroscuro of the mystery of Being. This dream-like consciousness emerges out of the unknown, slows down the quantitative speed of life and thought, wanders away from anything in particular, and keeps in touch with the oceanic experience. It constitutes the willingness to "listen to the voice of Being" (Heidegger), to remain "open for experience" (Rogers), to be "available" in creative receptivity (Marcel). This fundamental understanding of dreaming is practically synonymous with "musing" and "idling," if taken in their positive sense. This is why the following statements about idling and musing accurately describe the adolescent's situation. James Jarrett, in his *The Quest for Beauty,* remarks that "idling is sometimes the least idle of pursuits: it may be a wise passiveness in which the ideas germane to accomplishment are being engendered." (104, 66) And, according to Verhoeven, musing "is playing with possibilities, creating space around things." "Musing," he says, "is marking time, a retarded, iterative thought whose goal is not to arrive at certain conclusions but to restore the lost intimacy with things." (214, 194)

The adolescent's musing and dreaming is his playful transition from observation to participation, from a world of work and functions to a world of leisure and celebration. The early adolescent discovers the possibility of true leisure for the first time, and begins to playfully enjoy it both in the solitude of his private room and in the spontaneous dialogues of the crowd. In order to understand the term "leisure" as it is used here, one has to overcome the functionalist prejudices of the world of "total work." In this world, leisure is usually interpreted in function of work. It is seen as a temporary freedom from the demands of work in order to be able to work better again, whether it is called spare time, a weekend off, a holiday, or a vacation. In contrast, true leisure is an altogether different phenomenon. It breaks the chain of utilitarian functions and work completely. True leisure is not even on the same existential level. True leisure is not the mere absence of work on the functional level, but rather the very presence of non-utilitarian values and meanings on the personal level.

True leisure is an existential attitude of openness to the whole of reality, which transcends the workaday world and allows the authentic and non-utilitarian phenomena to happen without any active interference or preoccupation on the part of man. The experiential awareness of the "happening" of these phenomena is "happiness." The elements of musing and creative dreaming are clearly recognizable here. True leisure is the existential attitude of silence before Being, which is the attitude of wonder. Silence as the primordial response to Being is not the mere absence of speech, but rather the lasting source of authentic language. Authentic silence is not the mere absence of noise, but rather the undisturbed listening to the voice of Being. And listening, according to Heidegger, is man's "existential way of Being-open as Being-with for Others." (88, 206) Leisure as authentic silence is the creative listening of man as Self-presence to the totality of Being. This is precisely why the playful discovery of true leisure is a developmental task of early adolescence. Josef Pieper remarks rightly that "leisure is only possible . . . to a man at one with himself, but who is also at one with the world." (172, 54) The implication is that true leisure is a happy affirmation of one's Self-presence to the totality of Being, or a joyful assent to reality as a whole. This "Yes" to life as a whole is the essence of celebration. "The soul of leisure," says Pieper, "lies in celebration." (172, 71)

Whereas the earlier, undifferentiated phase of the discovery of leisure often finds its expression in the adolescent diary, the later, socially differentiated phase is revealed in the life of the crowd. Before the adolescent is able to share his musing and Self-discovery with other persons, he often finds a natural way of expressing himself in the literary form of the diary. The adolescent diary accurately reflects the structural characteristics of early adolescence. This diary is an intimate, secret, and literary document in which the adolescent engages in a spontaneous conversation with himself about what is happening to him. It is a playful experimentation or musing dialogue with the authentic values of life in a personal, unique, and aesthetic way. The diary becomes a confidant, an ever-ready listener who supports the tentative Self without ever criticizing it.

Gradually, the adolescent's Self begins to differentiate into a small and spontaneous social group of interpersonal relationships which is usually referred to as "the crowd." The crowd constitutes the social life of early adolescents and characteristically corresponds to their way of Being-in-the-world. As contrasted with the earlier club and gang, the crowd has no organization, no structure, no rules, no officers. The crowd is not organized, but it happens, and is held together exclusively on the basis of personal relations. This is why its unity is spontaneous, profound, and creative. The adolescent's world becomes a shared world. Through the recognition of the other person as an end in himself, the adolescent's Self can no longer pretend to be the sole arbiter of value and meaning in the world. His solitude becomes, paradoxically, a shared solitude. He shares his leisure, his musing, his playful discovery of authentic values, his very Self. And even the experience of sharing itself is a new discovery that has to be experimented with. The authentic values of life are Being-values (Maslow), all-encompassing and personal, and, therefore, only given in persons. But persons are only fully persons in their interpersonal I-Thou relationships, in their togetherness of co-Being. This is why the spontaneous and unorganized discussions of the crowd serve no useful purpose outside themselves, but have a supreme significance in themselves. These discussions include such issues as: attitudes towards life, philosophical, psychological, and moral problems, religion, love, sex, art, world events, culture, etc. They are part of the playful discovery of the Self, and of the non-utilitarian values of life. The crowd is the mutual Self-discovery of early adolescents through their shared musing, their shared leisure, and their shared probing into the mysteries of authentic existence.

The most important interpersonal relationship that emerges during this period is the adolescent's personal love and friendship. This love, to be sure, is only the original perception of personal love, and has all the structural characteristics of early adolescence. Nonetheless, it is personal and differs radically from any previous form of love. According to Fromm, love is "the achievement of personal union." (58, 18) Philosophically speaking, love, as the achievement of personal union, is man's Self-presence to the whole of Being as co-Being. In genuine love, the partners share their participation in the mystery of Being. The intimacy of their mutual Self-presence transcends the subject-object dichotomy, and constitutes the authentic *We* of their I-Thou relationship.

One's concern here is to understand the first experience of personal love as it manifests itself in early adolescence, both in terms of friendship and in terms of heterosexual love. What seems strange, and is often frowned upon, is that the early adolescent's friendship shows a great similarity to romantic love, the first beginning of heterosexuality. For instance, it is a well-known fact that youth friends have a profound need for intimacy, and that their friendship contains a strong erotic element. However, when these facts are viewed in the light of the foregoing discussion of early adolescence, they cease to be strange or objectionable. On the contrary, true intimacy and erotic love are literally among the most beauti-ful and wonder-ful phenomena of human existence.

When the early adolescent begins to discover his authentic Self, he has to co-discover another Self, for there can be no complete Self without the Thou. His youth friendship, as a mutual Self-discovery, is an integral constituent of his Self-discovery, which is the developmental task of this period. His innermost Self becomes present to the innermost Self of the friend, and it is the first time that his friendship is based on personal intimacy (*intimus*—innermost), on the inner life of the friends. Friendships of children are rather determined by extrinsic conditions such as usefulness, pleasantness, living in the same neighborhood, being in the same class, being playmates, etc. Youth friends seek one another's presence as something of supreme value, as something to be enjoyed and appreciated for its own sake.

The philosophical foundation of their mutual confidence is the fact that both friends share the trustworthiness of primordial Being. Without this basic trust in the whole of Being, without the interpersonal confidence of a love relationship, no true Self-confidence is possible. Similarly, the mutual respect and admiration created by the interpersonal intimacy of youth friends find their philosophical foundation in the revelation of wonder as co-wonder (*ad, mirari*—to wonder at, to admire).

But how does the erotic element come into the picture? What does erotic love have to do with a healthy friendship between two men or two women? The answer is that it constitutes its beautiful beginning during early adolescence. This cannot be understood, however, as long as erotic love is mistaken for "eroticism" in the sense of genital arousal, sexual titillation, or lust. Lust is the experiential aspect of genital love on the bodily level. Genital love is a drive or instinct like hunger and thirst, and depends on the proper functioning of the sexual glands. As a drive, genital love is biological in nature and aims at the satisfaction of a particular need of the organism. The goal of genital love is the release of genital tension and the pleasurable satisfaction that accompanies it. This satisfaction remains restricted to the individual who feels it.

Erotic love is essentially different. As contrasted with genital love, erotic love seeks interpersonal intimacy rather than relief of tension; it seeks to prolong and increase itself rather than to satisfy itself; it seeks beauty rather than mere lust. Ever since Plato, *eros* has been regarded as a "spirit" *(daimoon)* rather than the functioning of an organ. It is the "desirous longing" of the soul in its ascent to the contemplation of the perfect good for the beauty of the body and the beauty of the soul in their undifferentiated unity. Erotic love transcends sensuous love, not by denying it, but by incorporating it in the spiritual openness of personal love. In other words, erotic love is beautiful love, and, therefore, the original perception of personal love.

Since the world of early adolescents is the world of beauty, their beginning interpersonal love is erotic. Consequently, what I said about their aesthetic perception applies, *mutatis mutandis,* to their experience of erotic love. The philosophical meaning of this can be summarized by the following quotation from my *Existential Thinking:*

The *ontological significance* of erotic love is that it presents the phenomenon of personal love in its *original givenness.* Erotic love is *beautiful love,* it is the experiential, wonder-ful and undifferentiated beginning of personal love. In the beauty of erotic love the lovers encounter one another in the sym-bolic union between the wonder-ful Being and its visible embodiment. In erotic love the lovers love one another's body not as an object of lust, of dark passion or unholy sensuality, but rather as the "holy" incarnation of spirituality of their personal Being. In erotic love the lovers love one another with their *whole body* and *whole soul* in an *undifferentiated unity.* (19, 248–49)

In their erotic love, the adolescents reveal to one another the beauty of their personal truth and goodness as embodied in their male or female existence. They stand fascinated and enraptured, and momentarily feel as if they had found the whole of Being. This erotic element is characteristic of the beginning friendships during early adolescence. As Edward Spranger points out, these "homo-erotic" friendships between adolescent boys or between adolescent girls constitute a perfectly healthy period of transition, and are at least as common as their beginning heterosexual loves. (198, 80) And, in fact, these beginning heterosexual loves are also manifestations of the adolescent world of beauty; they are also erotic loves. This erotic heterosexuality is what is commonly called "romantic love." The homo-erotic friendships and the hetero-erotic romantic loves of early adolescence have in common that they seek beauty, tenderness, and intimacy. The differences between these two kinds of love become more explicit when the world of early adolescence begins to differentiate into more mature love relationships.

If one thing has become evident from this long, but important, section, it is that the criterion of beginning maturity is not adjustment, efficiency, success, or functional usefulness, but wonder, beauty, and eros. This conclusion runs counter to the worldview of a technocratic age. With the rise of the organization man, one witnesses the decline of Being-values and of the creative achievement of self-identity, and with it the vanishment of both adolescence and culture. For without wonder, there is no true Self; without beauty, there is no original perception; without eros, there is no mutual creation of non-utilitarian, cultural values. "Eros," says Rollo May, "is the center of the vitality of a culture—its heart and soul. And when release of tension takes the place of creative eros, the downfall of the civilization is assured." (152, 98)

Under these conditions, it becomes increasingly difficult for the adolescent to *be* an adolescent. His world of wonder, beauty, eros, and leisure, in short, the bliss of Being, is by no means an unmixed blessing. In fact, genuine courage is required just to *be* an adolescent. For he has to face difficulties, dangers, and anxieties coming both from without and from within. The adult world has little patience with "this adolescent non-sense." In the triviality and publicity of everydayness, the adolescent is pressured by the "they" *(das Man)* to behave as everyone behaves, to think what everyone thinks. Both the common man and the functional organization man pressure him into conformism. If the adolescent is to function in the adult world at all, he is expected to participate in the deadly serious adult game of role-playing. He is offered acceptance, security, and happiness for abdicating the prerogatives of his newly discovered Self in favor of the social system. He is told that even his very survival depends on his adjustment to society. The adolescent wonders, however, how the deadening of the sense of Self could be called survival. He wonders how the depersonalized, standardized, and alienated existence of a prisoner of society could be called life. He needs great courage to remain faithful to his developmental task without being panicked into rebellion or conformism.

These difficulties are still further compounded by difficulties that arise from within. Totally unprepared, and without any help, he has to let go of all former certainties and to question all meanings and values that have served him thus far. And what is more, his joyful Self-affirmation is essentially permeated with a profound anxiety. For this Self-affirmation is the acceptance of his Self-presence to the mystery of Being as a Self-questioning question. He experiences the fascinating unconcealment of the truth of Being as concealed in the awesome void of authentic Nothingness. In other words, the joyful affirmation of Being brings man face to face with authentic Nothingness in the experience of existential anxiety, and has to be a courageous affirmation. For courage, according to Paul Tillich, "is self-affirmation 'in spite of,' namely in spite of nonbeing." (206, 66) Authentic joy and happiness, therefore, are not for the weak, but for the strong and the courageous.

In addition to all this, one should realize that psychological anxiety is a normal emotional response to anything new. And the early adolescent is precisely confronted with the total newness of a world which is awe-inspiring, unlimited, overwhelming, and mysterious. In this world, "typical areas of anxiety-provoking concern are such issues as religion, philosophy, politics, authority, independence, commitment, vocational choice, dating and sex, marriage." (162, 135) Also completely new is the experience that these issues reveal themselves in a profound unity and interdependence. The early adolescent is at first at a loss for answers to problems that cannot be objectified, classified, and dealt with separately. He does not know how to handle questions that encroach upon their own data, and that cannot be detached from their experiential interwovenness within his Self-presence to the mystery of Being. A radically new way of thinking presents itself.

Lastly, in all this, he is completely on his own. In the educational process of "help to Self-help" (Pestalozzi), he has arrived at the stage of Self-help. In his developmental task, he can no longer rely on any help other than his own Self-help rooted in the dreadful freedom of his trembling soul. It should be evident by now that, contrary to the common opinion, the characteristics of early adolescence cannot be regarded as symptoms of weakness or disorder, but should be seen as demanding genuine courage and strength.

LATE ADOLESCENCE PROPER: ACHIEVING PERSONAL INTEGRATION

There is no clear line of demarcation between early and late adolescence proper. For the developmental task of late adolescence is to work out the primordial inspiration received in early adolescence. This, again, demonstrates the continuity in discontinuity of human development. Between the ages of 18 and 22, one witnesses the period when the end of early adolescence marks the beginning of late adolescence which roughly lasts a decade (18-28 for women; 20-30 for men).

The developmental task of late adolescence is usually understood in terms of achieving adult status. This implies, apart from achieving legal adult status, vocational, marital, and sociocultural "adjustment." After the adolescent has "completed" his physiological and psychological development, there is only one more task to be performed in order to become fully integrated into the adult world. He has to forget all "adolescent nonsense," to "come down to reality," and to learn to play successfully the adult roles society expects him to play, particularly in the areas of vocation, sex, and sociocultural reality.

Of course, no one doubts that selecting a mate, establishing a home, acquiring a vocation, and integrating into one's adult sociocultural environment are among the most important tasks of this period. However, those who restrict the very meaning of late adolescence to the achievement of adult status through these forementioned tasks are seriously mistaken. For they mistake adulthood for maturity; they fail to see that maturity is rooted in wonder rather than in adjustment.

The fundamental question is not so much how effectively the late adolescent performs his various tasks of adjustment, but rather how effectively he puts these adjustments at the service of his newly discovered personal Self. The late adolescent is not outgrowing the primordial inspiration of early adolescence, but working it out and orchestrating it into the symphony of a mature existence. The undifferentiated and all-encompassing phenomenon of wonder is an inexhaustible and unending process of birth. The late adolescent does not leave this process behind without ceasing to be mature at all. He does not leave it behind, but he differentiates it, and fulfills his differentiated tasks and functions within its creative dynamism and cosmic universality. Again, the basic question is not how perfectly the late adolescent adjusts, but how well he achieves his personal integration.

From the foregoing, it should be evident that the actual transition from early to late adolescence is the most decisive moment in the birth of the young personality. The word "decisive" here is taken both in its etymological sense and with all its connotations. The word "de-cision" is etymologically derived from the Latin *decidere* which means: to cut off, to separate, to decide (*de*—off, from; *caedere*—to cut).

The world of early adolescence is the fundamental sym-bol of wonder which invites the adolescent to explore and penetrate the ambiguity of its enigma. Wonder as a question and a quest is both thought-provoking and growth-provoking. The adolescent begins to wonder at wonder. And it is precisely in this beginning re-flection or bending-back upon wonder in thought and action that he first achieves his differentiated ex-sistence of late adolescence.

When the adolescent begins to bend-back upon wonder in thought and action, something interesting happens. The global, undifferentiated, and cosmic mystery of Being differentiates into a multidimensional structure, into a unitary but articulated phenomenon. His reflection on wonder ex-plicates or un-folds this undifferentiated experience into the unitary structure of his authentic ex-sistence. He finds-his-Self-Being-together-with-others-in-the-world.

The adolescent no longer perceives himself as if he had become the whole of Being, but he begins to become explicitly aware of phenomena that are other than himself, that are original data given in their own right. He becomes aware that he is only participating in the whole of Being. He becomes aware that others are unique too, and have meaning and responsibility in their own right. He becomes aware that he has to make a vocational decision, and to adjust himself to the sociocultural pattern of his adult environment, if for no other reason than that he will be asked very soon to enter the mainstream of life. Whereas early adolescence responds to the undifferentiated inspiration of wonder, late adolescence responds to the dialectical Self-manifestation of wonder (*logos*). And it is here that one encounters the actual beginning of maturity. For whereas wonder is still an implicit, unlimited potentiality, in late adolescence it has to become actualized in a "definite" situation. To remain in a state of unincarnated idealism is to be of no use to oneself or others. Important, and often irrevocable, decisions have to be made. But de-cisions cut off other possibilities, and have a limiting effect on the whole of our potentialities. To marry *this* woman implies the elimination of more than half of humanity. To make one's home in Chicago excludes San Antonio, Amsterdam, and Melbourne as actual places of residence. To become a physician greatly reduces the possibility of ever becoming a professional football player. Yet, during late adolescence these important decisions are not so much experienced as sources of limitation, but rather as the joyful adventure of a playful experimentation.

The transition from early to late adolescence is not without possible dangers and conflicts. This transition, therefore, is also decisive in the sense of critical or dangerous. Fears from within or pressures from without may affect the actual birth of maturity which is the separation from the womb of primordial wonder. This actual birth is a critical turning point, a crisis fraught with danger, a moment which decides upon the very authenticity and the future course of the maturational process.

The adolescent's sense of unlimited response-ability must be given reality in a definite situation. As a result, he may refuse to differentiate and incarnate, because he is afraid that the necessity to accept limitations compromises his integrity and prevents him from being true to himself. He begins to suffer from what Sam Keen calls "Dionysian pathology." "The psychic condition of the anomic individual is one of undifferentiated, diffuse, total possibility. He recognizes no inner limits, because he has made no de-cisions." (119, 177) He remains fixated in early adolescence. "When enthusiasm is not tempered with judgment, man loses his rootedness in the limitations of the present, and he soars into the situationlessness of pretended onmipotence." (119, 176)

Or the opposite may happen when the "adult" world pressures him into jumping into the mainstream of life, before he is able to swim or find his own sense of direction. This may frighten him into abdicating his personal freedom and creativity in favor of the security of societal systems. He begins to suffer from what Keen calls "Apollonian pathology," which turns his world into a cosmic prison. (119, 172) He wants to "play it safe," and, therefore, has to play the roles society expects him to play. His world is completely governed by the rules, customs, and taboos of his sociocultural environment that "conspire to destroy wonder and freedom by picturing the world as a closed system which may be understood and explained without remainder." (119, 167) When this happens, the adolescent regresses, surrenders his true Self in favor of impersonal structures, and becomes fixated at the level of puberty.

That, indeed, it is difficult to avoid these pathological conditions is shown by Robert Nixon in his *The Art of Growing* (162, xiii-xxiii). He calls those who are fixated in either of these perilous alternatives respectively "rebels" and "conformers." Rebels and conformers respond to the challenge of late adolescence in diametrically opposite ways. Rebels refuse to adjust to their sociocultural environment, whereas conformers completely adjust to it. Yet, fundamentally speaking, both responses make the same mistake, for both responses are uncritical, unquestioning, and final. Both result in a fixation which terminates the process of maturation and prevents adolescents from being true growers. Both distort the primary data and original unity of authentic human existence by reducing them to either a world-less Self or a Self-less world. But what particularly demonstrates the perilousness of this period is the fact that the rebels and conformers outnumber the growers to such an extent that rebellion and adjustment, rather than growth, seem to be the major issues of adolescence.

"Until fairly recently," says Nixon, "we believed that virtually all young people were either rebels or conformers. The few who apparently fitted neither of these common patterns [the "growers"] . . . seemed to be so very few as to be without statistical significance." (162, xvii) Yet the statistically insignificant minority might precisely be the normal ones in the sense of healthy. And the growers *are,* despite the psychological tradition that equates "average" with "normal." This tradition itself is a victim of the Apollonian pathology, where psychology has turned into the "pathology of normality" (Keen), or the "psychopathology of the average" (Maslow). Only the growers are normal adolescents in the sense of "healthy." For only the growers are strictly faithful to the authentic principles of human development. Only the growers develop in accordance with the dynamism of human nature.

The process of the differentiation of the *person* into the young *personality* takes up the entire phase of late adolescence. Of course, the term "personality" is used here not in its merely psychological sense, but in its fundamental sense of dialogue between the individual world and the World of the person. This integration of his personal idealism into the realism of his workaday world compels the late adolescent to give up his "all or nothing" mentality, and to drop the absoluteness of his demands. He discovers that it is possible to make compromises without compromising his personal integrity. He no longer expects the good person to be a saint, and the bad person an all-out sinner. He begins to realize that the goals of life are not rectilinear and merely inspirational, but very complex and demanding, and that they can only be pursued through conflicts, hard work, and occasional failure. He realizes that it is necessary to have patience with himself and with others.

While integrating his former functional multiplicity into the unity of his personal Self, the late adolescent goes through a period of playful experimentation with the newly discovered possibility of orchestrating life. He often hesitates between two or more possible alternatives (L. *haesitare*—to get stuck, to be undecided). For instance, he wonders what is more important, reason or emotion, individualism or socialism, idealism or realism, etc. In the process of finding out, he may first playfully experiment with one extreme, and then contrast it with the opposite extreme. He may play the role of a rationalist, and then suddenly change into an emotional being. One minute he may exhibit extreme self-centeredness, only to appear a few minutes later as the paragon of self-sacrifice. This extremism is a playful experimentation with beginning integration characteristic of the late adolescent in his early twenties, and disappears in his late twenties when he has established his adult personality.

6

THE CRISIS OF THE LIMITS

By the late twenties, the turbulence has passed. Young men and women are more stable, more serious and sedate. They have established themselves as adult personalities in their sociocultural environment, in their home, in their occupation and lifestyle. The developmental task of adolescence has been fulfilled; the crisis is over. The road to maturity has come to an end.

However, contrary to the common belief, human development has not come to an end. The achievement of adult personality is at the same time the end of the road *to* maturity, and the beginning of the road *of* maturity. Maturity, as a road, is the process of the dialectical Self-manifestation of Being in man. This process is not simply a quantitative increase of experience and learning, or a qualitative growth in wisdom and judgment; the road *of* maturity, as the mature process of maturation, passes through existential stages and crises.

Once the late adolescent has established himself as an adult personality, he finds himself in a differentiated and integrated way on all levels of human existence. Adolescence has passed, but man keeps moving as a result of the creative dialogue between his personal world and the world of his workaday existence. However, he does not move towards another level of existence (where would he go?). Rather, he continues to build and integrate his world; he begins to stabilize it and to consolidate his previous gains. He enters a period of relative calm, and, yet, a period that often comprises the most productive years of his life.

This period (roughly for women from 27 to 35, and for men from 30 to 40 years of age) is usually called the period of early or young adulthood. This is, of course, correct insofar as one's viewpoint is restricted to observational and statistical thinking. Anyone between the ages of 21 and 40 can rightly be called a young adult, whether he is mature or not, whether he is a fixated rebel or conformer, or the

112

paragon of a growing personality. The term "adult" does not connote maturity, as does the use here of the term "personality." I, therefore, prefer to call this period the stage of "the adult personality," to indicate, on the one hand, the maturity of this phase, and, on the other, its emphasis on the adult values that are the goal of this first half of life. Moreover, the use of the term "adult personality" enables one to clearly distinguish the period that precedes "the crisis of the limits" from the stage of "the mature personality." This stage of the mature personality emerges from the crisis of the limits, and emphasizes personal fulfillment, which is the goal of the second half of life.

The pivotal importance of the crisis of the limits for the understanding of the mature personality is obvious. Whereas adolescence originates the adult personality, it is the crisis of the limits that gives birth to the mature personality. Interestingly enough, there is a remarkable resemblance between adolescence and the crisis of the limits. In fact, the crisis of the limits is adolescence renewed and reviewed on a higher level. Yet, despite its essential importance, the crisis of the limits is still largely an unknown in the understanding of human development.

THE STAGE OF THE ADULT PERSONALITY

The adult personality continues to develop in the direction that was started in late adolescence. Man continues to build and expand his world, and to actualize and assert himself as the living center of this world. All this is strongly experienced as a progressive expansion and realization of his own personal Self. But, although the adult personality is not moving to another level of existence, a basic change takes place during this period (women 27–35; men 30–40). This change is a basic shift in emphasis. Whatever the adult personality had created with playful experimentation as an extension of his inner Self, now begins to assume its own stability, to exist independently, and to become a thing-in-itself for which he becomes responsible. Whereas the late adolescent experiences his lifework as a personal and playful experimentation, to the adult personality it becomes more of an objective duty, only to turn into a real burden during the crisis of the limits.

For example, a young man who has received his degree from a school of business may have decided to open a hardware store. During late adolescence, his struggle to build up the store shares much of the playful experimentation so characteristic of this period. It enables him to apply the knowledge and skills he learned in college. It enables him for the first time to deal with employees, to be in charge of buying and selling, of financial management, of advertising, etc. But, most fascinating of all, it enables him to establish himself in the adult world, to make a living, and, as a result, to marry, to buy a home, to start a family, and to educate his children. It is through all this that he establishes himself as an adult personality and that he experiences his world as an extension of his expanding Self.

But when, by the early thirties, he has established himself, his world is no longer experienced as a mere extension of his personal Self. His world has become more differentiated, and his creations have assumed a reality in their own right, a reality that has to be respected for its own sake. His hardware store is there, his home is there, his wife and children are there. Although these realities are still part of his own world, they are so in a different way. They are no longer mere extensions of his own Self, but realities that have their own independent nature, their own laws, their own needs, their own demands. After having brought them into existence, he has to accept them as added responsibilities. He considers it his objective duty to care for them, regardless of his personal feelings, regardless of the work, the boredom, or pain it might involve.

With this change of emphasis, the more exploratory stage of late adolescence ends, and a more selective stage of the adult personality begins. Again, the boundaries between these stages are fluid, rather than sharply fixed. Yet, the goals and duties of the adult personality become more specific, more definite, and, therefore, more limited (L. finis—limit). This is also a necessary condition for the achievement of the goals of the first half of life. In short, the period of the adult personality is the period of organization, of stabilization and consolidation of life. It is a period of great productivity, of achievement and action.

In fact, many are so entirely absorbed in their work, and so eager to be in perfect control of things, that they emphasize their controlling will and calculative reason of the functional level at the expense of the cultivation of their personal world. As Jung writes, "We wholly overlook the essential fact that the achievements which society rewards are won at the cost of a diminution of personality. Many—far too many—aspects of life which should have been experienced lie in the lumber-room among dusty memories." (115, 119) Among these often-forgotten aspects of life are beauty, wonder, intimacy, tenderness, celebration, religion, and whatever belongs to the world of the true Self. John Gardner puts it succinctly where he states that "By middle life most of us are accomplished fugitives from ourselves." (62, 13)

Indeed, most people are so absorbed in the building of their surrounding world at this stage, that they become alienated from their own Self and from the building of their own personal world. Preoccupied by their own eagerness, by economic necessities, and society's demands to climb the heights of success, status, affluence, and power, they find that personal values frequently become casualties on the road. It seems that the increase of success, security, and comfort is directly proportional to the decrease of meaning, self-understanding, and personal happiness. The adult personality is at the peak of his achievement, yet he feels that everything has become routine. He is in perfect control of things, yet he finds that nothing makes any sense. He is about to fulfill the goals of his life, yet he begins to ask himself questions such as, "Is this all?" or "What is life all about?" When this happens, a new crisis has already announced itself.

THE SYNDROME OF THE MID-LIFE CRISIS

This new crisis is "the crisis of the limits" (roughly for women from 35–40, and for men from 40–45). In recent years certain symptoms of depression in middle-aged men and women have come to be recognized. Although people go through this stage of restlessness, frustration, and anxiety with varying degrees of intensity, this experience is quite common and normal. It should be obvious, however, from looking at the chronological ages, that one is not dealing here with the climacteric in men or the menopause in women. The crisis of the limits usually occurs long before these physiological changes take place (approximately at the age of 50).

At the beginning of this century, the menopausal problems occurred closer to the age of 40, and often coincided with the crisis of the limits. As a result, the "middle-age blues" were generally attributed to the menopause, and were not expected to occur in middle-aged men. It was nearly impossible, indeed, to realize that similar symptoms such as restlessness, anxiety, and depression could originate from radically different causes. This is one reason why it has taken so long to discover the crisis of the limits. Another reason is the static nature of the traditional conception of maturity in terms of perfect adjustment. To admit the occurrence of a developmental crisis at this age would have been tantamount to the acknowledgment of one's failure to grow up. It would also painfully impel the adult personality to re-evaluate his entire life, and to begin all over precisely at an age when he was on the verge of getting it all together.

Furthermore, the technocratic society does not exactly promote an interest in the crisis of the limits; its calculative thinking fails altogether to understand the meaning of this crisis. And its youth- and work-oriented mentality fails to reward any attempt to reflect on the deeper meaning of life. "Its prizes are always given for achievement and not for personality." (115, 118) And, finally, there is another interesting reason why it took so long to discover the crisis of the limits. Until recently, too few people even lived long enough to make the middle-age blues a serious problem for society to cope with. For, at the beginning of this century, the average life expectancy in the United States was approximately forty-five years. As a result, only 10 per cent of the population was in the middle-age bracket, a percentage so small that it could easily be neglected by the psychologists, who were then preoccupied with the discovery of adolescence.

The crisis of the limits is first and foremost an existential crisis in the birth-process of Being in man. "We are dealing here," says Oger, "with a crisis which is existential rather than merely physiological or psychological." (163, 20) Just as the crisis of adolescence is the existential transition from the world of the child to the world of the adult personality, so the crisis of the limits is the existential transition from the world of the adult personality to the world of the mature personality. It is the transition from the goals of the first half of life to those of the second half. The crisis of the limits is just as healthy and normal as the crisis of adolescence, and one should add, just as difficult. In fact, it *is* adolescence (*adolescere*—to grow into maturity), but on a higher level of Being.

In order to understand the fundamental meaning of this crisis as the fourth existential crisis in the birth-process of Being in man (after birth, the crisis of autonomy, and adolescence), I will give a brief phenomenological description of its symptoms. However, a mere listing of symptoms does not elucidate the fundamental meaning of the crisis until one coordinates the seemingly insignificant data in the primordial luminosity of the Being-process. And it is not until one has arrived at an existential understanding of its syndrome, that the outcome of the crisis of the limits can be evaluated. The basic questions, therefore, are: "What are some of the characteristic manifestations of this crisis?"; "What is the true meaning of this crisis?"; and "How can we overcome the crisis of the limits?"

There are certain physical changes occurring during this period that are so minor that they would remain largely unnoticed if it were not for their symbolic value. For instance, the first gray hairs may cause a sudden feeling of depression. One pictures oneself "sans teeth, sans eyes, sans taste, sans everything" (Shakespeare). Among men of this age, there is a gradual growth of stiff hair in the nose and the ears; women often experience an increase in growth of hair on the upper lip and chin. In both men and women, the skin begins to show some wrinkles; both become far-sighted and need glasses; both begin to gain weight in the area of the waistline. Both receive warnings from their doctors of the dangers of being overweight, and are advised to be moderate with respect to food, drinks, and exercise. They have a tendency to fatigue more easily precisely at an age when their duties and responsibilities, and the pressure to perform on the job, are at their peak. Although these physical changes taken singly are usually not too serious, their cumulative effect may give a sense of limitation and urgency to one's whole existence. What was a playful experimentation in late adolescence, and a duty for the adult personality, becomes a burden during the crisis of the limits.

But, more importantly, the physical changes tend to reinforce the psychological and existential changes taking place during this period. Life is at an intersection of past and future. On the basis of past experience, one is less optimistic about the future. "What have I really accomplished?" "What has happened to my great adolescent ideals?" "Was my life really worth living?" "Where have I been; where am I going?" One has experienced what it takes to accomplish anything worthwhile. "Who knows how long I will still be around?" "I may have my last chance to make it big, or to do something worthwhile in this world. But then I must hurry! I must do it now." Such are the musings of the mid-lifer.

Life, which promised so much in earlier years, has been profoundly disappointing; one is disillusioned. And this is certainly not because of a lack of success in life. For it is precisely when one has achieved success, status, affluence, and power that one asks, "Is this all?" It is precisely at the peak of achievement, that one discovers that all values are open to question, and that one asks, "What is the use?" It is precisely when one has acquired everything, that one feels unfulfilled, incomplete, and depressed. "By the age of forty," says Oger, "man becomes worried. He realizes that despite his efforts he has not accomplished the goal of his life." (163, 19) And, in the light of Jung's "two goals of life," this is true of course. For, according to Jung, the goals of the first half of life are the goals of nature, such as entrenchment in the outer world, professional achievement, procreation, the care of children, acquisition of wealth and social status. The goal of the second half of life is culture, by which he means personal fulfillment, spiritual life, or cosmic participation. (115, 126) It seems that in the process of achieving success, one has lost precisely those values that make success worth achieving.

During this mid-life crisis, one not only sees the goals of a lifetime crumble, one also experiences life itself as a dull and unpromising routine. Life has lost its novelty, its freshness, its fascination, and the future holds no surprises any more. One knows what the future will bring: "More of the same." By now one has gone through just about everything: work, struggle for life, love, indifference, misunderstandings, human encounters, etc. One knows how there is always much ado about nothing, and how important issues are often ignored. One knows how human beings behave, how conflicts arise, how human relations develop, how people try to play the roles they are expected to play. Things begin to repeat themselves, and the uniformity of life becomes boring, meaningless, and disgusting. The young man who started his hardware store full of playful experimentation succeeded very well, and founded two additional branches. Between thirty and forty, he began to experience the management of these stores as a serious responsibility, or even as a painful duty. At about forty, however, he may feel positively burdened by a business which demands more time and energy than he has, and keeps him from being himself and from really enjoying his own life. What is the use of managing three stores, when only one store would suffice to provide a comfortable income? What is the use of facing a future that promises absolutely nothing, but the same killing routine of selling more hammers and nails?

Moreover, by the time man arrives at this critical turning point in mid-life, experience has taught him some other limitations. Precisely when he is at the peak of power and achievement, and feels "in perfect control of things," he discovers the ultimate inefficacy of all his controls. There are in life events and phenomena that break in upon the mechanical course of events created by man's will to control, and that withstand any attempt on man's part to be in perfect control of things. Among these phenomena are birth and the lifelong drive towards self-actualization, death, sickness, accidents of every sort, existential boredom, the meaning of life as a whole, getting involved in conflicts and misunderstandings, the letting go of children, the struggle against decline and decay, love, anxiety, existential crises, the precariousness of human existence, etc.

During late adolescence, man sets out to build his world, to achieve success, status, wealth, power, and security, thinking that this will lead him to the promised land. But when he reaches the mid-thirties or forties, he discovers the failure of his achievements as a whole, despite their partial triumphs. The recognition of the ultimate inefficacy of all his achievements, coupled with the fact that he finds himself in a predicament with "no exit," disenchants him of all idealistic expectations. He is disillusioned with life as a whole. A profound disgust assails him (the classical *taedium vitae*), and he begins to despair over the meaning of life. All his achievements together do not even begin to answer the disturbing questions: "Who am I?" "Where am I going?" "What does life mean?" Possessing the whole world does not enable man to save himself. He experiences the radical limitedness of human life, and feels frustrated, useless, and inadequate. As a late adolescent, he embarked on a career with boundless energy, planning to change the entire world. But his work has brought him nowhere. When the middle-age crisis hits, he cannot even change the meaninglessness of his inner world. Life has come to a dead end.

Yet, change is what is desperately wanted. Life seems more promising elsewhere, but man doesn't know where that "elsewhere" is. He seeks answers through change. He is not getting anywhere here. Here he is in a rut. He has to get out of "here." But when he gets "there," he discovers to his dismay that it is just another "here," only elsewhere. He discovers that any achievement, any occupation, any person, any human relationship can become routinized and boring. This crisis is an all-pervasive thing; it affects all human activities and all human relationships. No matter what man does, where he goes, or whom he meets, it seems that life itself chokes him to death. Or, at least, its very meaning seems to elude him.

Being already closer to death than to birth, with no future to look forward to, man begins to experience life as a sort of living death. The enthusiastic involvements of earlier years are replaced by the empty experience of being not-yet-dead. He begins to realize that time-for-living is not forever. Moreover "time flies," although nothing really "happens." Birthdays begin to cause depression; autumns bring nostalgia. Man becomes painfully aware of the radical finitude of the human condition. He realizes that he is mortal and that life is no longer limitless. It was Romano Guardini who first gave this existential crisis the appropriate name of "crisis of the limits." (75) Jung called it the "turning point of life" *(Lebenswende);* Hurlock referred to it as the period of "self-evaluation"; Waterink named it "the manic-depressive period."

The intensity of the experience of the crisis of the limits varies greatly, and ranges all the way from moments of mild depression to suicidal tendencies. Many of the factors that modify the onset of adolescence, also influence the beginning and the quality of the crisis of the limits. For instance, women usually begin earlier than men. "Statistical tables," says Jung, "show a rise in the frequency of cases of mental depression in men about forty. In women the neurotic difficulties generally begin somewhat earlier." (115, 120) And, as Jung points out, the fact that a person's parents are still alive may delay the crisis, just as the death of a parent may trigger the sudden onset of the crisis of the limits. And, then, he adds "We see that in this phase of life—between thirty-five and forty—a significant change in the human psyche is in preparation." (115, 120) Although the existential experience of the crisis of the limits is basically the same for men and women, there are, of course, some differences due both to the polarity between the male and female psyche, and to the respective roles they are expected to play.

At about forty, a *man* meets his noon-day devil. "Everything suddenly comes under question: his professional life, his relations to his fellow men, his sexual life." (45, 7) He finds a few gray hairs, magnifies these incipient signs of old age, and realizes suddenly that he is not going to be the president of his company. He may refuse to accept his limitations, ignore his doctor's advice to slow down, and make a tremendous effort to carry on. He still attempts to climb to the top of his corporation, while at the same time competing with teen-agers in sports. Thus he strives to show that he can still "take it." Sooner or later, of course, it catches up with him. He may suffer a nervous breakdown, a stroke, or a heart attack, which is the greatest source of death for men between the ages of 35 and 60.

Another frequent reaction is that the man becomes extremely depressed by the discovery of his own limitations. He begins to suffer from fatigue, insomnia, and loss of appetite. He becomes irritable, anxious, and restless. He may even fear impending insanity and attempt to commit suicide. It is not uncommon for a psychiatrist to hear a man of forty complain about these symptoms. And it is not uncommon for the psychiatrist to be puzzled. For, on the one hand, the man is wealthy, he has a wonderful wife, lovely children, and owns a beautiful home. And, on the other hand, there are no indications of any physical or mental illness whatsoever.

The problems of this man, who is already emotionally drained from the mid-life crisis syndrome, are further compounded by younger men pushing him from lower positions. The younger generation becomes a threat to him, particularly in a youth-oriented society. The younger generation has more stamina, newer methods and techniques, and a much longer future. The middle-aged man feels pressured, realizes that his professional efficiency is decreasing, and may begin to worry about his job security. The new generation is moving up, while his own productivity and creativity are declining. He realizes that he is not indispensable. All this gives him periodic bouts of depression and makes him lose his self-confidence. According to Deeken, "these are the first external signs of the advancing crisis of aging. Interiorly, the chill is felt more deeply: 'Life goes on! Is it possible that someday I will be no longer needed?' " (45, 7–8)

And as if all this were not enough, the middle-aged man's sexual life also comes under question. When he hits the mid-life crisis, he begins to worry about his waning sexuality and is afraid that impotence is part of his getting older. This fear is still aggravated by other factors. It is through his masculinity that the man feels secure and in control of things. When his masculinity is threatened, his control and security are threatened. He discovers that there is no device that can control his being in control; he discovers the radical precariousness of his very existence. This is why his nagging fear of waning potency is an important factor in the growing awareness of his existential limitations. His alarm over this is magnified, since contemporary men have been conditioned by a technocratic society to worship depersonalized sexuality, to be preoccupied with sexual techniques and performance, and "to become machines even in bed." (152, 54) All this is reinforced by the fact that the mid-lifer's personal values have atrophied. In terms of sexuality, this means a decline of tenderness, of personal love, of intimacy, of feeling, and of sensitivity. His sexual life, too, has become a routine, a dutiful performance for his wife, or even a burden filled with anxiety about impotence. Here, too, he looks for a solution through change. Fearing that the tide of life may ebb, or trying to convince himself that his fears are groundless, he wants to take a last fling at new experiences while there is still time. This is why men at this age are apt to go astray.

The *woman*, on the other hand, because she can have at least physical intercourse regardless of her orgastic abilities, is not threatened in terms of sexual performance. In fact, at around the age of 35, her sexual desires are at their peak. But in the woman it is rather through her sexual attractiveness and feminine charms that she has a hold on the world. It is precisely during the crisis of the limits that she becomes aware that her physical presence no longer holds the same attraction, and that the bloom of her youth is fading. She is afraid that the gradual loss of her charms may drive her husband into the arms of a younger, more beautiful woman. "People," says Alfons Deeken, "may still value her abilities, her professional success and her good reputation, but this will appear to her as little more than a retirement pension." (45, 7) The woman may begin to suffer from insomnia, and become moody and restless. And, as Deeken beautifully puts it, "the mornings are losing the charm of newness, the noondays bring monotony, and the long evenings and nights are spent in loneliness." (45, 7)

Suddenly she may find herself without her children, without closeness to her husband, without a mission in life, without a future. And, yet, she still has about one half of her life to live. As Simone de Beauvoir puts it: "it seems to her that there will be nothing more for her to do than merely survive her better days; her body will promise nothing; the dreams, the longings she has not made good, will remain forever unfulfilled. . . . she is appalled at the narrow limitations life has imposed upon her." (43, 543) She may become acutely aware of the fact that she has been loved and appreciated for her functional services, rather than for who she is as a woman and as a person. She feels hurt, left alone, unloved, and unappreciated. "She makes," says de Beauvoir, "the discovery that her husband, her environment, her occupations were unworthy of her; she feels that she has not been appreciated." (43, 543)

Just as the man, so also the woman begins to look for a solution through change. Yet, it seems that she is doomed to face a future without meaning, a prey to loneliness, nostalgia, and boredom. She finds her freedom at a time when she is unable to make use of it, when time has become her enemy. This is why she feels doomed to spend her long future "killing time." To be sure, particular changes, particular objectives, particular involvements may temporarily relieve her boredom. But they fail to extend her influence on the world, to give meaning and fulfillment to her life, or even to justify her very existence. In fact, her partial successes may even seem to accentuate the uselessness of her personal life as a whole.

There is a great variety of ways in which the woman—just as the man —attempts to solve her mid-life crisis through change. For instance, the housewife may try to become a career woman, whereas the career woman may contemplate a second career. Unfortunately, women are often handicapped by the fact that "among a great part of our generation there is still the feeling that men *must* work in order to be 'real persons' and that women *may* work in order to 'keep busy.'" (137, 235)

De Beauvoir, in her book *The Second Sex,* presents us with an exhaustive picture of possible changes in the lives of women in their mid-life crisis. First of all, she often tries desperately to turn the clock back. For instance, she may take refuge in cosmetics, skin treatments, or plastic surgery. She may begin to keep an intimate diary and to dream of what might have been. If she is the "maternal type," she may attempt to have another child. If she is the "sensual woman," she may "endeavor to ensnare one more lover." If she is the "coquette," she will attempt everything to please the other sex. She begins to dress young, and may assume childish airs. The woman in her mid-life crisis may "try to realize all her wishes of childhood and adolescence before it is too late: she may go back to her piano, take up sculpture, writing, travel, she may learn skiing or study foreign languages." Erotic fantasies or a mystical dream-life may become forms of escape for her. Knitting has always been a customary way for the middle-aged woman to "kill time." But "its importance is trifling"—"the woman sadly weaves the very nothingness of her days." (43, 543–58)

The syndrome of the crisis of the limits presents a depressing picture of the middle-aged man and woman. Although its symptoms are experienced with a great variety in quality and intensity, there is something here for everyone to identify with. The symptoms of this mid-life crisis seem to indicate both that the beginning of the end of life has arrived, and that life itself has been a total failure. The mid-lifer sees the whole meaning of his world collapse, and begins to wonder if life is not ultimately "a tale told by an idiot."

The analogy between the crisis of the limits and the negative stage of adolescence is conspicuous. In both crises, life has become a meaningless repetition, a boring routine, an empty world. Both crises are characterized by boredom, restlessness, anxiety, and a desperate search for meaning and self-identity. Yet, whereas the negative stage occurs before the person has found his self-identity, the crisis of the limits takes place after he has established himself as an adult personality.

THE MEANING OF THE CRISIS OF THE LIMITS

As I have said, one understands the fundamental significance of an existential crisis when, within the perspective of existential thinking, one understands its place in the birth-process of Being a man. And it is only then that its characteristic phenomena or symptoms reveal their full significance as interdependent manifestations of the total configuration. In the previous chapter, I have shown that the negative stage of adolescence discovers the no-thing-ness of primordial Being without discovering Being itself. The negative stage is a limit-situation, and reveals the fundamental limits of any and all particular things, indicating that there is something more fundamental, without revealing as yet what that something more fundamental actually is. And since the symptoms of the crisis of the limits are remarkably similar to those of the negative stage, except that they occur on a higher stage of development, one wonders if the crisis of the limits is not also a limit-situation, but on a higher level of ex-sistence.

That, indeed, this is the case will become apparent from a philosophical reflection on this mid-life crisis. Despite the similarity of their negative features, the crisis of the limits and the negative stage of adolescence are ultimately not the same thing. For by the time the person arrives at his mid-life crisis, he already has transcended the negative stage; he already has found his personal Self-identity and established himself as an adult personality on all three levels of ex-sistence. If, therefore, the crisis of the limits is another limit-situation, but on a higher level, it can only mean that it reveals the fundamental limits of the adult personality, indicating thereby that there is something more fundamental. But how is that possible? How can there be anything beyond the full humanness of the adult personality? How can there be anything more fundamental than the three levels of human ex-sistence?

The foregoing reflections on the essence of human ex-sistence provide an answer to these questions. Man is "more than he is" as an open relation to Being. As a participant in the inexhaustible concreteness of the birth-process of Being, man cannot be encapsuled in a merely logical definition. These insights enable one to understand the crisis of the limits as a more fundamental limit-situation. Whereas the negative stage of adolescence revealed the no-thing-ness of the person (Being), the crisis of the limits reveals the not-mere-humanness of man. Philosophically, this means that an existential crisis occurs, a change in the level of Being, a transition from immanent integration in the world of adults to transcendent integration in the world of Being. The crisis of the limits constitutes the transition from the goals of the first half of life to those of the second half, from the adult personality to the mature personality.

The fundamental significance of the crisis of the limits, therefore, is that man cannot fulfill himself in his mere humanness, but only in his original integrity with the whole of Being. In the crisis of the limits, man discovers the radical limitedness of being "merely human," and his inability to unfold himself into the fullness of his Being unless he allows primordial Being to take the initiative. After having established himself as an adult personality, he now has to permit primordial Being to establish him as a mature personality. Through the crisis of the limits, man begins to realize that having achieved all the goals of the first half of life, or even having gained the entire world would ultimately remain meaningless unless he transcends all this in a courageous resolve to open up to Being in a creative act of Self-surrender as "releasement" unto Being. (*Gelassenheit*—Heidegger)

But haven't I said earlier that early adolescence is characterized by its openness to Being? This is true. But the openness of early adolescence is potential rather than actual. It is the still unreflective, implicit, and undifferentiated phenomenon of primordial wonder. There is no differentiation yet between man and Being, immanence and transcendence, implicit and explicit. Moreover, once the Self and wonder began to differentiate, the movement was predominantly outward. In fact, achieving the goals of the first half of life, and establishing oneself as an adult personality, usually entail a diminution of personal values and an atrophy of the sense of wonder. In other words, it is not until the crisis of the limits that man is challenged to achieve the fullness of his authenticity, to differentiate and explicate primordial wonder itself, and to listen to the voice of differentiated Being *(logos)*. In order to accomplish this, however, he may have to retrieve the original phenomenon of wonder as experienced twenty years earlier, during the period of early adolescence. For the sense of wonder, if not lost altogether, has become at best a phenomenon of secondary importance in the life of the adult personality.

One is now prepared to com-prehend the characteristic phenomena of the crisis of the limits in their original unity, as structural manifestations of the birth of the differentiated Self-presentation of Being *(logos)* in man. Or, to put it differently, one is now able to diagnose the symptoms of the crisis of the limits as constituting the syndrome of an existential crisis, namely the existential "turning point" from the world of the adult personality to the world of the mature personality. This diagnosis will also reveal that the negative symptoms of the crisis of the limits are fundamentally neither negative nor pathological at all. They are, despite the appearance to the contrary, positive and healthy affirmations of the not-mere-humanness of the mature personality.

As long as the crisis of the limits is approached from the everyday or functional levels of existence, or, for that matter, out of the very experience of the early crisis itself, the phenomenon seems to be entirely meaningless. There is nothing positive, nothing that makes any sense. In the foregoing discussion, however, I have shown that the crisis of the limits is a limit-situation, a phenomenon that receives its intelligibility in the light of its own transcendence, that receives its meaning directly from the primordial luminosity of the differentiated self-manifestation of Being *(logos)*. It is impossible, therefore, to explain the crisis of the limits in terms of merely physiological or psychological causes. For "we are dealing here with an existential crisis rather than a merely psychological or physiological one." (Oger) And as an existential crisis, the crisis of the limits is an all-pervasive phenomenon that affects all man's relationships and his entire being-in-the-world. It is the shift from involvement in particular goals, functions, and concerns to a way of life of the ultimate concern. This shift is a totality experience in which the whole man-in-his-world is placed under question.

Since "man is infinitely more than he is" as a participant in articulated Being *(logos)*, nothing merely human can satisfy his ultimate hunger. The middle-aged personality has mis-taken merely human values for ultimate values. If achieving one particular goal or owning some private property leaves his ultimate hunger unsatisfied, so will achieving success, wealth, and prestige or even owning the entire world. The early crisis of the limits is a limit-situation which reveals the fundamental limits of anything merely human. In the light of differentiated Being *(logos)* which announces itself without revealing itself, the adult personality experiences that ultimately nothing merely human makes any sense, without understanding the "why" of this experience. Not yet realizing that his very crisis points to the need of transcending his present situation, he sees the goals of a lifetime crumble, feels that he is in a dull routine, and considers himself, despite his successful achievements, a total failure in life.

As a limit-situation, the crisis of the limits transcends somehow the world of the adult personality, the world of mere humanness. For man experiences limits only when he "transcends" that which he experiences as limited. The crisis of the limits somehow reveals man's participation in the whole of Being, albeit in the negative way of dissatisfaction with the non-ultimacy of anything merely human. Fundamentally speaking, therefore, the crisis of the limits is not negative at all. What appears to be a failure of life is really a significant step in the development of the mature personality. The crisis of the limits reverses the outward movement of the adult personality by announcing the need for interiorizing Self-transcendency characteristic of the mature personality. (The initiated reader will recognize here the interior dynamics of the so-called "reversal" [*die Kehre*] in Heidegger's thought.)

When the successful mid-lifer, who is about to fulfill all his goals of life, begins to ask himself questions such as "Is this all?" "What is the use?" "Was my life really worth living?" he is, despite the appearance to the contrary, not experiencing a negative, but rather a very positive phenomenon. His feelings of frustration, disappointment, and disillusionment are fundamentally not symptoms of failure or disease at all. On the contrary, they are rather healthy indications that a new phase of growth is emerging. Fundamentally speaking, this experience of the radical impotence of any and all merely human achievements announces the emergence of an ultimate hunger, and the need to transcend the world of the adult personality.

The negative stage of the crisis of the limits, however, is a limit-situation. In other words, the emergence of a new transcendence announces itself without revealing itself. Consequently, the mid-lifer cannot understand his predicament as a limit-situation, as a beginning transcendence, and even less as a phase in the birth-process of Being. The true meaning of what is happening to him escapes him altogether. He cannot understand that his experience of failure, disillusionment, and meaninglessness in life are ultimately indications that his particular concerns and goals of the first half of life can no longer satisfy the emerging hunger for a new goal: the way of life of the ultimate concern. He will mistake these basic signs of healthy growth for symptoms of a mental disease, or for morbid indications that he is "falling apart," or that his life has been an actual failure.

And, of course, he will at least for the time being react accordingly. He may withdraw from people and reality because he is different from normal adults or has concluded that his life is over anyway. He withdraws from life, either psychologically or by committing suicide, because "he isn't getting anywhere," because he has decided he is "dead already." Or he may reinforce his attempt to make it big before it is too late. He may try to work harder, to improve his achievements, and to make things bigger and better. Or, again, he may attempt to solve his problems through change. He has to get "out of here." He has to find himself another home, another occupation, another woman, or another environment. "Here" it is dark; the stars are brighter "elsewhere."

In the light of the foregoing elucidations of the meaning of the crisis of the limits, it should be clear that these reactions don't get him anywhere either. In the first place, total withdrawal obviously doesn't get anybody anywhere. But more interestingly, even "trying harder" for success, trying to make things bigger and better, gets him nowhere. For no amount of success will satisfy his ultimate hunger or allow him to live a way of life of the ultimate concern. As Walter Stace puts it, in *Time and Eternity*, "How do you attain your end by making things bigger, or longer, or wider, or more this or more that? For they will still be *this* or *that*. And it is being this or that which is the disease of things." (199, 5)

Similarly, no amount of change will get him anywhere, as long as this change is within the world of "this" or "that," or within the domain of the merely human. To quote Stace again,

There is in your life much darkness—that much you will admit. But you think that though this thing, this place, this time, this experience is dark, yet that thing, that place, that time, that experience is, or will be, bright. But this is the great illusion. You must see that all things, all places, all times, all experiences are equally dark. You must see that all stars are black. Only out of the *total* darkness will the light dawn. (199, 6)

This total darkness is the crisis of the limits out of which the light of personal maturity will dawn. Personal maturity is the ultimate hunger which no "here" or "there," no success, no status or affluence, no comfort, no power, and no possession can ever satisfy.

As long as the mid-lifer's thinking is still dominated by the merely human values and goals of the first half of life, he cannot understand himself and the meaning and why of his predicament. He will experience the initial precipitation into this crisis in a merely negative way, as a threat of disintegration and destruction of everything he values. The very foundations upon which his life is based begin to crumble. But he cannot yet understand that precisely this undergoing of corrosion may be a genuine phase in his coming to himself. He cannot yet understand that his very anxiety is growth-provoking by liberating him from the ultimacy of merely human values, and freeing him for his most authentic potentialities that constitute the goal of the second half of life. As long as he still keeps looking for particular explanations or solutions, he will find his predicament to be a totally unintelligible and dreadful enigma. As long as the light of the *logos* has not yet dawned, he mistakes what is essentially a promise of rebirth for an omen of total disintegration.

Whether he comes out of the mid-life crisis reborn and with renewed interest in life, or spends the rest of his life trying to work through it, depends very much on whether he accepts or refuses to accept the dawning revelation of the *logos*. As soon as he begins to accept the emerging luminosity of differentiated Being, he begins to open up to a way of life of the ultimate concern. He begins to understand that his crisis and its symptoms have a positive meaning as a phase in the birth-process of Being. He begins to realize that his experience of frustration is not a meaningless phenomenon, but rather a positive purification of the illusion of the ultimacy of particular values and goals. He no longer mistakes his anxiety for a pathological symptom, but he recognizes it as a dreadful call out of a silent and unknown distance announcing the promise of genuine freedom.

In the light of the emergence of his explicit Self-presence to the whole of Being, even his experience of restlessness begins to make sense. For as soon as the way of life of the ultimate concern begins to announce itself, he experiences the exigence of transcendence, and no particular concerns can give him rest any more. However, as long as the realm of the ultimate concern does not yet reveal itself in this limit-situation, he doesn't know where to turn. He simply is unable to dwell anywhere in peace. No space, no time, no work, and no function can give rest to his searching soul. Nothing can fulfill him; nothing can satisfy him or give him peace. He feels the exigence of transcendence; he needs change; he has to get out of "here." But as long as he still mistakes his exigence of vertical transcendence for the horizontal transcendence within the world of particular goals and concerns, he will get nowhere. For he will keep restlessly changing every "here" for a "there," which is only another "here" but elsewhere. It is not until he finds an elsewhere that transcends the opposition between any "here" and any "there," that he will get somewhere. Now, this transcending "elsewhere" is the world of the person, which as the Self-presence to the whole of Being transcends any opposition between "here" and "there," and is the ultimate source of every possible "here," "there," or "elsewhere."

THE BIRTH OF THE MATURE PERSONALITY

The discovery of the true meaning of the crisis of the limits is the moment when the mature personality is born. As soon as the mid-lifer realizes that he cannot get out of his crisis by going to an external "elsewhere," but only by advancing towards the inner "elsewhere" of his personal Self-presence to the whole of Being, a new level of personal fulfillment emerges. As soon as he discovers that he gets nowhere by merely changing jobs or places, but only by seeking change within himself, the crisis of the limits comes to an end. "Coming to an end" does not merely mean here "termination"; rather, it means to have reached the apex of life, the period of full maturity and of personal fulfillment. It is interesting to note that the word "maturity" does not connote the emptiness of an ending, but rather the fullness of a beginning. The word "maturity" is etymologically derived from the Latin *maturus* which means: ripe, timely, early (related to *mane*—early, in the morning). To be "mature" is to be "ripe," i.e., having arrived at such a stage of development as to be ready for reaping (akin to O.E. *ripan*, to reap), or having advanced to the point of being in the best, most perfected condition, being completely developed as a person. Now, it is precisely through the crisis of the limits that man begins to achieve his way of life of the ultimate concern, and to unfold himself into the fullness of his own Being. It is, therefore, essentially through the crisis of the limits that the "mature" personality comes into existence.

This period of life is full of dangers and pitfalls. Whether man comes out of the crisis of the limits reborn, or spends the rest of his life trying to work through it, depends very much on his ability and willingness to convert to a more fundamental and personal way of life. Unfortunately, many people are either unable or unwilling to respond in a positive way to their mid-life crisis. These people escape in defense mechanisms and often become fixated in them. These negative reactions are merely pseudo-solutions, for they have one thing in common: they prevent the actual birth of the mature personality.

A great number of people in their mid-life crisis simply close their eyes to the evident facts and stick to the goals of the first half of life. They pretend that nothing has changed. They fail to recognize that, as Eda LeShan puts it, "the wonder of the crisis of middle age" is that "its challenges are the greatest opportunity one has ever had to become most truly alive and oneself." (137, 12) They fail to slow down, to relax, to reflect upon their own situation, and to develop into their own depths. They simply try to stay young, to keep active, and to continue to "raise the standard of living." They close their eyes to the fact that merely giving increase to the same old standards of the first half of life is getting them nowhere. They refuse to see that wealth, power, security, and reputation are achieved "at the cost of a diminution of personality" (Jung), and that it is precisely the crisis of the limits which reveals the ultimate impotence of the merely economic standards. Consequently, they are unable to arrive at the true solution of this mid-life crisis, which consists in "raising the standard of living" to a new level of ex-sistence, namely the level of the cosmic standard of man's Self-presence to the whole of Being.

There is, of course, a great variety of ways in which the mid-lifers may attempt to evade the real challenge of the crisis of the limits through pseudo-solutions. Some try desperately to turn back the clock. "They cling to youth as a caterpillar anxiously clings to a branch, refusing to become a butterfly that might swing itself into the new freedom of flight." (45, 11) They try to stay young forever by dressing young and acting young in ways that often border on the ridiculous. They would rather die than look their age. Others, to use the same simile, may prefer to remain within the protective covering of the cocoon rather than swinging themselves into the new freedom of flight. They want to remain within the protective security of wealth, power, and social acceptance, the standard of living of the first half of life. They want to stick to the schemes of thought and action of the preceding period, and gradually become fixated in a superficial life of comfort and security, or in the spiritual insignificance of the "rocking chair" philosophy.

Others, again, are unable to solve the crisis of the limits because they remain fixated in a chronic state of depression for the rest of their lives. They may turn grouchy, bitter, and resentful. They begrudge the young their joyful vitality. Their resentment against the young turns into a destructive attitude. "When I was young, we didn't do things like that." "The younger generation is good for nothing." Their well-known symbol, of course, is the old witch of the fairy tales who enjoys burning children to death in the oven. Some seek refuge from their depression in destructive scepticism, biting sarcasm, or bitter and unhealthy self-irony. Others, on the contrary, try to escape from their existential frustrations in a fake optimism, in the pretense of eternal youthfulness, or in a deliberate attempt to get doped so as to shut out the future. Theirs is the Epicurean *carpe diem* philosophy: "let us live it up today with wine, women, and songs, for there may not be a tomorrow to enjoy." And, finally, there are those who attempt to escape through busy work, hobbies, or continual change. Insofar, however, as these activities restrict themselves to particular concerns and to the goals of the first half of life, they prevent the mid-lifers from opening up to the whole of Being and the way of life of the ultimate concern. They may provide them with some temporary solace, but ultimately they get them nowhere. Instead of solving the crisis of the limits, these pseudo-solutions rather intensify and perpetuate the restlessness, the frustration, the anxiety, and depression that are so characteristic of this period of life.

The healthy outcome of this crisis is, of course, the birth of the mature personality. The middle-aged person begins to emerge from his mid-life crisis as soon as he experiences and accepts his participation in the whole of Being, and lets go of what was proper only to the first half of life. Instead of taking refuge in various escape mechanisms and pseudo-solutions, he begins to take an honest look at himself, his life, and his predicament.

On the one hand, this can be sobering. He may have to accept that he will never be the president of his corporation, that he will never be a wealthy landowner, or a winner of the Nobel Prize. He realizes that becoming human always means: becoming limited. He will have to accept that he is limited as a human being because of his sex, his heredity, his profession, his surroundings, and the very finitude of his existence. He is confined to a life of only a few decades on an infinitesimal speck in the universe, and his inevitable end is death. Yet, on the other hand, he begins to realize that by freely and consciously accepting these limits, he transcends them and becomes free in a much deeper and more comprehensive sense than ever before. For the acceptance of his limits removes any possible stagnation of the Self, and allows him to transcend his mere humanness into an all-encompassing presence to the whole of Being, and to experience this presence as both a mystery and a gift.

Instead of running away from himself and his problems, the mature personality realizes that the time has come to stop running, to slow down, to reflect on his situation, and to start developing his own depths. He gradually begins to open up to the emergence of a wonderful world of unexpected meaning and fulfillment. He becomes gratefully aware of his emerging participation in the whole of Being, and begins to experience this "cosmic participation" (Jung) and his very own existence within it as a wonder-ful gift.

One is here in the context of the birth-process of Being, where all causal interpretations are a mistake. One is dealing here with an unmotivated upsurge of a world of inspiration, and no one can control or predict its emergence. It always takes one by surprise. It cannot be caused or explained in terms of lower levels ("the principle of emergence"). The cosmic luminosity of Being begins to dawn out of the dark night of the crisis of the limits, and man responds with the faith that is total surrender to the trustworthiness of this cosmic revelation. This response arises from the very depths of his being, where he opens up to meaning and Being far beyond himself.

Here man achieves authentic Self-identity by his courageous resolve to open up to the whole of Being and to allow himself to be led by its cosmic luminosity in which he begins to participate. It is only through the creative act of Self-surrender *(Gelassenheit)* to the differentiated totality of Being that the crisis of the limits can be brought to a healthy solution. LeShan sums it up by saying that the middle-age crisis "can offer the greatest risks of all, but if you have the courage to take the necessary leap into faith, the adventure can be the most important and wonderful one that you can ever experience." (137, 22)

This positive solution can only be arrived at very gradually. In fact, this conversion from an anthropocentric (man-centered) into an onto-centric (Being-centered) way of Being-in-the-world is such a radical transformation that it takes the rest of one's life to accomplish it. The gradual achievement of an ontocentric World is the developmental task of the mature personality. Or, to put this in the terminology of Jung, the goal of the second half of life is "culture," in the sense of personal fulfillment, cosmic participation, or the cultivation of non-utilitarian values.

It is not until the mature personality emerges from the crisis of the limits that he is fully born into the essence of his ex-sistence, namely into his cosmic participation in the birth-process of Being. Whereas his life expectancy has diminished in the chronological sense, it has increased in the existential sense of anticipatory awareness of personal fulfillment. The mature personality expects less from life quantitatively, but more qualitatively. He experiences his life as a process of birth and growth into hitherto unknown dimensions.

But is one not hereby denying the importance of "the formative years"? The answer is that one is not in the least underestimating the importance of "the formative years," but that one is simply extending their duration to the entire course of human life. Growing is not the prerogative of childhood. "The impact of psychoanalysis," says Le-Shan, "with its explorations and insights into 'the formative years,' has tended to distort our vision, to lead us down the primrose path of absolute determinism." (137, 15) The childhood years determine only what is more or less "deterministic" in human life, namely the fixed behavior patterns of "character" and the fixated behavior patterns of "illness." Yet, it is the mature personality who discovers his true Self-identity as a participant in the birth-process of Being. It is not until this stage that his birth-process is fully born, and that his way of growing is full-grown. The developmental task of the mature personality is the achievement of an ontocentric World, and this task is even more dynamic, more comprehensive, and more meaningful than any tasks of his earlier development.

7

THE MATURE PERSONALITY: 1

The fundamental reflections on the crisis of the limits have made it abundantly clear that man does not achieve mature identity and final integration at the termination of adolescence, as is generally believed. Personal maturity is never an accomplished fact or a state of being that can be captured once and for all and retained as a permanent possession. On the contrary, personal maturity, as it emerges from the crisis of the limits, is not a thing but a happening, a coming-to-pass that dynamically continues, an occurrence which is always in the process of being achieved.

The mature personality emerges when the cosmic luminosity of Being begins to dawn out of the dark night of the crisis of the limits, and man responds with total surrender to its dialectical manifestation. Only by being "more than he is," only as a participant in the event of the *logos* does man fulfill his essential potentialities, actualize his authentic ex-sistence and achieve his personal maturity. This is also why the mature personality is fundamentally a unitary phenomenon that can only be studied in the cosmic context of the whole of Being.

FINAL INTEGRATION IN THE MATURE PERSONALITY

Every time man passes through an existential crisis, the ultimacy of his former world disintegrates, and a creative re-integration of his former ex-sistence into a higher world of being begins to take place. When the mid-lifer emerges from the crisis of the limits, his anthropo-centric world disintegrates, and a final re-integration into the ontocentric world becomes the developmental task of his mature personality.

Through this final process of re-integration, the mature personality achieves his Self-presence to the cosmic unity of all that is, and, thereby, the mature integration of his own personal ex-sistence. For, being more than he is, it is only from and in his presence to the all-encompassing unity of Being, that the mature personality first returns to his Self-presence for the fulfillment of his authentic potentialities. This entails that the self-assertion of the mature personality is never a rigid and aggressive insistence on his own importance and wishes, but rather a surrender to the transcending originality of the source of his own being.

The nature of the mature personality defies any attempt to give a strictly logical definition of it. For a logical definition expresses the static essence of a thing by fixing its limits, by setting it down in the closed boundaries of its proximate genus and specific difference or of the sum total of all its predicates.

Unlike the logical definition, however, the philosophical definition does not draw boundary lines that terminate all further discussion and become dead-ends on the way to the truth. On the contrary, the *logos,* as the differentiated self-manifestation of primordial wonder, sets all beings apart in their primordial unity of Being. And by setting all beings apart in this primordial horizon of fundamental meaning, the *logos* allows these beings to essentiate, i.e. to be (*esse*—to be) what they truly are, to present their essences as dynamic pre-sences, or to de-fine themselves within the proper limits (*finis*) of their own finality (*finis*) towards Being. Philosophical defining means "giving horizon to something," rather than merely "delimiting" (Gr. *horizoo*—to define). Philosophically defined essences are never static, definite, or abstract. They are not boundaries, but beacons. They are not dead-ends on the way to Being, but rather thought- and growth-provoking phenomena. Moreover, since each philosophical phenomenon gathers in its own way the totality of all that is, no philosophical essence can be defined in its isolation. Each philosophical essence is a part-whole and, in a sense, re-defines the whole of philosophy. In other words, philosophy as *logos*-thinking is basically the ever growing self-definition of its own essence.

It is impossible to define the mature personality unless one grasps the human person as a whole and understands his fundamental integration in the cosmic context of his meaningful relationships to the whole of Being. This is why it is just as impossible to define the mature personality in terms of one simple characteristic, as it is to define him in terms of a list of unrelated criteria. A structural characteristic of the mature personality is not a quality or property adhering to a static substance, but an authentic mode of Being-in-the-world, a differentiated manifestation of the *logos.* As differentiated self-manifestations of *Being*-in-the-world, the structural characteristics of the mature personality are interdependent, overlapping, and interchangeable. The com-prehension (grasping-together) of the *logos* con-stitutes (puts together) the unique nature of the maturity syn-drome (Gr. *syn* and *dramein*—to run together).

This unique and dynamic togetherness of the characteristics of the mature personality is itself a fundamental characteristic of maturity. It is the final process of integration which sets all characteristics apart in their primordial unity of Being and constitutes the ever growing self-definition of the mature personality. The primordial togetherness of the maturity syndrome allows the unitary but structured phenomenon of the mature personality to be what it truly is, to present its essence in the dynamic presence of Being. In the light of the logos, the mature personality is one who orchestrates his entire ex-sistence within the cosmic context of differentiated Being. This definition of the mature personality coincides, as is to be expected, with the definition given earlier of the authentic personality as the person who allows the workaday world of his subject-process *(ego)* to enter into an experiential dialogue with the cosmic World of the Being-process (Self). In short, the final integration in the mature personality is his mysterious, dynamic, concrete, and open-ended Self-definition in process.

Final integration is not a characteristic among other characteristics, but the fundamental and all-encompassing characteristic that ascertains the maturity of a personality as a whole, and of the particular characteristics in the light of the whole. Here is the single over-all criterion of maturity, which eludes all fragmentary thinking. However, I shall delay discussion of this over-all criterion until the following chapter; what is the main concern here is to understand the final integration of the mature personality as his Self-definition in the light of the *logos,* to understand the mature personality as a whole.

The findings thus far have provided some basic insights into the nature and structure of personal maturity. What is characteristic of mature integration is characteristic of the integral maturity of a personality. Mature integration is not a quality or property of a person, but rather his authentic Being-with-others-in-the-world. Mature integration is not a state of being, but a dynamic process; it is not an accomplished fact, but a developmental task; it is not a static schematism, but rather a permanent adventure. Mature integration is not being "organized to death," but being the origin of authentic life; it is not the end of growing, but rather the full-grown way of growing. Mature integration is never an established reality that can be captured once and for all and retained as a permanent possession, but an inexhaustible happening, an occurrence which is always in the process of being achieved.

Mature integration does not organize the personality into the fixity of a perfectly adjusted world, but it orchestrates his life into the existential harmony of creative conflicts. Mature integration, finally, is not an attempt to get things under control, but rather a response to the primordial gift of the *logos,* and an attempt to let beings become what they are, by allowing them to share in this primordial gift of Being.

In short, personal maturity as a whole is an authentic way of Being-in-the-world, a creative integration, a developmental task, and a response to a primordial gift. But if maturity is an unending process that never reaches its ultimate goal, then nobody can achieve full maturity; nobody can successfully terminate his search for self-identity; nobody can ever find a final answer to the question, "Who am I?"

Does one have to conclude from the foregoing that true maturity is essentially unattainable, and that one cannot call a person mature at any stage of his existence? Of course not. Only those who fail to see the rootedness of personal maturity in the inexhaustible dynamism of primordial Being fail to understand it as a process, much less as a never-ending process. This, for example, is the position of Robert Nixon in the "Conclusion" of his otherwise thought-provoking book, *The Art of Growing.* Some people, he says, "speak of an endless process of maturing: one is forever approaching or moving in the direction of maturity, but the goal is never reached. For these people there is a *process* of psychological maturation, but no such thing as a *state* of psychological maturity." (162, 139)

Nixon still sees life after adolescence too much as one long plateau. He is aware of the road to maturity, but not of the road of maturity. He still bases his argument on the unexamined conception of the person as an unchanging *ego,* which holds together the changing experiences throughout the continuity of life. "The psychologically mature person," he says, "knows who he is at twenty-five, he knows who he is at forty-five, and he still knows who he is at seventy-five. He has a sense of sameness, of continuity, of basic identity, which remains constant despite the passage of time, the variety of experience, the growing accumulation of wisdom." (162, 141) In short, by approximately twenty-five, a person is mature when he has established his *ego* as an unchanging "I-substance" underlying changing properties, or as a permanent core that holds together the varying experiences of life.

Earlier, I rejected this unexamined common sense conception of self-identity in terms of a self-evident, static *ego*-substance. The *ego* is not a static entity, but a subject-process. And, what is more, the ordinary conception of personal self-identity fails to differentiate between

the *ego* and the Self. As a result, it accounts for the unifying permanency of the *ego* in terms of an *ego*-thing that has "a sense of sameness,
of continuity, of basic identity which remains constant despite . . . the
variety of experience." In other words, the sameness, permanence, and
constancy of mature self-identity are based on the thing-like nature of
a state of being. There can be a process of maturation, but only a state
of maturity.

As contrasted with this static view, I have shown maturity to be a
coming-to-pass that dynamically continues, an occurrence which is
always in the process of being achieved. The unifying permanency of
personal maturity is not based on a thing-like state of being, but on the
very nature of the authentic Self as a participant in the cosmic process
of Being. The unifying permanence of the mature Self is rooted in the
emergence and abiding of primordial Being as the process that sets all
things apart in their original one-ness. And this is precisely the process
of final integration which characterizes the mature personality as a
whole. One agrees, of course, with Nixon, that the unifying permanence
of maturity can be won. (162, 142) It can be won, however, not as a
state of being, but as an enduring process of final integration. It can be
won not at twenty-five, but whenever the person emerges from the crisis
of the limits. It can be won, not through a final answer to the problem
of self-identity, but by entering the mystery of one's own creative self-
presence to primordial Being.

"The perennial maturer has," says Nixon, "for his central core, the
eternal question 'Who am I?' and his life is dedicated to a never-finished
search for the answer." (162, 141) Here, again, the failure to differentiate between the *ego* and the Self is manifest. For, within limits, the
problem of the psychological and functional self-identity can be solved.
The mature Self, however, participates in the mystery of Being, and is
essentially involved in an inexhaustible self-questioning. To be dedicated to a never-ending search for the answer to the fundamental
question "Who am I?" is not a sign of immaturity, but rather a criterion
of genuine maturity.

The achievement of mature integration, and, therefore, of maturity
itself, is a never-ending task, an ideal which is always in the process of
being realized, and a dynamic response to the inexhaustible gift of the
logos. All this entails, however, that maturity as a whole is essentially
finite, limited, incomplete. In other words, final integration is a phenomenon which is not fully what it is, which is not perfectly identical
with itself. This means that maturity as a whole is a kaleidoscopic
whole. Of interest here is the differentiation of maturity into aspects,

which is characteristic of a whole as finite. Not being perfectly one with itself, maturity as a whole manifests itself in an oscillating variety of different appearances. Maturity as a whole can be looked at from the aspect (L. *aspicere*—to look at) of integration, of integrity, of health, of holiness, and of peace.

It is most interesting to realize, not only that these aspects have always been regarded as fundamental characteristics of the mature personality, but also that, etymologically, all these terms are derived from words that mean "whole." The terms "integration" and "integrity" are derived from the Latin *integer,* which means "whole." The terms holy, whole, health, hale, and healing all relate, etymologically, to the O.E. *hāl* which also means "whole." And the English word "peace" can be traced to the Greek verb *pegnumi,* "to make into a whole." Although all these terms refer to the "integral" personality, albeit from a different perspective, they do not signify maturity as a whole, unless they are understood as aspects of the primordial whole, as manifestations of the achievement of final integration in the mature personality. These aspects are the final integration insofar as this comes to pass in an oscillating variety of perspectives that are interdependent and complementary, but never completely interchangeable. Everything that can be said about the achievement of final integration applies, *mutatis mutandis,* to each of its differentiated manifestations. If man's response to the *logos* is a task, a creative process, and a gift, then so is his integration, or his health, or his holiness, or his peace.

It should be emphasized again that these aspects of wholeness are not qualities or properties of the mature personality, but rather ways of Being that involve his entire Being-with-others-in-the-world. The achievement of final integration in the mature personality is a finite and polymorphous phenomenon which comes to pass in an oscillating emphasis on the various aspects of his response to the *logos.* Final integration in the mature personality can occur with emphasis on one of the following aspects: a harmony of psychic forces (integration); a unifying attitude towards life (integrity); a unifying outlook upon life (holistic thinking); a participation in the whole of Being (health); a surrender to the ultimate way of life (holiness); a harmonious dis-position (peace).

MATURE PSYCHOLOGICAL INTEGRATION

It is generally agreed that a mature personality is well-integrated. The term "integration" here is taken in its usual, psychological sense of "the harmony of psychic forces," or "the organization of the constituent elements of the personality into a coordinated, harmonious whole." It is important, however, to realize that these merely psychological formulae fail to define the final integration in the mature personality. For it is impossible to define mature integration unless it is understood within the cosmic context of man's participation in the *logos* as that which sets all things apart (differentiation) in their original unity of Being (integration). The original unity (integration) of the mature personality is the dynamic unity of the Being-process.

The just-mentioned usual definitions of integration are certainly useful within restricted areas of psychological behavior. Yet, they do not define mature psychological integration, for they fail to define mature psychological integration as an aspect of the fundamental integration in the *logos*. "An harmonious organization of psychic forces or constituent elements" can still be immature, as long as this organization is not rooted in the person's Self-presence to the whole of Being. Without this philosophical rootedness, the human personality does not reveal the original unity of his fundamental integration, but is supposed to be made up out of simple, irreducible elements. The human personality is at best a mere aggregate of isolated traits, or at worst a mere construct tied together by a proper name.

The usual psychological definition of integration, in terms of an organization of psychic forces or constituent elements, contradicts the original integration of human ex-sistence, and is based on an atomistic pseudo-philosophy of the personality. Moreover, if integration is an organization of independent forces, of isolated, simple elements, it has to be achieved by control from without. Otherwise, these elements would not be simple or isolated, but, somehow, they would be already integrated. Again, it matters little whether the controlling force is the reason, the *ego,* the Superego, habit-formation, or self-control. What matters is that integration is supposed to be achieved by a controlling force at all.

It is precisely this controlling orientation which underlies the usual interpretation of integration in terms of an organization of independent elements. For, man's controlling will and calculative thinking can only deal with reality by reducing it to quantifiable objects, and by becoming handmaidens in the service of an atomistic and mechanical view of the world. According to this mechanistic pseudo-philosophy, a well-integrated person is one who has everything under control and is perfectly organized, one who has reduced all his conflicts and anxieties and is perfectly adjusted, one who has achieved an inner consistency that keeps him permanently in a perfect balance. This mechanistic conception of integration closely resembles the physiological concept of "homeostasis," from which, in fact, it is borrowed. Homeostasis is the root-tendency of an organism to maintain its integrity and internal stability by restoring the equilibrium of its normal functioning when this is disturbed in the communication with its surroundings. The similarity between homeostasis and the mechanistic conception of integration is obvious.

But it should be equally obvious that this mechanistic model cannot account for all man's everyday integrations, let alone his mature psychological integration. To be sure, insofar as man has an organic body, the law of homeostatic equilibrium or "the wisdom of the body" applies. Within limits, this homeostatic equilibrium can be modified and controlled from without by conditioning reflexes, by reinforcing (rewarding) correct actions, or simply by giving an additional supply of oxygen to someone who has difficulty breathing. Yet, despite its validity on the physiological level, and the fascinating intricacy of its functioning, homeostasis remains a more or less mechanical principle.

But man is more than a merely physiological organism. He is a psychological being of existential nature, a being-in-the-world. The human individual in his usual, workaday world is a unifying subject-process that gathers all objects in their functional unity of the workaday world. The everyday individual is a world-forming subject-process, an integrating dialogue between the *ego* and its surrounding world. This everyday integration far transcends the mere homeostatic equilibrium. To be sure, the idea of homeostasis can effectively be used as a working definition for a part of man's psychological functioning. After all, his needs and drives, reflexes and mechanisms, instinctual life and pleasure principle, belong to the physiological substructure of his existence, and are impersonal, mechanical, and deterministic by nature.

But, above all, man is a personality, a spirit incarnate, an open relation to the totality of all that is. As such, he far transcends the world of his environment. And his final integration transcends his everyday integration. This does not mean that man leaves his surrounding world behind and enters the World of Being, or that these worlds are ever given as separate worlds. On the contrary, when man transcends his surrounding world, this usual world opens up into the unusual World of Being as "its own beyond." The workaday world widens and deepens its own horizon by meeting the otherness of the *logos* as the mysterious translucency of its own depth. The immanent, everyday integration in the workaday world and the transcendent, final integration in the World of the *logos* do not exist or signify separately, since both worlds are thrown together into the primal con-flict (L. *confligere*—to throw together) of their fundamental sym-bolism (Gr. *syn, balloo*—to throw together).

Consequently, a mature personality is psychologically well-integrated, not because he has perfectly organized his world, but because he allows his world to participate in the World of the *logos*. Mature integration, as the fulfilling of man's integrative potentialities, does not restrict itself to the functional level of control, mastery, and organization, but opens up in creative surrender to the process by which beings are set apart in their primordial unity of Being. This is the philosophical foundation of Andras Angyal's conception of the interplay of two distinct orientations in man: *"self-determination"* and *"self-surrender."* Marie Jahoda, in her book *Current Concepts of Positive Mental Health,* quotes Angyal as saying that the goal of the former (leading towards increased autonomy) is "to organize . . . the objects and the events of his world, to bring them under his own jurisdiction and government." Whereas the goal of the latter is "to surrender himself willingly, to seek a home for himself in and *to become an organic part of something that he conceives as greater than* himself." (101, 48)

Moreover, Angyal, too, emphasizes the fact that the mature and healthy personality always and essentially lives in both worlds at the same time. "It is only," he says, "in the counterfeit, the unhealthy behavior that one or the other of these basic orientations is partially obliterated; in a well-integrated person the behavioral items always manifest both orientations in varying degrees." (101, 48) The well-integrated, mature personality does not consist of two separate integrations: a functional or merely psychological integration, plus a final integration in the cosmic reality of Being. Psychological integration is only mature insofar as it is integrated into the final integration, insofar as it becomes an organic part of something transcending itself, or insofar as it becomes the immanent aspect of the primal conflict between everyday integration and fundamental integration in the *logos*. Mature psychological integration is not only horizontal, but also vertical; not only functional but also inspirational; not only a "doing" but also a "letting happen." Mature integration is never an accomplished fact, but rather an occurrence which is always in the process of being achieved.

A mature personality is not only well-integrated, but also well-adjusted and Self-consistent. Adjustment and consistency have always been regarded as essential components of integration, connoting its harmony respectively with the external world, and within the inner world of the Self. However, taken by themselves, i.e., apart from the final integration in the *logos,* neither adjustment nor consistency can function as criteria for maturity. The mature personality is well-adjusted. Adjusted to what? Crime, drug addiction, eccentricity? How well adjusted? Perfectly?—conformism? And, then, there are consistent liars, consistent burglars, and even consistently inconsistent people.

Adjustment and consistency, as structural characteristics of the mature personality, can only be discussed within the cosmic context of his final integration. Yet it is precisely this context which is conspicuously absent from most of the usual definitions of adjustment and consistency. The common denominator of current definitions of adjustment reads: "A satisfactory adaptation to the demands of the environment and a reduction of inner needs and conflicts." This definition has already appeared as part of the mechanistic conception of integration, which, despite its limited validity in an existential substructure, fails to define healthy and mature integration. Similarly, the mechanistic conception of adjustment may effectively serve as a working definition within the mechanisms of the workaday world, but it fails to define the adjustment of the mature personality.

The definition of mature adjustment as "a satisfactory adaptation to the demands of the environment and a reduction of inner needs and conflicts" is not only inadequate, it is positively false. It reduces authentic integration to homeostatic equilibrium, and ignores altogether the uniqueness, the mystery, the creativity, and cosmic openness of the personal Self. It leads up to the dehumanizing conformism of a robot, and causes rather than cures immature fixations and existential neurosis. There is a growing awareness, especially among psychotherapists, of the fact that many contemporary disorders or maladjustments have emerged not so much idiosyncratically, but rather sociologically and existentially. In order to solve the problem of social acceptance, man is forced by societal controls (violence, indoctrination, ridicule, fraud, fear of ostracism and occupational control) to live in total conformity with certain social habits, rules, customs, and taboos that keep him within the assigned coordinates of the social roles he is expected to play. Here man is maladjusted, not because he is not perfectly adjusted, but precisely because he is forced into the fallacy of perfect adjustment. Man is supposed to do things the way an impersonal "they" (*das Man* —Heidegger) wants them done. According to Laing, matters have gone so far that society takes away man's personal responsibility and he calls it security; it gives man violence and he calls it protection; it takes away man's sense of wonder, of eros, of transcendence, and of playfulness, and he calls it adjustment or down-to-earth realism. (131, Ch. 3) Society even alienates man from his very awareness of being alienated to such a degree that he comes to want what his society wants him to want.

This standardized and alienated existence results in a despair over the meaning of life as a whole, an existential despair which Frankl calls "nooneurosis" or "existential neurosis." "In this sense," he says, "despair over the meaning of life may be called an *existential neurosis* as opposed to *clinical neurosis.* Just as sexual frustration may . . . lead to neuroses it is conceivable that frustration of the will-to-meaning may also lead to neurosis. I call this frustration *existential frustration.*" (56, xi) No wonder that modern man feels frustrated when he is forced to live in a mechanized world which leaves no room for personal freedom and creativity, in which he has been degraded to a replaceable function or to an anonymous part of a cosmic machine. Modern man is promised perfect happiness for his perfect adjustment to a perfect network of functional relationships. Yet, modern man feels "perfectly" empty, despairs over the meaning of life, and wonders if life is worth living. Says Marcel, "Life in a world centered on function is liable to despair because in reality this world is empty." (141, 3) Bugental, speaking as a psychotherapist to his colleagues, agrees with my diagnosis by stating that their patients suffer as much from the cultural fallacy of perfect adjustment as from their individual disorders. "To aid the patient," he says, "to a 'passive' acceptance of social values and avoidance of conflict may well be to assist him in making rigid a character disorder that extinguishes his very humanity and assures an end to his creativity. Clearly such an objective is totally inconsistent with the concept of existential authenticity." (27, 33)

Perfect adjustment is totally inconsistent with the mature personality. For the world in which the concept of perfect adjustment has a limited application is set in the larger World of the person's Self-presence to the whole of Being. In this personal World of Being, which transcends the subject-object split or I-world dichotomy, the very term "adjustment" is inaccurate, and should be replaced by more appropriate terms such as "presence," "relation" or "participation." In fact, it would be self-contradictory to speak of being adjusted, let alone perfectly adjusted, to the mystery of Being, to a creative process, to the sense of wonder or to an all-encompassing phenomenon.

The usual world of everyday and functional adjustments and the unusual World of Being never exist separately in the mature personality. Mature adjustment to the environment takes place within the unique and creative world of the authentic personality. It is never impersonal and merely mechanical, but always "personalized." The mature personality is well-adjusted, not because he is "perfectly" adjusted, but because he is creatively adjusted, i.e., because his adjustment participates in the creative process of final integration, and promotes rather than blocks this developmental task of achieving an ontocentric world.

The mature person who is well-integrated and well-adjusted is ipso facto Self-consistent. For he has achieved a unification of his existence and a harmony with reality that give his behavior the stability, the permanency, and coherence of a consistent personality. Mature consistency encompasses man's response to the World of the *logos:* its ontological tensions, its existential anxiety, and its creative process of integration. Mature consistency *is* the consistency of final integration, the standing together (L. *consistere*—to stand together) of the authentic personality characteristics in the primordial process of differentiated Being. This is why mature consistency is never static, unchangeable, and closed in upon itself, but always open and expanding, deepening and growing. Again, the stability, the permanency and coherence of mature consistency are not based on a rock-like, immovable structure, but on the authentic Self as a creative response to the abiding emergence of differentiated Being.

Mature consistency is creative Self-consistency, rather than a rigid adherence to static structures and external principles. The mature personality is consistent when he remains himself in success and in failure, in his professional function, through the vicissitudes of life. He does not substitute clichés or stereotyped behavior for his personal integrity. He remains independent of the typical model created by his professional or social function. He does not use the stereotype of the professional man or the functional man as a defense mechanism to camouflage the insecurity of his own personal insignificance. He does not suffer from the professional deformation of the typical doctor, the typical artist, the typical bishop, the typical professor, the typical sales person, the typical executive, etc. Nor does he ever totally identify himself with any organization, institution, party, or corporation, or with the status quo of any establishment. When a person abdicates his free and responsible Self in favor of mechanical roles or rigid systems and structures, his behavior becomes no doubt consistent. But it is the "foolish consistency" Emerson objected to. (51, 57) It is the immature, fixated, unauthentic consistency of petty minds; it is the static, thing-like consistency of stereotypes, marked by stiffness, rigidity, formality, and the inability to listen, to change, to grow, or to benefit from any new experience or encounter.

The person who abdicates his free Self in favor of stereotypes is even alienated from himself, and lives in "bad faith" (Sartre).

The Self-consistency of the mature personality, on the other hand, con-sists in this: that he is true to himself. He does not substitute stereotypes or structures for his personal Self. Of course, the mechanistic conception of consistency is also true to itself to the extent that it displays identical behavior in different situations. On this level, one is true to oneself if one perpetuates an unchanging conformity to a static pattern of behavior or principles. But this type of consistency is inconsistent with the Self-consistency of the mature personality. The mature personality is true to himself when he is true to his true Self, when he transcends all static consistencies, stereotypes, and fixities in favor of his creative Self-presence to the totality of Being.

One may note in passing that it would be inaccurate, if not outright contradictory, to speak of "typical" maturity. For the "type" is totally inconsistent with the uniqueness, the creativity, and cosmic openness of the mature personality. There is no uniqueness, creativity, or openness in the fixated adjustment and consistency of a mechanical existence. The type has no life outside his role, no flexibility. One typical personality resembles another of the same kind much more closely than one mature personality resembles another. Yet, there is something typical in everyone to the extent that his existential substructure is subjected to routine habits, mannerisms, social customs, taboos, folkways, etc. Therefore, there is something typical even in the most mature personality. The typical characteristics of his sociocultural environment are recognizable even in the greatest achievements of his creative personality. He is still "a child of his time."

Yet, what is typical in the mature personality is precisely not what is mature in the mature personality. What is typical is his sociocultural heritage; what is mature is the fact that he both accepts and transcends this heritage. A person who totally accepts and adjusts himself to the immanency of his heritage, abandons his true Self and becomes a typical conformist. On the other hand, a person who totally rejects and transcends his sociocultural heritage, abandons his usual world and becomes a typical eccentric. Only the mature personality is able to avoid either horn of this dilemma by transcending the dichotomy between both worlds and incorporating them into the primal con-flict of his authentic ex-sistence. Thus he accepts his heritage, not in a passive way, but by integrating it into the creative context of his final integration.

The mature personality transcends the typical behavior patterns of both the conformist and the eccentric. He rises above complete determinism, not by rejecting the typical mechanisms of his character, his instinctual life, and his sociocultural heritage, but by integrating them into the cosmic process of his final integration. Being true to his authentic Self, the mature personality is both determined and Self-determining; both society-controlled, and transcending; both typical and uniquely creative. He is essentially an interplay between the world of freedom and the world of determinism, and his freedom is always a freedom in the process of freeing itself. And this is the very essence of the phenomenon of play. Play, therefore, is essentially more than a mere function, a property, a quality, or a particular activity. Play is a structural characteristic of authentic Being-in-the-world, and a genuine criterion for personal maturity. Play, according to Sadler, "is a mode of being in the world whereby the workaday world with its sense of gravity is left behind. In the moment of play, the serious cause-effect order of work is forgotten as one finds a freedom beyond the confinements of ordinary concerns. Play is definitely a form of freedom, a mode of transcendence, a genuine existential possibility." (185, 212) This is why, as contrasted with the conformist and the eccentric, the mature personality is not a deadly serious, but rather, by definition, a playful human being.

This fundamental significance of play as a structural characteristic of the authentic personality has rarely been understood. Usually play is seen as a separate function in human life, relegated to the children's playground where it serves to work off surplus energy, to prepare for life, and to provide recreation. Afterwards, it becomes subordinated to the serious business of adult functioning. However, no phenomenon taken by itself and isolated from the final process of integration can be understood in its essence or function as a criterion for maturity. Earlier, I have shown play to be the "interplay" between the world of determinism and the growing world of freedom, or the freedom of the authentic personality in the process of freeing itself. This means, in terms of the process of final integration, the creative interplay between the subject-process of environmental integration and the Being-process of cosmic integration. To think that the prototype of play is found in childhood, and that the phenomenon of playfulness in adulthood is a leftover from childhood for which one has to apologize is to be mistaken. Just as the child is a mature personality *in statu nascendi,* so also is his way of playing authentic playfulness in a primitive stage of development. Mature integration, adjustment, and consistency are playful phenomena. This, however, is not to say that they are not serious phenomena. On the level of mature existence, the dichotomy between seriousness and playfulness is transcended. This dichotomy exists only in those fixated forms where seriousness is "deadly" serious, and playfulness a mere "playing at."

Since play is a structural characteristic of man's authentic co-Being-in-the-world, it is more than a merely juvenile or a merely individual activity. It is a cultural and social phenomenon through which the creative transcendency of man's mature co-Being-in-the-world takes place. Sadler quotes Huizinga as saying that it is through "playing that society expresses its interpretation of life and the world." (185, 215) And, showing the all-pervasive nature of play, he adds that culture "does not come *from* play like a babe detaching itself from the womb; it arises *in* and *as* play, and never leaves it." (185, 216) Play is not a superficial activity; as the interplay between the freedom and the determinism of man's Being-together-with-others-in-the-world, it brings his whole existence and his whole society "into play."

Play, therefore, profoundly affects man's historicity, which is his World-building Being-process within the dimensions of authentic temporality. Discussing Gustav Bally's study on freedom as play, Sadler states: "Man plays his whole life, and his play has to do with his search for a sense of historical identity in a human world. . . . In play man engages himself totally in his world and thus may recover an awareness of his wholeness [integration]." (185, 217) It is through the creative process of playfulness that the mature personality continually frees himself from the sociocultural determinisms in order to free himself for a growing realization of the meaning and the freedom of his historical Self-identity. This playful historicity is the drama of civilization. Civilization is the ensemble of man's physical, technological, artistic, and spiritual creations put at the service of his personal growth, or his cultural heritage being integrated into the historical process of final integration. In this dramatic interplay of personal freedom and sociocultural determinisms, both are actor and audience. The role the mature personality plays in the theater of civilization has nothing to do with the mechanical role-playing of puppets, but has very much to do with the creative activity of the artist. Just as the artist mobilizes his tools and techniques, and allows his inspiration to execute the work of art through them, so also the mature personality mobilizes the typical mechanisms of his cultural heritage, and allows his playful freedom to create the work of civilization through them. Civilization is not the wall of his imprisonment in history, but rather the playground of his emerging freedom. "The history of civilization is none other than the growing awareness of freedom" (Hegel).

To return to the Self-consistency of the mature personality: it is easy to see that a person cannot be Self-consistent if he is not well-balanced. "It is no sign of maturity," says Symonds, "to lead a will-o'-the-wisp, flighty existence, to dabble, to touch experience lightly, to be here today and gone tomorrow." (203, 577) On the other hand, it is no sign of maturity either to remain permanently in a rigid balance, to live in a state of perfect equilibrium. People that are perfectly balanced have grown into their own statue. They suffer from arrested development, from immaturity, insensitivity, and superficiality. Again, the literal-mindedness of this mechanistic conception of balance reminds one too much of the "homeostatic equilibrium" of the body. And, what is worse, it reminds one literally of the state of equilibrium due to the equal distribution of weight on the scales of a balance. This is the rigid and inflexible conception of balance of those who follow "the golden mean" and always avoid extremes. It is the equilibrium of those who have adopted a middle-of-the-road position in any situation.

Although the unbalanced person and the perfectly balanced person may seem to be diametrical opposites, fundamentally speaking they are only similar. Whereas the unbalanced person lacks stability, the perfectly balanced person lacks flexibility. What both lack, however, is the ability to experience the flexible stability of their authentic Self as a response to the abiding and differentiating emergence of the *logos*. What both also lack is the ability to experience the unity-in-opposition of their authentic ex-sistence, to hold any tension between these polarities and to endure its mysterious blend of existential anxiety and fascination. Let me illustrate this with the example of the tennis court: a tennis player who never leaves the center mark of the tennis court is not a balanced player; he is not a tennis player at all. Nor can he enjoy the fascinating tension of the game. The player who rushes to the extreme corners of the court to return a ball is not an extremist, but a versatile player—unless, of course, he never returns from his extreme position. According to Sydney Harris, "Holding the polarities in tension means finding the optimum point at which they work together best; and this is not necessarily in the middle." (80, 41) Inflexibly following the principle of "the golden mean" leads to "mediocrity." A mature personality can be well-balanced even if he goes to extremes, as long as this remains within the playful context of final integration.

A mature personality is well-balanced. This does not mean that he lives in a state of perfect equilibrium or takes a middle-of-the-road position in every situation. On the contrary, mature balance is characterized by its playful seriousness, its flexible stability, and its creative faithfulness to the final process of integration. Mature balance is final integration, insofar as it keeps the polar tension between two opposite movements, the movement of differentiation, exteriorization, and objectification on the one hand, and the movement of integration, interiorization, and transcendency on the other, in the proper di-stance of their primal con-flict. Mature balance is final integration, insofar as it prevents a person from losing himself in a chaos of meaningless moments or from becoming frozen into the monolithic fixity of a dead system. Mature balance is final integration, insofar as it puts things in their proper order and perspective.

Before bringing this section to a close, I should briefly mention two other dimensions of final integration. In the first place, authentic existence stands out or is differentiated into the three "ecstases" of authentic temporality. It is by coming towards (future) its primary data (past) that the Self presents (present) the ecstatic unity (integration) of its authentic ex-sistence. The true Self, therefore, is not in time, but it is temporalizing. This creative and circular process of temporalization is final integration, insofar as it sets apart the authentic past, present, and future in their primordial unity of the World-forming Being-process. "This world-building," says Heidegger, "is history in the authentic sense." (89, 62) To say that in the mature process of integration, man discloses the historicity of his authentic existence, is by no means to equate history with the past or to reduce the mature personality to a museum piece. On the contrary, the temporalizing process of creative integration is a profoundly historical process in which the mature personality discloses and actualizes his authentic existence.

The temporalizing process of final integration transcends the ordinary time-for of the workaday world, and even more the abstractive conception of time in terms of an infinite succession of now-moments. Final integration holds together (integrates) the life of the mature personality from the beginning to the end. This authentic holding together (integration) transcends the mere continuous way in which the *ego* holds together (steadfastness, *sameness*) man's changing experiences from the moment of birth to the moment of death, and every moment in between (steadiness, *permanence*). The final integration of the mature personality as historizing is the creative Self-constancy of the true Self which from the beginning to the end holds together (integrates) the three differentiations of authentic temporality. From the beginning to the end no longer means between the separate moments of man's birth and death, but rather the equiprimordiality and interdependence of his authentic past, present, and future. It is precisely in this highly dynamic process of coming to (future) his having-been (past), that the mature personality presents (present) the progressive Self-disclosure and Self-actualization of his authentic ex-sistence. The historizing Self is "between" the authentic beginning and end of his creative involvements. And the constancy of this historizing process of final integration is no longer the static constancy of mechanical continuity, but the creative and existential Self-constancy of the authentic person's Self-presence to the abiding and emerging phenomenon of primordial Being.

At this point a clarification seems to be in order. Isn't creativity a prerogative of God, and analogously of men endowed with special talents? Doesn't this fact, together with the assertion that creativeness is an essential characteristic of personal maturity put some undue restrictions on this maturity concept? Who can claim to be God or a Michelangelo? This reduces for most men the chances of ever becoming mature. So it seems. However, it should be obvious that the creativeness of the mature personality is different from both God's absolute creativeness and man's special-talent creativeness. Maslow states, on the basis of his experimental research, that creativeness "is a universal characteristic of all [self-actualizing] people studied or observed. There is no exception." (149, 223) And then he adds unambiguously that this creativeness "is different from the special-talent creativeness of the Mozart type." (149, 223)

When one calls the mature personality "Self-creative," one is not ascribing divine powers or special talents to him. In order to avoid these misconceptions, it must be kept in mind that givenness and cosmic openness are among the essential characteristics of the true Self. In the first place, the temporalizing process of coming to his having-been, through which the Self discloses and actualizes his co-Being-in-the-world, is truly Self-enriching and creative. However, the creativity of this process does not start from zero, but presupposes the primary data as already given, as having-been, as thrown. Consequently, by mistaking this process of relative Self-creation for an act of absolute creation, one contradicts the primary data of the mature Self. As Heidegger puts it, "All projection—and, consequently, even man's 'creative' activity—is *thrown.*" (87, 244)

Furthermore, the all-encompassing experience of primordial wonder is not the prerogative of a special talent, but of man as man. This is why the creativeness of the mature person as a response to differentiated wonder is not a special-talent creativeness, but the prerogative of any mature personality regardless of his talents, occupation, or special interests. Mature creativeness, therefore, is revealed in an emanation of the personality, rather than in the writing of books, the production of

works of art, or the making of inventions. Mature creativeness, as
Maslow aptly puts it, "touches whatever activity the person is engaged
in," (149, 223) including, of course, his special-talent activities.

These brief elucidations of mature creativity have also provided the
key to a mature understanding of being true to one's Self, which characterizes mature Self-consistency, mature integration, and, therefore, personal maturity itself. The creative process of maturity develops in un-
deviating conformity to its principles neither by accepting its original
data with rigid and unchanging fidelity, nor by producing them in an
act of absolute creativity, but by adhering to its primary data with
"creative fidelity." (Marcel) Those who are conformists and have substituted for creative fidelity an uncreative conformity to past patterns
are as unfaithful to their mature Self as are those who want to play God
and have substituted for creative fidelity a pretense of absolute
creativity. A mature personality is true to himself not when he merely
keeps fidelity, but when his fidelity to his authentic Self, and to his
commitments and involvements, becomes more and more faithful in
depth and in quality. A mature personality is true to himself only when
his very fidelity participates in the creative Being-process.

VARIATIONS ON THE THEME OF FINAL INTEGRATION

I have discussed final integration in the mature personality as mature
integration; I now propose to discuss the same final integration in the
form of integrity, holistic thinking, holiness, mental health, and existential peace. All these phenomena, as aspects of authentic wholeness, of
final integration, are fundamental ways of Being-in-the-world, and not
mere qualities or properties of the mature personality. These aspects are
final integration itself, insofar as this, due to the finitude of its creative
process, fails to achieve perfect self-identity, and comes to pass in an
oscillating variety of complementary perspectives. In other words, final
integration never occurs by itself, but only in the form of ethical integrity, psychological integration, mental health, etc. Each of these aspects
is final integration, but in a different way and with a different emphasis
on man's response to the *logos*.

Here one has come upon the philosophical elucidation of something
that has always puzzled the psychologists: the fact that although maturity, mental health, integrity, etc. are practically synonyms, they are not
completely interchangeable. It is by reason of the fundamental finitude
of man's response to the *logos* that final integration differentiates into
an oscillating variety of or a creative tension between these integrative

responses. All this implies that whatever can be said about one of these aspects, can be said, *mutatis mutandis,* about all the others. This is not at all to suggest, however, that the aspects to be discussed in this section are characteristics of mature integration. In fact, mature integration, mental health, integrity, etc. are, strictly speaking, not characteristics at all. These equiprimordial perspectives are the entire mature personality in the oscillating plurality of his finite Self-disclosure.

Let me begin with the perspective of integrity. A mature personality is not only well-integrated, he also has integrity. Whereas the term "integration" refers to psychological wholeness, the term integrity denotes ethical wholeness. The way man achieves authenticity oscillates between a thinking and an ethical way of responding to the gift of Being. Again, due to the finitude of this responding to primordial Being, a certain tension or differentiation reveals itself between the phenomenon of Being and the Being of this phenomenon. It is this polar tension which underlies the classical distinction between essence (what-ness) and existence (that-ness). Man's achievement of authenticity will, of course, preserve this polar tension.

In other words, man's response to the dialectical Self-presentation of Being takes place in an oscillating duality between the Self-revelation of Being on the one hand, and the Self-actualization of Being on the other. The word "presentation" connotes both "bringing to light" and "making present." Man achieves authenticity in a thinking way and in an ethical way. Both ways of achieving authenticity are interdependent and complementary, but never completely interchangeable. Both ways involve the whole of our authentic ex-sistence (final integration), but with the respective emphasis on either its "bringing to light" or its "making present" of the cosmic Self-presentation of Being.

Now, final integration as the whole of our ethical Self-actualization is integrity. Or, to put it differently, integrity is final integration insofar as it unifies man's highest and specifically human activities, or his authentic and Self-actualizing behavior in accordance with the *logos.* The word "ethical" is derived from the Greek word *ethos*—dwelling place, abode, man's characteristic place or disposition in which he "holds his own" in the world. The way man authentically "holds his own" is by holding himself in Being, by "behaving" in response to the *logos.* To be-have (M.E. *be*—thoroughly, and *have*—to hold oneself, to act) means to have oneself in hand, to hold one's own, to achieve one's own authenticity, to be authentically. Authentic behavior, therefore, as man's response to the *logos,* is essentially ethical. And integrity is the integral abode of man with Being.

From all this it follows that the mature personality has integrity, or, more correctly, is integrity. This integrity, therefore, is none of the following: an accomplished fact, a rigid adherence to moral principles, a state of being complete or perfect, or an attitude of self-righteousness. These attributes contradict the very nature of integrity as man's abode with Being. As authentic behavior in accordance with the *logos,* integrity is not an accomplished fact, but an occurrence which is always in the process of being achieved. Mature integrity is not a state of being, but a developmental task, an inexhaustible ideal, a creative acceptance of a primordial gift. No human being is ever complete, no mature personality is absolutely perfect.

The mature personality has integrity. This also means that he is "a man of principle." This is usually understood in terms of "a steadfast adherence to a static set of moral rules or principles." Again, this mechanistic conception of integrity fails to comprehend man's true ethical life since it leaves his abode with Being *(ethos)* unthought. These moral principles are the so-called "objective" norms, external codes that are both understood and supposed to exist apart from their living source (L. *principium*—beginning, source). However, apart from personal integrity these principles are uprooted, lifeless, and abstract, and cannot possibly function as norms for mature ethical behavior. They are either surreptitiously borrowed from theology, or else they are attained by absolutizing *ethos* in the derivative sense of the term: regional customs (L. *mores*), usage, or folkways.

A mature person has integrity, not because he rigidly conforms to a static set of moral principles, but because of his creative fidelity to the originative process of final integration. He does not primarily concern himself with doing the right thing, but with being the true Person. Marcel puts it aptly when he says that "Fidelity to a principle as a principle [i.e., apart from one's Self-presence to Being] is idolatry in the etymological sense of the word." (141, 22) It worships the idol of the letter that kills, rather than the spirit that gives life. This rigid adherence to a static set of moral principles makes man abdicate freedom, playfulness, and creative fidelity in favor of determinism. This creates a "deadly" serious situation, indeed. For it deadens our sense of Self; it reduces creative fidelity to "bad faith," Self-actualization to self-betrayal, creative integrity to self-righteous perfectionism, and ethical excellence to routine habits.

It is his creative integrity and not a set of routine habits, or the so-called good habits, that constitutes the virtuousness of the mature personality. Creative integrity as authentic behavior in accordance with the *logos* ethicizes authentic ex-sistence and makes human life virtuous in the sense of "endowed with ethical excellence" (L. *virtus*—excellence). Virtue, therefore, is neither the one nor the many, but a polar tension between the one and the many. Nothing is virtuous apart from integrity as the ethical aspect of final integration. Virtue is in the whole. However, good habits in the sense of routine habits are not in the whole. They are not in accordance with the *logos,* but only in conformity with abstract principles, or merely external codes, norms, and customs. Yet it seems that a routine habit and virtuous behavior have identical characteristics. Both are acquired by a repetition of the same acts which makes these acts more and more effortless, more and more rooted in a permanent disposition.

However, this is where the comparison ends. Careful philosophical reflection shows that there is a radical difference between good habits and virtuous behavior. Good habits are acquired by the repetition of a series of identical acts which makes the acts less and less voluntary, less and less conscious, and more and more mechanical. These routine habits become progressively effortless to the extent that they become ingrained in the permanent disposition of the mechanisms of man's physiological substructures and their automatic stimulus-response situations. The homeostatic integrity of the "settled" man resembles the perfection of a machine much more than that of a real person; this static, rock-like integrity of the moral conformist is the ethical equivalent of the perfect integration of the psychologically perfectly adjusted conformist. Mature integrity, on the other hand, shows quite a different picture.

Mature integrity as authentic behavior in response to the *logos* is also acquired by re-petition of the same act. But unlike the mechanical repetition of routine habits, the re-petition of virtuous behavior is a historizing Self-actualization (present) which creatively seeks again (future) its having-been (past) (L. *re*—again; *petere*—to seek). Mature integrity is a historizing process by which the person re-peats his original data in the creative way of a self-enriching ad-venture. Mature integrity consists in a creative act of Self-repetition or Self-actualization which, as contrasted with routine habits, makes this Self-actualization more and more free, more and more conscious, less and less mechanical. Just like routine habits, virtuous behavior becomes progressively effortless. But unlike routine habits, its effortlessness and permanency are not due to a gradual mechanization, but rather to its rootedness in the abiding emergence of primordial Being. It should be noted here that when medieval philosophers used the word "habit" (L. *habitus*) in its ethical context, it meant "authentic behavior" (derived from L. *sese habere*—to "be") rather than "routine habit" (from L. *habere*—to "have").

Of course, this is not to say that routine habits and conformity with external rules, principles, customs or laws have no place in mature ethical ex-sistence. The findings concerning final integration also hold true for ethical integrity. A person of mature integrity both accepts and transcends his routine habits by integrating them into the primal conflict of his authentic ex-sistence. Mature integrity is the interplay between the world of freedom and the world of mechanisms. Routine habits are as necessary in virtuous behavior as the rules of grammar are in literature, the beating of time in music, or the rituals in celebration. Yet, taken by themselves, these routine habits, rules, and mechanical procedures remain meaningless. Just as the artist puts his tools and technical skills at the service of his inspiration, so also does the ethical personality put his routine habits at the service of his creative response to the *logos*. Mature integrity is much more a matter of artistic creativity than of correct procedures.

What conformism is to mature integration, "formalism" is to mature integrity. Moral formalism observes the correct form, the rigid adherence to external principles, the formation of routine habits, but it fails to understand mature integrity as virtuous behavior in accordance with the *logos*. Formalism obeys the law to the letter, but it ignores its spirit. Formalism brings ethical behavior down to the functional level of the controlling will and calculative thinking. The formalist wants to get everything "under perfect control," and can do so only by reducing all reality to quantifiable objects. As a result, he reduces his ethical integrity to an automatic, problemless, and perfect conformity to a static set of isolated rules and principles, and calls it "perfection." His impersonal and abstractive conformism has universal validity and becomes a universal moral norm for everyone. The formalist, therefore, automatically displays his own rigid conformism and stereotyped perfectionism, his pious mannerisms and smugly moralistic behavior as a norm for others, and calls it "giving a good example."

This good example is literally an object, a blueprint, a flashcard that the formalist holds up in front of others for observation and unquestioning imitation. Yet, by allowing his behavior to be reduced to the condition of things, the formalist has only one way to get in touch with others, and that way is collision. This is why the moral exhibitionism of his good example, instead of being inspirational, is literally repulsive to others. The formalist, in turn, finds anyone who dares to deviate from his own rigid behavior patterns repulsive and threatening. And, of course, he feels particularly threatened by mature virtuous behavior, and reacts with a self-righteous attitude of intolerance, condemnation, and aggression whenever he is confronted with the creative and playful integrity of the mature personality.

As contrasted with the formalist and legalist, the mature personality hardly thinks of giving an example. He does not give an example, but he is an example, almost in spite of himself. In fact, he doesn't even think of himself as "a good man" in the perfectionist sense of the term. The formalist may be "perfect," but he is a perfect machine. He is, in the words of Mark Twain, "a good man in the worst sense of the term." The mature personality knows that absolute perfection is not attainable. His authentic virtuous behavior reveals this to him in a variety of ways. He knows that his integrity is essentially imperfect. He knows that his integrity is never an accomplished fact, but an occurrence which is always in the process of being achieved. He knows the radical finitude, the givenness, and mystery of his own integrity. And, what is more, his authentic integrity is always and essentially involved in the primal conflict with the determinisms of his cultural and temperamental heritage.

Sociologically, according to Erving Goffman in his provocative book *Stigma* (70), all men find themselves in situations where they are compelled to play the social game. In order to solve the problem of social acceptance and survive as human beings at all, men may have to wear masks, use techniques of information control, engage in phoniness or "con" artistry. This seems to be the sociological equivalent of the "dirty hands" theory in modern philosophy, and of "original sin" in theology. The society into which one is born determines one not only with its virtues, but also with its vices. Indifference, dishonesty, prejudice, and violence are absorbed by the child long before he has the maturity of freedom to transcend these cultural determinations. And even the mature personality does not transcend this cultural heritage in the sense of leaving it behind, but by integrating it into the primal conflict of mature integration. Improbity, evil, and imperfection are integral constituents of genuine integrity. Nobody can fully transcend the lazy, impatient, or passionate nature of his own temperament. Nobody can fully transcend the prejudices, indifference, or violence of his cultural heritage. Only by admitting the presence of these dark recesses in his existence, can man be true to himself and have integrity. Only by integrating these negative modes of his existence into the primal conflict of his final integration, can his freedom be authentic, i.e., freedom in the process of freeing itself, freedom as the "interplay" between the subhuman and the superhuman.

It is both interesting and paradoxical that the example of "perfect" integrity which the formalist gives is repulsive, and that the example of "imperfect" integrity which the mature personality is proves to be inspiring and edifying. The edifying example of mature integrity has nothing in common with the external decorum and pious mannerisms of the perfectionist. On the contrary, the mature personality's creative integrity as a historizing or world-building process is edifying in both the philosophical and etymological sense of the term (L. *aedificare*— to build). Mature integrity is edifying because it is a world-building Being-process. Mature integrity is edifying because it literally builds up, actualizes, and gives increase to man's authentic co-Being-in-the-world.

And it is here that one comes upon the meaning of mature authority. Etymologically, an authority is one who is an "author," one who originates something. The word "author" is derived from the Latin word *augere* which means "to give increase," to author something, rather than to command. Mature authority is man's most fundamental and authentic way of originating something, of giving increase to his co-Being-in-the-world. And this is the edifying process of mature integrity as the creative response to the whole of Being. In other words, mature authority is the integrity of the mature personality's creative abode with Being. Mature authority, therefore, instead of suppressing freedom and stifling initiative, is an inspirational and wondcr-ful phenomenon that creates openness and respect, and is the very source of authentic freedom and initiative. Mature authority is never an accomplished fact or an unchanging state of being, but rather a never-ending task, an inexhaustible gift, and an occurrence which is always in the process of being achieved. Mature authority is not a means to create order, but it is the cosmic order (integration, integrity) itself in its creative aspect.

Moreover, mature authority is never unilateral authority. Since man's authentic Being is essentially co-Being, mature authority is essentially co-authority, or shared authority. Within the world of mature authority, nobody has absolute authority over the community or over any of its members. But every member is in authority; every member gives increase to the whole of the community, and to the personal initiative of each of its members. Instead of suppressing personal or group initiative, mature authority is their lasting source and inspiration. Even he who is in supreme authority is not merely ruling his people in the functional and legalistic sense. He is rather the supreme inspirer who gives increase to the initiative of his co-authorities.

It is interesting to see that mature authority cannot exist without mature obedience, and that mature obedience cannot be unilateral either. For one cannot creatively respond to Being without listening to the voice of Being. Mature authority is creative obedience to the Self-actualization of primordial Being in man. The term "obedience," here, is taken in both its fundamental and its etymological sense of listening to the transcending voice of the *logos* (L. *ob* and *audire*—to listen to that which transcends or is superior). In other words, to be in authority is also to obey, to listen, and to obey is also to be in authority, to give increase. And, since authority is co-authority, obedience is co-obedience, a mutual listening to the voice of Being in others, in ourselves, and in all that is. Mature authority not only has to obey the authority of those who obey, but it also has to obey its own authority.

Of course, mature personal authority cannot be achieved apart from the more or less mechanical functional world. Again, personal authority and functional authority do not exist as separate authorities in the mature personality. By functional authority is meant the right to control, to prescribe laws and rules, and to command obedience by enforcing law and order. This functional authority is immersed in the everyday world and its more or less mechanical structures, its utilitarian values, its social functions and organizations. This impersonal and functional authority, however, is no more unworthy of mature, personal authority and human freedom than the rules of a language are unworthy of creative writing and free expression.

Again, mature authority is possible only as the interplay of personal authority and functional authority within the primal conflict between the workaday world and the world of primordial Being. In the terminology of Maslow, personal authority would be an "end in itself," a "growth need" or "Being value," whereas functional authority would be a "means to an end," and function on the level of "deficiency needs." The order created by personal authority is the cosmic harmony of all that is within the unifying process of primordial Being. The order created by functional authority is the objectified and controllable order of the functional world, the order of the "law and order" type. The order created by mature authority is the interplay of cosmic order and functional order within the fundamental symbolism of their primal conflict. The creativity of the mature authority closely resembles the creativity of the artist to the extent that he puts the tools, skills, and techniques of his functional authority at the service of the primordial inspiration of his personal authority.

Whereas mature authority promotes freedom and increases the initiative and creativity of the community and its members, autocracy suppresses this freedom and initiative, and reduces all creativeness to mechanical conformity. Autocracy is immature authority which is fixated on the functional level. It divorces the legal motive from the ethical motive and believes in the absolute supremacy of functional authority. The autocrat wants to have everything and everybody under perfect control; he wants to be the sole and absolute ruler with unlimited authority over others (Gr. *autos*—self, alone; *kratein*—to rule). And he can only become an absolute ruler by setting himself up as the absolute center of his universe, by restricting the creative will-to-be of his personal authority to the controlling will-to-power of a merely functional authority, and by reducing persons to the reality of mere objects. He demands the absolute submission or unquestioning obedience of mechanical conformity. This, however, not only takes the joy out of obedience, it even takes the "listening" (obedience) out of obedience. Objects cannot listen and conformity is by definition not obedience. The autocrat literally petrifies others by not respecting their capacity and their right to self-direction.

And, of course, the same holds true when the authority to be obeyed is the authoritative voice of one's own mature conscience. Mature, authoritative conscience is the consciousness of ethical integrity as the mature personality's creative abode with Being, and corresponds to mature authority. Immature, authoritarian conscience is the interiorization of some external authority, and corresponds to autocratic authority. Mature conscience as the consciousness of man's response to the dialectical self-actualization of Being is creative, all-encompassing, inspirational, and directive rather than keeping in check, controlling, forbidding, and inhibiting. Mature conscience, therefore, is none of the following: a special faculty, a moral sense, an interiorization of external authority, a conformity, a set of rules, a stern sense of duty, an inner voice, or a fear of punishment.

Mature good conscience registers man's well-being when he behaves in accordance with his personal integrity. Mature guilty conscience registers an existential discomfort or dis-ease when man's behavior is injurious to his personal integrity. Mature conscience, according to Fromm, is "the guardian of our integrity." (59, 163) On the other hand immature, authoritarian conscience is "the voice of an internalized external authority, the parents, the state, or whoever the authorities in a culture happen to be." (59, 148) As Fromm points out, "the authoritarian conscience is what Freud has described as the Super-Ego." (59, 149) The theory of the Super-Ego is the weakest and most immature element in Freud's personality theory. For the dictates of one's authoritarian conscience are not determined by the nature and structure of one's personal integrity or by one's own personal value judgments, but merely by dictates coming from external authorities.

Immature good conscience, therefore, is "consciousness of pleasing the (external and internalized) authority," which "produces a feeling of well-being and security, for it implies approval by, and greater closeness to, the authority." (59, 150) Immature guilty conscience is "the consciousness of displeasing [the external and internalized authority], producing fear and insecurity, because acting against the will of the authority implies the danger of being punished and, what is worse, of being deserted by the authority." (59, 150) These immature and false guilt feelings underlie almost every psychoneurosis. Instead of enjoying the creative order of mature integrity, the neurotic suffers from an existential dis-order in which feelings of anxiety and impotence, obsessional thoughts and compulsive behavior weaken or paralyze the freedom and originality of his self-actualization. Subconsciously, the neurotic still tries to be the "good boy" or "nice girl" who attempts to live up to an irrealistic *ego*-ideal in automatic obedience and perfect adjustment to parental, ecclesiastical, or societal expectations. The world of the neurotic is narrow, rigid, and empty. He suffers from a general feeling of inferiority and worthlessness, and from an inherent lack of interest and enthusiasm. He is restless, unable to relax, and constantly tired, weary, and exhausted. His immature and fixated conscience resists any change, and blocks his growth tendency towards maturity and full humanness.

From all this it follows that the neurotic fails to be open to the Self-actualization of his co-Being-in-the-world. He is unable to relate, to share his very Being with others, and to be intimate on the personal level. In other words, he is unable to understand his mature ethical integrity in terms of mature personal love. Indeed, it requires a high degree of personal openness and maturity to realize that the Self-actualization of man's Being-together-with-others-in-the-world (mature integrity) constitutes the very essence of mature human and personal love. Authentic human love establishes a profound, experiential, interpersonal union between the partners. "Mature *love,*" says Fromm, "is *union under the condition of preserving one's integrity.*" (58, 20) Mature love is one's mature integrity. For, as an interpersonal union, mature human love is, philosophically speaking, a shared Self-presence to the totality of Being, or a mutual Self-actualization of authentic ex-sistence as co-Being-in-the-world. But this is precisely what ethicizes mature ex-sistence, and what constitutes its authentic integrity. Consequently, it is in his commitment to the fundamental life-style of ethical love, and not in his legalistic adherence to rules, principles, and establishments that the mature personality finds the source of his true integrity, and thereby of his creativity, his stability, his happiness, and fulfillment.

Since personal love constitutes mature integrity, it is personal love that ethicizes authentic existence in its entirety. Mature personal love is behavior in accordance with the *logos,* and is the very life of man's integral will-to-Being. Mature personal love, therefore, constitutes the virtuousness of his mature integrity, of the Self-actualization of his co-Being in its entirety. Mature virtue is in the whole. In other words, mature personal love is not one particular virtue among others, but rather that which ethicizes man's mature personality as a whole; and constitutes the ultimate virtuousness of any particular virtue. It is this insight which Aquinas expressed where he said "Love is the form of all virtues." In each virtue and in every virtuous act, man's whole integrity is at stake.

To be sure, authentic human love manifests itself in a variety of forms: love of one's neighbor (brotherly love), love of friendship, parental love, heterosexual love, religious love, etc. Yet, despite their morphological differences, these various forms of mature personal love have basic structural characteristics in common. It is interesting to see how one's understanding of mature integrity elucidates the nature and structure of mature personal love. A complete philosophy of love is, of course, beyond the scope of this study. I merely want to discuss some structural characteristics of mature love in their fundamental meaning and primordial unity as constituent features of mature integrity.

Mature integrity is the integral abode of man with Being, or man's Self-actualization as co-Being in-the-world. But this was also found to be mature love. The interpersonal union of mature love, therefore, is never merely a bond between two human subjects on the *ego* level, or a merely subjective, emotional togetherness, or the relation between a loving subject and a loved object. For the person as Self-presence to the whole of Being transcends the very subject-object dichotomy. The intimacy of mature love opens up the new dimension of an interpersonal "we," the existential togetherness of man's original Being-with, his co-participation in the all-encompassing mystery of the Being-process. To embrace a person in his Being is to love him. Mature love, therefore, opens up the primordial context of experiential oneness with all Being, and reveals man's original integrity with the totality of all that is.

This is why the interpersonal union of mature love does not isolate the partners from the rest of the world. On the contrary, although their I-Thou relationship is unique, it transfigures and enlivens their whole world and it promotes the actualization of their Being-with-others in this world. "If I truly love one person," says Fromm, "I love all persons, I love the world, I love life. If I can say to somebody else, 'I love you,' I must be able to say, 'I love in you everybody, I love through you the world, I love in you also myself.' " (58, 46)

In the same transcendency of interpersonal love, one finds the phenomenon of brotherly love, or love of one's neighbor. The word neighbor here means a person who lives near, one's fellow human being (O.E. *neahgebur*—one who dwells near). Human beings are closest to one another, not when they live in merely physical closeness, but as co-participants in the *logos,* when they dwell in the neighborhood of primordial Being. Says Fromm, "In brotherly love there is the experience of union with all men, of human solidarity, of human at-onement. Brotherly love is based on the experience that we are all one. The differences in talents, intelligence, knowledge are negligible in comparison with the identity of the human core common to all men." (58, 47) Brotherly love is the cosmic dimension of mature personal love. It is man's universal love for humanity. This, of course, is not to be understood in an immature way as the generalized love for all the nameless individuals of the human species, nor as the undifferentiated and anonymous instinctual love for what could be called the human herd. On the contrary, brotherly love emerges precisely by transcending the zoological definition of man. It is not until man achieves his final integration and attains a fundamental state of oneness, his original integrity with all that is, that he experiences himself as a unique representative of humanity.

Mature personal love as the mutual Self-actualization of persons in accordance with the *logos* is never an unchanging state of being, or an accomplished fact that can be taken for granted. On the contrary, mature interpersonal love is essentially creative; it is an occurrence which is always in the process of being achieved. Mature love is the never-ending process of reciprocal giving and receiving through which both partners achieve their ever-growing integrity. Mature love is authoritative love, for in this process of reciprocal giving and receiving the partners give increase to one another's Being and to the intimacy of their personal union. True love, however, is never given to the autocrat whose controlling and possessive love is dominated by the will to power.

The autocrat is unable to transcend the functional and utilitarian level of his existence and cannot make room for the other in his own personal Self. He lacks what Marcel calls spiritual availability *(disponibilité),* which he equates with genuine love. (141, 25) This immature, fixated, and self-centered person is incapable of responding to the other as other. He remains unavailable, for, as Marcel puts it, "he remains shut up in himself, in the petty circle of his private experience, which forms a kind of hard shell round him that he is incapable of breaking through." (146, 201) He remains incapable of giving and receiving on the personal level, and concentrates only on useful relationships. The other as other does not really interest him. Even when the autocrat seems to listen, he gives the impression that he is not present, that he does not really care, that he is preoccupied with himself. "There is a way of listening," says Marcel, "which is a way of giving, and another way of listening which is a way of refusing, of refusing *oneself.*" (141, 26) This refusal characterizes the autocrat who tolerates no contradiction, expects others to be submissive to him, and has no respect for the person of others. He becomes a threat to their integrity. And, of course, others avoid him instinctively.

Mature love, therefore, does not arise on the functional level, the level of controlling activity and calculative thinking. It rather emerges unexpectedly as a personal response to the mutuality of the primordial gift of Being. Only in the humble openness of man's existence in its entirety can he creatively receive the overwhelming originality of this mutual inspiration. True love is graced, and can never be pre-programmed. Man does not choose love; he surrenders before it. Authentic love always comes as a mutual surprise, and strikes man with a sudden feeling of wonder at the unexpected and overwhelming gift of Self.

Every gift given in love is first and foremost a gift of Self. For without the gift of Self, a gift loses its symbolic significance, and becomes a purely physical action or even a mere locomotion. A true gift is a fundamental symbol in which the gift of the personal Self is embodied in a bouquet of flowers, a smile, a handshake, a kiss, a word, or a gesture. The gift of love is a fundamental sym-bol in which personal presence and its visible expression are not independent constituents, signifying in their own right. The gift of love is not a symbol that refers to or stands for the presence of love; it is not a referential symbol. On the contrary, it is only within the symbolic gift of love that the actual presence of the loving person becomes visible. "Presence," says Marcel, "is something which reveals itself immediately and unmistakably in a look, a smile, an intonation or a handshake." (141, 26) It is within the material gift or visible expression, not as object, but as fundamental symbol, that one immediately perceives the loving presence of the other. In the context of Cartesian dualism, which reduces the human body to a mere object, there is, of course, no room for fundamental symbolism or for the phenomenon of interpersonal encounter. The fact that one can immediately perceive the presence of a person in his look, his smile, or his handshake is simply explained away by Cartesianism. And yet, as William Luijpen puts it succinctly, "When human eyes look at each other, human beings encounter each other. Their presence to each other is not the 'presence' of lenses, or of things." (139, 278)

To be mature means to be open not merely to one's own possibilities, but to those of others as well. In terms of interpersonal love, this implies that the partners are not merely participating in the Self-gift of one another's Being, but also in the Self-project of one another's ex-sistence. It is the never-ending task of both partners to give increase to each other's ex-sistence through their mutual Self-discovery and Self-creativity. There one finds interpersonal love as a temporalizing process which discloses the historicity of mature integrity. Mature integrity is an occurrence and not a static conformity. As an occurrence, it is a profoundly historical process in which those who love build their future world together. Through their mature interpersonal love the partners are not only giving increase to one another's integrity, but to the common future integrity of all humanity as well. By participating in the Self-process of one another's Being, they are participating in the very historicity of the World-building Being-process. This understanding of mature personal love is far removed from the common conception of love as a merely subjective emotion.

It should be evident that the characteristics of mature love are the same as those of mature integrity. Mature personal love is not a state of being, but a process, an event, a happening. Personal love is not mature because of its conformist fidelity to the status quo, to a static set of principles, or to the use of correct procedures, but because of its creative fidelity to the Self-gift of a person's Being. Mature love is not primarily concerned with doing the "correct" thing, but with giving increase to a person's Being, with affirming his personality, and respecting his uniqueness and Self-direction. Mature love as authentic integrity is the most fundamental integrating factor in the life of the person and in the life of humanity. True love is the achievement of final integration.

Consequently, it is mature love which is the source of real peace both in the life of the person and in the life of humanity. For mature love as the achievement of final integration makes both the person and humanity into a whole, makes them live in *peace* (Gr. *pegnumi*—"to make into a whole"). Peace is another aspect of the process of final integration. It is the achievement of final integration as a harmonious dis-position, as a primordial mood, as an experiential awareness of feeling at home. True peace is only given to a person when he feels at one with his Self-presence to the whole of Being. True peace, therefore, is not merely the absence of conflict, or a permanent state of undisturbed tranquility. On the contrary, the true peace of the mature personality is the ongoing orchestration of life into the existential harmony of creative conflicts. Mature peace includes even the primal conflict between inner harmony on the one hand, and the dis-order of pain, fixation, perplexity, sin, alienation, hatred, and violence on the other. This is why social justice will always be necessary to preserve the minimum of love and peace in the world. Mature peace is never attained once and for all, it is never an accomplished fact, but rather an occurrence which is always in the process of being achieved. Mature peace is essentially a process of reconciliation.

There is no peace except interior peace. Peace cannot be imposed upon one, it cannot be organized or preprogrammed. The world is unifying itself, and people everywhere are becoming more and more conscious of their natural oneness. However, what people are not sufficiently aware of yet is that the outcome of this unifying process depends entirely on the level in which the integration takes place. If the unification takes place exclusively on the abstractive level of science, technique, functions, organizations, and structures, then man falls a victim to what Marcel rightly calls the "techniques of degradation." For the only way man can relate to another man on the abstractive level is by depersonalizing and degrading him to a thing, or an ob-ject. And, of course, when man allows himself to be reduced to a thing, he assumes the characteristics of things. He allows himself to be controlled, used, and manipulated. He is out of touch as a human being, and remains side-by-side of and impenetrable to others.

Unfortunately, this absolutism of the abstractive level is the dominant persuasion today. Marcel calls it "the spirit of abstraction" and considers it to be "a factor making for war." (145, 114) "It is impossible," he says, "to build true peace on abstractions." (145, 3) This "is a world," says Rollo May, "in which, amid all the vastly developed means of communication that bombard us on all sides, actual personal communication is exceedingly difficult and rare." (152, 22) Modern man is alienated from his neighbor, from himself, and even from nature which has been reduced to raw material for industry. Unifying the world without man, however, is unifying the world against man. Modern man feels ill at ease in a world which degrades him to a replaceable function, to an anonymous part of a cosmic machine. He feels alienated, empty, lonesome, and "homeless." It is, therefore, not to be wondered at that today one finds a growing interest in ecology and ecumenism— both derived from the Greek word *oikos* meaning "home."

Even the home as the dwelling place of the family suffers from the same alienations. The "home" has been reduced to a "house," a building, a merely physical shelter in which individuals of the same family remain out of touch as persons, and grow side by side from childhood into adulthood without any intimacy, without ever affecting one another in their Being. A "home," on the other hand, is "a house with a soul," a place where human beings grow as persons, where members of the same family grow together from immaturity into maturity. And, where giving increase (authority) and listening (obedience) are mutually interdependent characteristics of the entire family as the hierarchical co-Being of parents and children in the shared adventure of their common dwelling.

One can only be fundamentally "at home" or "at peace" with oneself in the home or on earth in the process of final integration, i.e., when one dwells in the neighborhood of Being. But to dwell in the neighborhood of Being is to co-participate in the world-building Being-process. It is here that one is truly oneself, that one finds authentic identity, and reveals the very Being of one's ex-sistence. In his profound essay "Building, Dwelling, Thinking," Heidegger recalls that the word "to build" originally means "to dwell" (O.E. *buan*—to dwell), and is even etymologically related to the word "to be." (91, 146–147) Genuine building, therefore, can only be understood as the sym-bolic union between the erecting of buildings or structures on the one hand, and authentic dwelling or World-building on the other.

Consequently, universal peace will never be brought about by mere techniques, institutions, organizations, programs, or blueprints, but by the personal process of final integration in mature and loving personalities. "It can never be too strongly emphasized," says Marcel, "that the crisis which Western man is undergoing to-day is a metaphysical one; there is probably no more dangerous illusion than that of imagining that some readjustment of social or institutional conditions could suffice of itself to appease a contemporary sense of disquiet which rises, in fact, from the very depths of man's being." (145, 27) The World Community is built through the personal decision of each member to dwell in the neighborhood of Being, and to promote the reality of universal peace by sharing the riches of his brotherly love. No one can make this decision for another. By now the pivotal importance of personal maturity both for the achievement of a durable world peace and for the future destiny of humanity should be obvious.

Returning to the discussion of mature personal love, it is easy to see why true love makes man happy. For happiness is the experiential awareness of the "happening" of primordial Being. Mature lovers share the experiential happening of the wonder-ful event of primordial Being and give increase to one another's happiness. Yet, the bliss of mature love is not an unmixed blessing. For the fascination with the happening of Being is a fascination with the mystery of Being. In addition, mature love cannot be achieved without the pain of its primal conflict with indifference, hatred, alienation, egoism, fixation, prejudice, etc. A mature person can have integrity even though he stumbles. Mature peace, love, and happiness can only be attained at the cost of a lifetime of self-discipline, constant struggle, arduous effort, and even occasional failure.

It should be noted here that mature love transcends many of the usual dichotomies and oppositions. Thus far I have shown how mature personal love transcends the dichotomy between subject and object, between man and the world, between giving and receiving, between happiness and anxiety, between peace and conflict. And it is not to be wondered at that particularly personal love reveals the resolution of dichotomies in the mature personality. For personal love, as the actualization of man's co-Being-in-the-world, achieves his primordial oneness in Being. Maslow derives the same important insight from his study of self-actualizing people. "At the higher levels of human maturation," he says, "many dichotomies, polarities, and conflicts are fused, transcended and resolved." (150, 86) Apart from the aforementioned dichotomies, mature personal love transcends several other dichotomies and oppositions in the mature personality.

At first glance, it seems to be a contradiction to say that in mature love, the lovers create a profound interpersonal union, and at the same time maintain their own Self-identity, and even intensify their own uniqueness and autonomy. But on the level of personal maturity this is only an apparent contradiction. For mature love transcends the opposition between physical closeness and physical distance altogether. Paradoxically, true intimacy presupposes difference, distance. This distance, however, is not physical, but respectful distance. To respect a person is to let him be who he is, to esteem him for his unique personality, to allow him to be different, to admire his integrity, and to be concerned with the self-project of his Being. Respect, therefore, implies the absence of exploitation, the absence of possessive closeness, of the desire to possess (sadism) or to be possessed (masochism). Intimacy is not possessive closeness, since this would be an immature love, a fusion without integrity, a symbiotic union, a union from which at least one of the persons remains absent.

Mature love can only exist in the intimacy of an interpersonal union. This is a union in which both partners retain their personal integrity while sharing the respective Self-project of their innermost Being (L. *intimus*—innermost). This is why Fromm rightly supplements his definition of mature love as "an interpersonal union" with the observation that this is a union "under the condition of preserving one's integrity." (58, 20)

Another dichotomy which is transcended in mature love (and, therefore, in mature, self-actualizing people) is the usual dichotomy between spontaneity and motivation. Spontaneity and motivation are usually understood as antithetical. Spontaneity is a natural, unmotivated, uncontrolled, and self-acting activity. Whereas motivation indicates an activity which is provided with certain motives. And a motive is a particular reason or incentive that prompts a person to act in a certain way (L. *movere*—to move). One can now raise the question: Is mature personal love spontaneous or motivated? The answer to this question will depend on one's understanding of spontaneity and motivation. If these terms are taken in their usual, unauthentic sense, mature love is neither spontaneous nor motivated. But if these terms are employed in their authentic meaning, things are different. Mature love is not only spontaneous and motivated, but it also resolves the dichotomy between these terms.

The term spontaneity in its ordinary, unauthentic sense indicates an unmotivated, uncontrolled involuntary action which can be impulsive, instinctive, or automatic. This involuntary spontaneity contradicts the spontaneity of personal love which, as the will-to-co-Being, is spontaneity in the *authentic* sense of *voluntary* action, of freedom-to-be, of letting the event of Being happen (L. *sponte*—of free will). The spontaneity of personal love participates in the primordial spontaneity of the process of Being, or in what Merleau-Ponty calls "the unmotivated upsurge of the world." (156, xiv) The all-encompassing phenomenon of Being cannot be motivated by anything other than itself, and its emergence escapes all control and calculation. The primordial phenomenon of interpersonal love comes as a mutual surprise, or as a primordial inspiration. And the authentic spontaneity of this primordial inspiration is an essential constituent of mature existence.

To say that the spontaneity of mature personal love is unmotivated is true as long as one understands the term "motive" in its usual, unauthentic sense of a particular reason or incentive. For, indeed, no "particular" reason or motive is great enough an incentive to induce a person to enter into the all-encompassing universality of a mature love relationship. This is not to say, however, that mature love is not motivated at all, or that particular motives don't play a role in mature motivation. Mature interpersonal love is motivated. But what motivates it transcends any exclusive preoccupation with merely particular motives. Mature love is not motivated by anything other than itself. What motivates man to love is love itself, the very spontaneity of its primordial inspiration. Mature love is its own motivation and its own reward. Mature love, therefore, transcends the dichotomy between spontaneity and motivation by transcending the unauthentic use of these terms. It is the primordial spontaneity of love itself which moves man to the core of his Being (*movere*—to set in motion; to affect with emotion).

Indeed, man is profoundly "moved" by the experience of personal love, and it affects him with overwhelming emotions. Yet mature love is motivated by the all-encompassing spontaneity of mature love, and this spontaneity is never a merely subjective or particular motive. Consequently, genuine love is none of the following: a being attracted to certain qualities of a person, a warm feeling for somebody, a passive emotion, enamoredness, a mere "being" loved, a passion, a compulsively being driven, or a surface fascination with visible features. In other words, mature love also transcends the dichotomy between motives as objective reasons and motives as subjective emotions. For the true motivation to love, which is the primordial spontaneity of love itself, brings man in tune with the whole of Being (G. *Stimmung*—tuning; mood, disposition), and affects his entire ex-sistence.

This primordial affectedness is man's being-tuned-in to the all-encompassing phenomenon of Being, and cannot possibly be a particular or merely subjective feeling, mood, or emotion. On the contrary, personal love is motivated by the primordial phenomenon of wonder, or by what Heidegger calls "primordial mood" *(Befindlichkeit)*. (88, 712) Eugen Fink speaks in this connection of "primordial enthusiasm" (Gr. *en* and *theos*—being possessed by supreme Being, being-in-transcendent Being). (55) The creative affection of mature lovers is not a subjective feeling, but a creative response to their being affected by their mutual Self-presence to the openness or truth of Being. In their creative affection, therefore, mature lovers participate in the primordial enthusiasm of one another's ex-sistence. And since primordial enthusiasm places them in the very dynamism of the Being-process, it is precisely through this primordial spontaneity of enthusiasm that lovers influence one another and the world.

Of course, by saying that mature personal love is not motivated by anything other than itself, and that what motivates man to love is the very spontaneity of its primordial enthusiasm, one is not suggesting that particular motives don't play a role at all. By saying that the Self-motivation of mature love transcends any particular motivations, one is not implying that in personal love, or for that matter in personal maturity, man remains totally unmoved by particular motives, ordinary feelings, or bodily qualities. For this would not only contradict the philosophical meaning of "transcending," but also one's actual experience of personal love.

Man cannot remain indifferent to the visible appearance and to the especially attractive features of his beloved ones. He is sensitive to charm, physical beauty, strength of body and mind, appealing idiosyncracies of personality. Transcending these particular motives in personal love does not mean that man does not allow himself to be affected by them at all, but rather that he breaks with his acceptance of them as the only and most fundamental motives of personal love. In mature love, particular motives become integrated into the final integration of the mature personality. Taken by themselves, particular motives are never mature. They become mature only insofar as one accepts them as co-motives of love's Self-moving spontaneity, only insofar as one integrates them into the primordial inspiration of personal love. This is what constitutes the integrity of a loving personality.

One is now prepared to comprehend the true meaning of emotional maturity. The insights into the nature of mature personal love have provided the key to an understanding of emotional maturity. Mature love transcends any particular motives, and, therefore, any particular feelings, passions, and emotions. This does not mean that personal love is not also moved by particular feelings, but only that these particular feelings are not accepted as the exclusive and basic motives of personal love. Particular emotions or feelings are not mature when taken by themselves, but only insofar as they become co-motives of the self-moving spontaneity of primordial Being. Mature emotions are emotions that are integrated into the primordial mood of wonder, enthusiasm, and inspiration, which is neither a particular, nor a merely subjective phenomenon. Emotional maturity is the creative interplay of primordial wonder and particular emotions within the context of final integration. Emotional maturity is a matter of the integral personality.

Consequently, it is impossible to understand emotional maturity by equating it with one of its constituent elements, such as balance, stability, adjustment or control. Earlier I have shown how these characteristics, when taken out of context, become rigid, static, and immature features that fixate rather than define the process of mature integrity. For instance, it is said that a person is emotionally mature when he is emotionally balanced. This is too often interpreted, however, in terms of homeostatic equilibrium. To be sure, a mature personality does not blindly follow his first impulses; he does not give way to uncontrolled outbursts of anger or passion; he is not exclusively preoccupied with particular emotions; he does not overreact, or try to meet his frustrations with temper tantrums or self-pity. On the other hand, the mature personality is not always even-tempered either. His emotional balance is not the colorless, desensitized existence of one who has cut off his ability to feel, to wonder, and to experience enthusiasm. His emotional balance is not the static equilibrium and rigid stability of stoic resignation, of holy indifference, or of deadly seriousness. On the contrary, his emotional balance and stability are characterized by playful seriousness, flexible stability, and creative faithfulness to the final process of integration. Emotional maturity is final integration insofar as it integrates particular feelings and emotions into their common *ethos* of primordial wonder. Emotional maturity is final integration insofar as it allows the primordial inspiration of personal love to orchestrate the passions, feelings, and emotions into the living symphony of a mature and wonder-ful personality.

And, finally, the usual understanding of emotional maturity in terms of self-control, implies that the one way of dealing with emotions is to squelch them. For one can only control things or objects. And if one wants to control emotions and feelings, one must reduce them to things and objects that are hard and solid, but don't have feelings. According to this interpretation, to be emotionally mature means to be hard, to petrify one's feelings, to be staunch, strong and tough, to put all one's emotions in a strait-jacket, to be consistently cool, indifferent, and insensitive. Can there be emotional maturity after the emotions have been killed and cease to be? The rigidity of the controlling will-to-power has nothing to do with the playful, flexible, and creative interplay of primordial inspiration and particular emotions that orchestrates the entire personality. Consequently, a person is emotionally mature, not when he merely controls his emotions or keeps a lid on his feelings, but rather when he is able to accept his integral emotional resources in a healthy, creative and spontaneous way.

Emotional maturity, then, is the ability to let one's feelings and emotions fulfill themselves in accordance with the *logos*. It is Self-fulfillment rather than self-control; it is freedom to feel, rather than a manipulation of one's emotional life that constitutes emotional maturity. This freedom-to-feel is, of course, not to be construed as license or irresponsibility. License does not respond to the *logos*. License is irresponsible, acts on impulse, and creates chaos and anarchy. Mature freedom, on the other hand, responds to the *logos,* responds to the final process of integration, and is response-able.

The mature personality is the author of his own responses to his particular feelings, passions, and emotions. He is capable of gradations of his emotional responses; he is capable of delaying his responses, and does not have to act impulsively. He can be even-tempered or go to "a golden extreme"; he can be on the defense for values, angry, aggressive, but always wants his response to be meaningful and constructive rather than destructive. His emotional life shows a sense of proportion, for he allows it to participate in the creative process of final integration.

This results in a fusion of the id, the *ego,* and the authentic Self, or in an orchestration of the personality into a living synthesis of, respectively, the pleasure principle, the reality principle, and the principle of meaning. This is why the emotional behavior of the mature personality is marked by wholeheartedness, uniqueness, integrity, simplicity, naturalness, spontaneity, and expressiveness, and by the absence of artificiality, pretense, or affectation. The mature personality doesn't have to hide his emotions behind a solemn face; he doesn't have to play roles or wear masks. Instead of concealing his emotional life, the mature personality accepts it in spontaneous simplicity. And it is through the depth and warmth of his feelings, and through the contagiousness of his enthusiasm, that he touches the lives of others, and that the charm of his personality becomes tangible.

8

THE MATURE PERSONALITY: 2

MORE VARIATIONS ON
THE THEME OF FINAL INTEGRATION

Man achieves his authenticity by responding to the whole of Being. However, due to man's basic finitude, this responding comes to pass in a variety of oscillating perspectives. Each of these perspectives is final integration or the whole of maturity, but with a difference of emphasis. Whereas, for instance, ethical integrity participates in the dialectical Self-presentation of Being as Self-actualization, authentic thinking participates in the same process of Being, but as Self-manifestation. Authentic thinking is Self-thinking, is personal thinking. And since the true Self is man's Self-presence to the whole of Being, authentic or mature thinking is thinking in response to the *logos*. Mature thinking is the thinking of the primordial phenomenon of Being and of particular beings in the light of this primordial phenomenon. Mature thinking transcends the workaday world and the world of abstractive thinking, and comes to pass only in the total openness of the personality in his entirety.

Mature thinking, therefore, is none of the following: a particular characteristic of maturity, the functioning of a particular faculty, abstractive, functional, or logical thinking, classifying or calculative thinking, the professional thinking of an expert or specialist. All this fails to transcend the world of particular beings and, as a result, fails to think in the widest possible frame of reference: the all-encompassing World of primordial Being. This is not to say, of course, that impersonal, abstractive, logical, or professional thinking are invalid ways of thinking, or even that they are immature in the fixated and pejorative sense of the term. All I am saying is that taken by themselves, and without reference to final integration, these kinds of thinking cannot be regarded as authentic and mature. It is not man's ability to generalize, to deal with abstractions and to apply abstract and logical principles, but rather his ability to respond to the light of the *logos* that constitutes the maturity of his thinking.

Mature thinking is not intellectual maturity in the sense of a quality of a special faculty, but it is one of the oscillating modes of the very process of final integration. It is the thinking way of achieving final integration. Mature thinking is thinking in accordance with the *logos*. Mature thinking, therefore, is not the activity of a particular faculty of the human subject. It is rather the creative response of the openness of one's ex-sistence in its entirety; it is a thinking with mind, heart and hands. Mature thinking is existential and holistic thinking. It is precisely upon this thinking that I have reflected in my comprehensive study, *Existential Thinking*. (19)

Mature thinking is thinking in accordance with the Being-process. Mature thinking, therefore, is never an accomplished fact, is never finished thought *(pensée pensée)*, but always thinking thought *(pensée pensante)*. Mature thinking is an unending task, an inexhaustible ideal, an occurrence which is always in the process of being achieved.

As final integration, mature thinking presents the unifying philosophy of life which one finds on Allport's list of proposed criteria of maturity. (4, 294) Again, taken by itself and without reference to the *logos,* even a unifying philosophy of life cannot qualify as a criterion of maturity. For instance, a mechanistic *Weltanschauung* is certainly a unifying philosophy of life, but not a mature philosophy of life. This mechanistic worldview is literally a "looking at" the world, an objectification of the world, and a unification of the world in terms of functional and mathematical relationships. Its unifying conception of the world fails to include the whole human personality, and it fails to think Being and the final process of integration. The *logos* as the primordial horizon of fundamental meaning allows beings to "essentiate," i.e., to be (*esse* —to be) what they truly are, to reveal their true essences as insights, as dynamic presences within the unifying light of the mystery of Being. Mature thinking, therefore, as *logos*-thinking is the mysterious, dynamic, experiential, and open-ended Self-definition of its own essence. Consequently, mature insights are never static, definite, or abstract. They are not boundaries but beacons; they are not dead-ends on the road to fulfillment, but rather thought- and growth-provoking phenomena. The mature thinker is not afraid of the unknown or the mysterious, but actually attracted by it. As Einstein said, "the most beautiful thing we can experience is the mysterious. It is the source of all art and science."

The truth achieved by mature thinking is neither the truth of conformity, nor the truth of coherency, but the truth of revelation, or of unconcealment. Both the truth of conformity and the truth of consistency presuppose a still more fundamental truth: the openness or unconcealment of the World of Being. What defines the veracity of the truth as it is achieved in mature thinking is the reliability (O.E. *treowth*—reliability, trustworthiness) of its revelation, rather than its conformity or the consistency of its structure. Mature thinking achieves the truth when its conformity is creative fidelity to the dynamic unconcealment of primordial Being, and when its con-sistency is the creative *standing* -together of its experiential insights (phenomena) in the primordial luminosity of the Being-process.

From all this it follows that the mature personality is a balanced thinker. Again, this is not to be understood in the static or rigid sense of a person who lacks all flexibility. Primordial wonder, which is both the beginning and the lasting inspiration of holistic thinking, is the source of both the unity and the openness of its dynamic process. It is primordial wonder that puts mature thinking at the proper distance between chaos and fixity, between intellectual anarchy and the autocracy of a one-track mind, between naïve realism and absolute idealism, between under-distanced and over-distanced perception of the world, etc.

The way a person perceives the world has always been regarded as an important criterion of personal maturity, and, for that matter, of mental health. A mature personality, as it is said, has an objective acceptance of reality, or a realistic perception of himself and the world. The importance of authentic perception for mature and holistic thinking is obvious. For man's thinking never begins from zero. Thinking is a re-flection in the etymological sense of the world, a "bending-back upon" that which is immediately given to one's conscious ex-sistence, or perceived in one's pre-reflective presence to the world *(Lebenswelt)*. According to Albert Dondeyne, "Human consciousness is not originally and primarily a 'knowing' one in the narrow intellectualist sense of this word; it is first and foremost 'being-with,' a lived experience of presence." (46, 18) Consequently, it is of the greatest importance to ascertain the accuracy of pre-reflective perception to avoid a distortion of reflective thinking.

It is evident that mature thinking as holistic thinking has to originate in a holistic perception. This holistic perception is the all-encompassing phenomenon of primordial wonder. In wonder, man transcends his exclusive concern with particular beings and viewpoints, with useful functions and external purposes. In wonder, man opens up to a way of life of the ultimate concern. We do not wonder "in order that." Since wonder is only perceived in the total openness of man's whole personality, it is an holistic and experiential perception that transcends the empirical world of mere sensory perception and the experimental world of scientific perception. Consequently, wonder transcends the subject-object dichotomy, and, *a fortiori,* any kind of bias, prejudice, or mental construct.

From all this it follows that the mere statement that the mature person has "an objective perception of reality" cannot, taken by itself, function as a criterion for maturity. For as long as one merely means by "objectivity," correspondence to "objects" (L. *objicere*), and by "reality," the existence of "things" (L. *res*) independently of the mind, one fails to transcend the subject-object dichotomy and to understand the pluralism of human thinking. By stating that perception is mature (and mentally healthy) when it corresponds to what is "really" there, one implies that there is only one correct way of perceiving what is really there. In my book on *Existential Thinking,* I have exposed this viewpoint as the myth of "pure facts." (19, 74–77) "Pure facts" would be facts that reveal themselves independently of the mind, which not only is self-contradictory, but also ignores the pluralism of perception. Since perception is a lived experience of presence, the way of perceiving depends on one's mode of being-in-the-world. There is not one correct way of perceiving that relegates all other ways to the realm of subjectivism. For instance, when in the workaday world, one perceives water as a colorless, odorless, tasteless, and transparent liquid that can be used for washing and drinking, then one perceives what is "really" there. But when the chemist in his world of chemistry perceives it as a compound of hydrogen and oxygen (H_2O), then he too perceives what is "really" there. So does the philosopher, who perceives water in the light of Being as a material intra-worldly reality. All these perceptions are "correct" and correspond to what is "really" there. Yet, they are irreducible ways of perceiving corresponding to the pluralistic nature of human existence. It is possible, therefore, that a person who has the "correct" perception of his own restricted world is still immature or lacking in mental health due to his inability or to his unwillingness to perceive the validity of other possible perceptions.

Marie Jahoda agrees with this finding that " 'correctness' of perception cannot mean that there is one and only one right way of looking at the world around us." (101, 51) This is one reason why, taken by itself, it cannot be used as a criterion of maturity and mental health. However, her solution for this difficulty, interesting and important as it is, still remains too negative and incomplete. She writes: "To avoid the connotation that there is one correct way of seeing the world, the effort has been made to eliminate the word 'correct' altogether from the mental health criterion and replace it by 'relative freedom from need-distortion'." (101, 51) Indeed, since perception is conscious presence to reality, it can be distorted by whatever prevents us from being present to reality or open to experience. Among the factors that tend to interfere with healthy perception are: wishful thinking, prejudice, fear of the unknown, neurosis, psychosis, egoism, mental constructs, passion, bias, fixation, dogmatism, fanaticism, rationalism, dualism, and, for that matter, almost any "ism." It is obvious that one cannot arrive at healthy perception unless one tries to free oneself from these impediments.

But this is not the whole story. A person may have a healthy perception of, say, his surrounding world without being able to perceive his own true Self-presence to the World of Being. He may simply be a healthy child on the road to maturity, one who is mature for his age. But it is also possible that he is an adult whose *Weltanschauung* is that of down-to-earth realism. He perceives and accepts the things *(res)* in his environment correctly, but he has said "no" to his true Self and the authentic dimension of his existence. Original or authentic perception, on the other hand, reveals beings as they truly are. This means that original perception allows beings to essentiate in the primordial presence of wonder, or to reveal their truth within the reliable revelation of the Being-process.

Correct perception taken by itself, therefore, even when it is relatively free from need-distortion, is never mature. A mature personality's perceptions are mature not because he has correct perceptions relatively free from distortions, but when his correct perceptions are integrated into the true perception of differentiated wonder *(logos)*. Mature perception always perceives the interplay of inner reality and outer reality. The mature personality is at home both with himself and with external reality. Mature perception in wonder is a creative affirmation of life as a whole. Neither the realist nor the psychotic is able to perceive or affirm life as a whole. The former, because he is out of touch with his inner world; the latter, because he is out of touch with the outer world. "Both are sick," says Fromm. "The sickness of the psychotic who has lost contact with reality is such that he cannot function socially. The sickness of the 'realist' impoverishes him as a human being." (59, 96) The true opposite of down-to-earth realism is not insanity, but mature, holistic perception. Or, as Fromm puts it " *'Realism' seems to be the very opposite of insanity and yet it is only its complement.*" (59, 97)

Since mature perception takes place within the cosmic consciousness of the all-encompassing phenomenon of wonder, the mature personality has a more intimate perception of reality and more comfortable relations with it. Reality is not something to be attacked, but something to enter into a constructive dialogue with. The mature personality can perceive things in their own intrinsic nature, rather than merely in terms of subjective needs, social customs, or public opinion. Perceiving his Self and all that is in the cosmic context of Being, he is Being-centered rather than *ego*-centered as insecure people are. He gives himself to great ideals, and is primarily concerned with the basic and universal issues in the world, rather than with the petty details of his own private life. He can be true to himself without becoming a mere opportunist; he can accept criticism without being crushed; he can accept himself with all his limitations, shortcomings, and evils without anxiety or shame or apology.

The mature personality perceives the real world of nature in its original, pre-reflective uniqueness because he perceives it in the light of nature in its original Greek sense of the term *physis* meaning "the emergence of the all-encompassing phenomenon of primordial wonder." (19, 197–200) It is because of this original perception that the mature personality can perceive beings as they are in their original presence to the "natural world" (in its original sense), relatively free from need-distortion, and from the dogmatic prejudices, mental constructs, and stereotypes of scientism. This is confirmed by Maslow's finding that Self-actualizing people "live more in the real world of nature than in the man-made mass of concepts, abstractions, expectations, beliefs, and stereotypes that most people confuse with the world." (149, 205)

What is usually called "knowing" is merely a kind of classifying or categorizing perception, a placing of experience in a system of concepts or functional relationships. To the mature personality, however, whose original perception allows beings to emerge in their original unity and uniqueness, it is obvious that classifying perception blocks rather than promotes this original access to reality. According to Maslow, "it was found that self-actualizing people distinguished far more easily than most the fresh, concrete, and idiographic from the generic, abstract and rubricized." (149, 205) And, of course, it is characteristic of the mature personality that he himself resists being classified or categorized. Moreover, since his original perception participates in the creative process of Being, he has the ability to see something as if he were seeing it for the first time. Maslow, employing the terminology of Herbert Read, calls this "the innocent eye." (149, 205) "Self-actualizing people," says Maslow, "have the wonderful capacity to appreciate again and again, freshly and naïvely, the basic goods of life, with awe, pleasure, wonder, and even ecstasy, however stale these experiences may have become to others." (149, 215)

To return to the topic of mature thinking, it is obvious that the insights into the nature of original perception will further elucidate this thinking. Since mature thinking deepens and differentiates the all-encompassing phenomenon of original perception, the thinker is involved with his entire ex-sistence in his process of thinking. Mature thinking is holistic and experiential. Mature thinking is sapiential thinking, i.e., a thinking which is not abstractive, but a thinking which is characterized by wisdom (L. *sapientia*—wisdom; from *sapere*—to taste). And wisdom is lived insight or personal participation in the truth of revelation. In other words, the mature thinker is one who is personally present to the happening of the truth of Being; one who testifies with his very existence to the veracity of his insights; one who bears witness to the truth of his thinking. The mature thinker is a lover of wisdom (Gr. *philo-sophos*). Though he is not necessarily a philosopher in the professional sense of the word, he does not take anything for granted, is intrigued by the mystery of all that is, and has the wonderful freedom to develop a unifying philosophy of life. The mature personality is thought-ful.

And, of course, mature thinking is historizing. As a re-flection or bending back upon primordial wonder, mature thinking projects itself into its authentic past, throws light ahead of itself into its origin, or goes out into its past as something to come (G. *Zukunft*—future). In mature thinking, the personality is coming towards (future) his primary data (past) as the dis-closure of his fundamental presence to the Being-process (present). The thought-fulness of the mature personality presents itself (present) as always being ahead-of-itself (future) into its own original potentiality *(past)*. In other words, mature thinking is the Self-enriching ad-venture of man's participation in the historizing dis-closure (truth) of the Being-process. (19, 59–62; 188–189)

As the progressive Self-disclosure of all that is, mature thinking is an event of the Being-process, rather than a merely human activity. It is a thanking-thinking rather than a merely calculative-thinking. Mature thinking is a response to the primordial word of Being *(logos)*. This is why the word of Being is the source of authentic or mature human language.

Usually language is understood as a means of communication between human beings. This presupposes, however, that prior to the communication that which is to be communicated is already dis-closed in language, and in the openness of a world. As a result, "language," according to Heidegger, "is not only and not primarily an audible and written expression of what is communicated." (91, 73) Moreover, words and language are never written or spoken entities that can either exist apart from or be attached to previously existing meanings. This view contradicts the primary data of human existence, and presupposes the fallacy of Cartesian dualism. Meaning does not pre-exist as a static essence that merely needs to be brought into contact with a word-thing, nor is it some property of such a word-thing. Meaning, as I have shown in *Existential Thinking,* arises as a dialectical mode of man's being-in-the-world. (19, 94) It is in language that the disclosure of Being takes place. "Language alone," says Heidegger, "brings what is, as something that is, into the Open for the first time." (91, 73) It is here that one discovers the philosophical foundation of a phenomenon that was found to be characteristic of the crisis of autonomy, namely the "naming mania." By naming ob-jects, the budding child brings them, as something standing-over-against him, into the openness of his surrounding world for the first time. And, of course, the authentic language of the mature personality who thinks and builds the World of Being is initiated by the soundless voice of this all-encompassing phenomenon. Authentic language holds together the usual language of the everyday world and the unusual language of the World of Being in the creative conflict of their fundamental sym-bolism. Authentic language is an art in the aesthetic rather than in the technical sense of the term. Words are put at the service of the primordial inspiration of the spirit, and language is composed as an artist composes a poem or a symphony. In this sense one can say that the mature personality is his language.

Similarly, the authentic thinking of the mature personality holds together the dis-closure of the truth of Being, and its concealment in particular preoccupations, errors, and ambiguities in the primal conflict of their fundamental sym-bolism. And, again, this is why the art of mature thinking resembles the art of an artist rather than that of a technician. "Truth," says Heidegger, "as the clearing and concealing of what is, happens in being composed, as a poet composes a poem." (91, 72) When one says that the mature person is "composed," one means that he is calm, tranquil, serene. In the light of the foregoing elucidations, however, it is obvious that this is not to be interpreted in terms of static tranquility, stoic calm, or deadly seriousness. The mature personality is composed because he is able to get the personal World of Being and his usual, workaday world to work in concert. He composes his authentic identity by orchestrating his ex-sistence into the primal conflict of its fundamental sym-bolism. The mature personality is composed, not because he becomes solemn or stoic, but because he composes his life as the artist composes a symphony.

As to the remaining modes of final integration, a few basic observations will suffice. The mature personality is mentally healthy, or, as one usually calls it, "normal." Personal maturity cannot be understood by psychology alone. Mental health, therefore, as a mode of final integration, cannot be interpreted as a merely psychological category either. This is why even the concept of normality, taken by itself, apart from man's final integration, cannot possibly function as a criterion of maturity. This is what Allport is saying when he states that "psychologists cannot tell us what *normality, health,* or *maturity* of personality mean." (4, 307)

Usually the concept of normality is a static one, and is tested by criteria of efficiency, conformism, success, freedom from conflicts, social customs, down-to-earth realism, or statistical average. Taken in this sense, however, normality cannot function as a standard of mature mental health. For it remains restricted to man's unauthentic existence; it includes the average, immature, neurotic, and fixated forms of behavior, but excludes the final process of integration. Indeed, a person may be normal in the sense of being able to cope with his motivated behavior in terms of seeking need gratifications, without being able to respond to the unmotivated upsurge of the Being-process and its concomitant self-validating end-experiences. It is against this exclusive understanding of normality in terms of statistical average, perfect adjustment and need-motivation that Maslow has directed the main thrust of his work. Speaking of his chapter on "Cognition of Being in the Peak-Experiences," he writes: "This is then a chapter in the 'positive psychology,' or 'ortho-psychology,' of the future in that it deals with fully functioning and healthy human beings, and not alone with normally sick ones. It is, therefore, not in contradiction to psychology as a 'psychopathology of the average'; it transcends it and can in theory incorporate all its findings in a more inclusive and comprehensive structure which includes both the sick and the healthy, both deficiency, Becoming and Being. I call it Being-psychology because it concerns itself with ends rather than means, i.e., with end-experiences, end-values, end-cognitions, with people as ends." (150, 69)

The mental health of the mature personality, therefore, is not to be understood as normality in the sense of conforming to the usual standard of average psychological behavior. The mental health of the mature personality is rather his authentic behavior in accordance with the unusual, self-validating standard of the Being-process. Jahoda states that "the attempts to give meaning to the idea of mental health are efforts to grapple with the nature of man as he ought to or could be." (101, 4) In the light of my previous observations on the nature of man, mental health can be defined as "living in accordance with the *logos,*" or "the ability and willingness to enter into a living relationship with the whole of Being." Or, to put it differently, mental health is man's ability and readiness to become what he potentially is, or to respond fully to the demands of reality in its entirety.

It should be noted here that this definition of mental health coincides with the definition of maturity as the process of final integration. Interestingly enough, the various criteria for positive mental health discussed by Jahoda are in fact the criteria for personal maturity as listed by psychologists such as Allport, Rogers, Angyal, Fromm, Maslow, and others. (101, 22–64) Yet, mental health does not exhaust the very richness of final integration. "We suggest," says Jahoda, "that mental health is one goal among many." (101, 78) All this becomes intelligible when one understands mental health as one of the oscillating aspects or modes in which the final process of integration comes to pass.

For instance, in both existential peace and mental health, man achieves his wholeness through his living relationship with the whole of Being. But whereas in peace, the gift of Being to man is emphasized, in mental health the stress is laid upon man's response to the gift of Being. In peace, it is the gift of Being that places man in a harmonious disposition, and makes him feel at home with others, with himself, and with the world. In mental health, it is man's ability and willingness to accept the gift of Being, his readiness to respond to the demands of reality and to enter into a living relationship with the whole of Being that constitutes his existential whole-someness, and makes him feel at ease with himself and the world. The opposite of peace is homelessness, alienation, warfare; the opposite of mental health is dis-ease, dis-order, illness.

It is evident that mental health as one of the basic ways in which the final process of integration comes to pass is none of the following: a state of being, a blueprint for action, statistically average psychological behavior, the mere absence of mental illness or conflicts, the presence of merely emotional well-being. Mental health is not a state of being, but a lifelong process. It is never attained once and for all, but always remains an occurrence which is in the process of being achieved. Moreover, this process is not characterized by the mere absence of illness or conflicts, but rather by its inclusion of the primal conflict between the integrating process of mental health on the one hand, and disease, frustration, and conflict on the other.

The difference between mentally healthy and mentally sick persons does not lie in the respective absence or presence of conflicts, but in the way these conflicts are handled. "All authors," says Jahoda, "who talk about this aspect [conflict, tension] agree that tension, anxiety, frustration, or unhappiness occur in normal and in sick persons. The difference lies not in the presence of symptoms but rather in whether these symptoms can seriously unbalance the degree of integration an individual has achieved." (101, 42) In other words, the mentally healthy personality has essentially and simultaneously healthy and sick components. Mental health is not the absence of conflicts and anxieties, but the presence of existential and creative conflicts and anxieties in their primal conflict with pathological and destructive conflicts and anxieties in the existence of man.

Since mental health is the ability and willingness to respond to the whole of Being, this response has to be a response of the whole personality, rather than of any of its particular faculties or behavior patterns. Mental health, therefore, or, more accurately, "personality health" (Sidney Jourard) cannot be equated with the mere presence of emotional well-being, at least if this is understood in the subjective sense of fleeting states of euphoria, of superficial contentment, or of "feeling grand." But if by emotional "well-being" one means happi-ness as well-Being, as the primordial dis-position or experiential awareness of the happening of the Being-process, it can be regarded as a criterion for mental health. I have discussed how true happiness cannot exist without courage and without conflicts. But it cannot exist without inspiration either, since the gift or inspiration of Being occurs without prevision. It is particularly this inspirational nature of mental health which is usually overlooked by modern Mental Health Organizations. There are no techniques that automatically lead up to successful mental health; its emergence cannot be controlled or predicted; one cannot make a blueprint of this creative adventure, nor can one pre-program mental health any more than one can pre-program love, happiness, or celebration. Any attempt to get mental health under perfect control may very well become a source of what Frankl calls "nooneurosis" or "existential neurosis," which is the despair over the meaning of life.

Whereas in mental health the tendency to integrate is prevalent, in mental illness the tendency to dis-integrate is predominant. Let me clarify this with the example of the chronic, undifferentiated type of schizophrenia which as a blend of the various types of schizophrenia presents something like an overall view of this psychosis. Although, of course, the etiology of schizophrenia is unknown, an understanding of its characteristic phenomena in the light of the Being-process will elucidate the basic meaning and coherency of its seemingly incoherent agglomeration of symptoms. Indeed, one can understand the schizophrenic patient's regression as a withdrawal, as a living backwards, as a reversion of the Being-process. This withdrawal is first and foremost not a withdrawal from any particular objects or persons, but from the very mainspring of life itself, i.e., from the Being-process. Rogers calls this mainspring of life "the tendency to move forward to maturity." (182, 995)

Schizophrenic regression as a withdrawal from the mainspring of life, as a reversion of the Being-process, is the very opposite of self-actualization. The opposite of self-actualization is, of course, the process of progressive reduction to passivity for which Frankl coined the term "passivizing." In his book *The Abnormal Personality*, Robert White refers to Frankl's concept of "passivizing." "Frankl," he says, "has called attention to a very general characteristic of schizophrenic experience which he calls the 'passivizing of the psychic functions.' The patient feels helpless, observed, photographed, influenced, the passive object of things happening around him." (218, 529) As the reversion of self-actualization, passivizing is not a symptom among other symptoms, but rather, as Frankl calls it, "a *universal law* of the psychology of schizophrenia" which explains the syndrome of this psychosis.

The mentally healthy personality is self-actualizing; he creatively builds and unifies his Self-presence to the whole of Being, and experiences himself to be the author of his thoughts, his actions, and his feelings. Schizophrenic passivizing, on the other hand, reduces the person to the mere passivity of a hap-less existence. The person becomes a patient both in the sense of one who suffers from a dis-order, and in the sense of one who passively undergoes actions from without (L. *patior*—to suffer, to undergo, to be passive). The patient is no longer a Self-acting person. He becomes a passive plaything of the outside world, a pure object controlled and acted upon by external forces. Frankl calls this phenomenon "the experience of pure objectness." "All

the phenomena," he says, "that come under the headings of 'sense of
being influenced' or 'observation delusion' or 'persecution delusion' can
be thought of as special forms of a more general experience of pure
objectness. The schizophrenic experiences himself as the object of the
observing or persecuting intentions of his fellow men." (56, 249) The
schizophrenic patient has constant delusions of being manipulated,
observed, persecuted, or talked about by the outside world. He may
even suffer from hallucinations and begin to hear voices. Frankl explains also this phenomenon in terms of passivizing regression. "The
normal person's thinking," he says, "is accompanied by more or less
conscious 'internal speech.' These acoustic elements are experienced in
passive form by the schizophrenic; he feels that his thoughts come from
outside himself and so 'hears voices,' experiences his thoughts as if they
were perceptions." (56, 252)

Whereas the self-actualization of the healthy personality is unifying,
integrating, responsible, involved, creative, and self-determining, the
passivizing regression of the schizophrenic patient turns all this into its
opposite. This is why the schizophrenic personality dis-integrates, and
why his thought and language become more and more disorderly,
unstructured, and incoherent. This is also why he has increasing difficulty con-centrating, or drawing things together into the unifying center of the self, and why he is easily dis-tracted (L. *distrahere*—to pull
apart) by the many stimuli coming from the outside world. His passivizing regression results in a loss of Being, a loss of initiative, of response-
ability, and of interest. He gradually lapses into a state of apathy. His
freedom declines to the extent that he becomes dependent on the mechanical forces of the external world, or wrapped up in the fantasies,
mannerisms, stereotypes, and automatic obedience of his own autistic
world.

It is obvious that the therapeutic treatment of the schizophrenic
patient should consist in reversing the direction of passivizing, and in
assisting the patient in his attempts to live forwards, and to accept the
self-actualizing mainspring of his life again. This, however, cannot be
accomplished with merely impersonal techniques or mechanical methods, but rather on the basis of interpersonal relationships. "By providing the genuine reality which is in me," says Rogers, "the patient can
successfully seek the reality which is in him." (182, 955) Truly therapeutic power is not the prerogative of technological experts, but rather
of human beings in their full-humanness. The growth-provoking power
of the mentally healthy and mature personality constitutes what Paul
Tournier calls "the medicine of the person." Learning to live as a

person takes place through interaction with other persons. Only a person can move a person.

And this brings me finally to the last mode of final integration to be mentioned here: holiness. Holiness is one of the oscillating aspects or modes in which the final process of integration comes to pass. In both integration and holiness, man achieves his wholeness in response to the differentiated whole of Being *(logos)*. But whereas in psychological integration the immanency of final integration is emphasized, in holiness the stress is laid upon its transcendency. Our findings concerning the other aspects of final integration (maturity) apply, *mutatis mutandis,* to the aspect of holiness.

Holiness is wholeness as a way of life of the ultimate concern. Holiness, therefore, involves the whole personality in his willingness to surrender himself to transcendent reality, whether this be a personal God, a cosmic ground of all that is, a mystical experience, the sense of wonder, or the experience of oneness with the All. Holiness is the self-actualization of the whole mature personality with the emphasis on his religious mode of being. "My religious mode of being," says van Kaam, "is a standing-out in reverence and surrender toward a Being whom I experience as the personal Transcendent, the ultimate ground of all that is and, therefore, of my own being. Being religious is a mode of existence; it is not merely a feeling, a thought, a style of behavior, or a moral code." (213, 120) Holiness, as one of the oscillating modes of final integration, incorporates the whole mature personality insofar as he lives the religious mode of existence as his central mode of being. Holiness, therefore, incorporates all the other, previously discussed, aspects of final integration and all the characteristics of the mature personality.

It follows that mature holiness is none of the following: a state of being, conformity to a doctrine, to a set of rules, or to an establishment, the function of a special faculty or talent, pious mannerisms or external decorum, deadly seriousness, or otherworldliness. Holiness as the creative surrender *(Gelassenheit)* to the transcendent reality of the whole of Being is never an accomplished fact, but rather an occurrence which is always in the process of being achieved. Holiness is a creative adventure; it is the ongoing process of achieving one's ontocentric world. The person who restricts his holiness to perfect conformity to a body of doctrine, a static set of rules or the status quo of an establishment lives according to the letter that kills, rather than according to the spirit that gives life. Mature holiness is not primarily concerned with doing the right thing, but rather with becoming the genuine person. As a creative surrender to the transcendent reality of the whole of Being, mature holiness is graced and can be received as a gift only by the openness of the whole personality. Holiness cannot be acquired by any particular faculty or special talent; its emergence cannot be controlled or predicted, and no technique can automatically produce this phenomenon.

In his classic study, *The Idea of the Holy,* Rudolf Otto calls the moments of "awefulness" and of "fascination" in the mystery of Being the "numinous" which is man's experience of the holy. (164, 136–142) It is in primordial wonder that the all-encompassing totality or the primordial wholeness of the mystery of Being first reveals itself. Wonder is the first bestowal of the gift of Being, and places man in the primordial openness of his authentic Self. Wonder also places man in his primordial mood. The "awefulness" and "fascination" of wonder constitute man's primordial mood which is self-validating, non-utilitarian, and deserving to be respected for its own sake. In other words, primordial wonder is the first revelation of the holy or the sacred. "There is," says Sam Keen, "no substantial difference between wonder and the experience of the holy." (119, 35) And since authentic ex-sistence is the differentiated self-manifestation and self-actualization of primordial wonder, mature holiness is the progressive emergence in man of the primordial twilight of the very mystery of Being (spirit, *logos*).

By describing holiness as the creative surrender to the transcendent reality of Being one is not, of course, suggesting that the holy personality goes beyond his usual, workaday world in the sense of going outside it or leaving it behind. This interpretation would flatly contradict the nature of holiness as a mode of final integration, and presupposes an unacceptable dualistic philosophy of man. The angelic view of holiness as a purely spiritual perfection dehumanizes the human personality, detotalizes his wholeness, and coagulates his dynamism into the fixity of a material entity. According to the well-known words of Pascal, "Who wants to become an angel becomes an animal." This unholy otherworldliness and its static, closed, unfeeling and unloving perfectionism, which was once called "holy indifference," is a far cry from genuine holiness. It is the holiness of those who have lost their center of gravity in the creative stability and trustworthiness of the Being-process for which they substitute perfect conformity to rules, laws, structures, and blueprints. These people have to play it safe and can take no risks. They achieve their pseudo-security through non-involvement and perfect control. They do not want to get involved in any risk, danger, conflict, change, or in anything personal or inspirational; they call this state of non-involvement "holy indifference" or "detachment." Moreover, they want to have their perfection (i.e., "conformism") under perfect control, and try to achieve their state of holiness once and for all so that they can sit back and enjoy their pathological world of deadly serious ritualism with perfect security and complacency.

Primordial wonder as man's first revelation of the holy transcends the everyday world of work and functions. This means that the world of the holy or the sacred transcends the world of the profane. This does not mean that the sacred goes outside the profane or leaves it behind. The world of the holy is not to be understood as a separate entity hovering over the profane world of work and functions. This would contradict the *all*-encompassing phenomenon of wonder, and result in the unholy otherworldliness which was just rejected. Wonder does not withdraw from the workaday world, but merely from the usual meaning attached to it by revealing it in the un-usual, wonder-ful depth of a primordial perspective. Similarly, the holy does not detach itself from the profane, but it detaches itself from whatever prevents it from surrending itself to the whole of Being.

In other words, in wonder the world of the sacred and the world of the profane are not given and do not signify separately, but the usual world opens up into the unusual world as its own beyond. The profane world widens and deepens its own horizon by meeting the otherness of the holy as the translucency of its own inwardness. The holy and the profane are essentially thrown together in the primal con-flict of their fundamental sym-bolism. Consequently, whatever is destructive of personal maturity is destructive of holiness. The holier the person, the more truly human must he be. The trouble with the unholy otherworldliness is precisely that it is not worldly enough. Hence, the contemporary tendency towards secularization. Important as this movement is, particularly in a technocratic society, there is the danger of the opposite extreme, that of "secularism," which is unholy worldliness that has lost the sense of wonder and the sense of the sacred.

Mature holiness as a mode of the final process of integration is at the very core of man's struggle for wholeness. Mature holiness is the primal conflict between the holy on the one hand, and the non-holy and unholy on the other. Holiness is not the exclusive prerogative of the saints, any more than evil is the exclusive prerogative of sinners. Man was born into a body and into a society with imperfections and evils long before he had the freedom to do anything about it. The holiness of the mature personality is freedom in the process of freeing itself from the negative modes of existence. This is why mature holiness is not deadly serious, but rather playful, flexible, and relaxed. One must admit that jealousy, egoism, pride, laziness, or aggressiveness are really part of one's existence without being ashamed of it or feeling the need to apologize for it. Says van Kaam, "Our personal inclinations to certain types of sin and imperfection will be with us as long as we live. They are rooted in our unique nature and in the dark recesses of our past." (213, 14) Mature holiness is not perfectionism, or holiness without conflict, failure, imperfection, and sin, but rather the very presence of the primal con-flict between the sym-bolic (*sun, balloo*—to throw together) and the dia-bolic (*dia, balloo*—to throw apart). Mature holiness *is* the lifelong struggle between the process of ultimate integration (wholeness, holiness) and the presence of ultimate dis-integration (evil, sin). It is in this context that Rollo May aptly remarks: "The saints were not talking nonsense when they called themselves the greatest sinners." (152, 139) Mature holiness can never be taken for granted, but it remains at stake at every moment and in every decision. Mature holiness keeps the spirit of wonder alive which "keeps us aware that ours is a holy place." (119, 211)

THE CRITERIA OF MATURITY

It is the com-prehension (grasping together) of the *logos* that constitutes (puts together) the unique nature of the maturity syn-drome (to run together). Maturity is this final process of integration which sets all characteristics apart in their primordial unity of Being. And, as such, the final process of integration *is* the dynamic, mysterious, experiential, and open-ended Self-definition of the mature personality. Moreover, this process of final integration or of Self-defining maturity comes to pass in an oscillating variety of modes, each of which comprises the whole of maturity, but in a different way.

It is, of course, within the philosophical perspective of these findings that any explicit discussion of the criteria of maturity has to take place. Consequently, whether or not one is in the presence of genuine maturity cannot be adequately decided upon or ascertained (Gr. *krinoo*—to decide upon, to ascertain) by the traditional objective criteria, in the sense of testing on the basis of observation, measurement, and experimental verification. These so-called "objective criteria" become a certain set of specifics, some sort of a checklist of particular, isolated standards for testing the maturity of a person. But it is here that the genus and species syndrome blocks access to an insight into the genuine maturity syn-drome.

The all-encompassing truth of Being cannot be checked against any external norm, or any particular principle or procedure. The criterion of maturity, therefore, is not something free-floating which is "outside of" or "other than" maturity. But it is the dynamic self-verification of maturity itself (L. *verum, facere*—to make the truth truer). The mature person as the Self-presence to the whole of Being is the bearer of the *treowth,* the truth and trustworthiness of this primordial self-evidence. As the primordial self-evidence of the truth and trustworthiness of Being, maturity cannot and need not be verified by anything other than itself. Personal maturity is its own solid ground, and he who feels a constant need to prove either to himself or to others how mature he is, proves only one thing: his immaturity.

Yet, this solid ground is, of course, not the rock-like solidity of a static certainty, of unshakable facts or final concepts. On the contrary, the solid ground of the process of final integration is itself an occurrence which is always in the process of being achieved. It is a process of progressive self-verification; it is a self-grounding ground (*Grundlegendes Aufweisen*—Heidegger). It should be obvious by now why the traditional objective criteria fail. No particular standard or criterion can, taken by itself, function as a criterion for maturity. Only in the context of the whole of maturity, in the light of the *logos,* can a particular criterion function as a criterion for maturity. A simple listing of the criteria of maturity is always and essentially a listing out of context. A mature personality is well-adjusted. True. But how well? Perfectly? Adjusted to what? Burglary? If one looks for particular criteria (measures) for maturity, one errs. For it is maturity itself which provides the standard by which one measures the particular criteria for maturity. When the observational criteria are viewed in the experiential light of the spirit (the whole of Being), they cease to be classifiable and additive, and begin to present insurmountable obstacles to the merely classifying frame of mind.

These obstacles were even felt by the non-classifying mind of Maslow, who pioneered the research into self-actualizing people. "I consider the problem of psychological health," he says, "to be so pressing, that *any* bits of data, however moot, are endowed with great heuristic value. This kind of research is in principle so difficult—involving as it does a kind of lifting oneself by one's axiological bootstraps—that if we were to wait for conventionally reliable data, we should have to wait forever." (149, 199) And this is literally true. For no particular, external and merely empirical criterion can ever function as a criterion for the all-encompassing, experiential, and self-validating phenomenon of maturity. Maturity, as the dynamic wholeness of the authentic personality, cannot be measured by any of its parts, nor can its growth be measured by fixity. In other words, the practical criteria that one applies to test the maturity of a given person remain meaningless unless one applies them within the experiential context of the fundamental self-validating criteria of the meaning of maturity itself.

Indeed, the method used by Maslow correctly combines the search for practical and fundamental criteria. The practical criteria that Maslow applies in the testing of his self-actualizing subjects are at the same time the fundamental criteria of the maturity concept itself, which becomes progressively elucidated during the process of "iteration." Maslow uses the technique of iteration, which is reminiscent of Husserl's technique of "ideation" (149, 26–27): he starts with a vaguely grasped whole, examines more closely the structural parts in the light of the whole, reorganizes and redefines the whole, etc., in a never-ending spiral-like process of self-correction and self-elucidation. Yet, despite the great depth and acuity of his phenomenological observations, Maslow fails to see these phenomena as dialectical self-manifestations of primordial Being. His technique of iteration still lacks the ontological and dialectical dimensions of the final process of integration as the dialectical Self-manifestation of Being.

It is of essential importance for a genuine understanding of the criteria of maturity that the particular or merely psychological criteria are grasped in their primal conflict with the self-validating criterion of final integration. In other words, the single, over-all criterion of maturity is neither the one nor the many, but a primal conflict between the one and the many. It is neither one monolithic philosophical criterion, nor a sum-total of many, unrelated psychological criteria, but rather the self-validating maturity syn-drome itself as a dynamic, mysterious, and differentiated criterion in process. In short, the only way to arrive at a well-founded understanding of the criteria of maturity is in a living dialogue between philosophical and psychological ways of thinking and researching.

This explains why a discussion of the particular criteria had to become a constituent part of this elucidation of maturity as a whole. In fact, practically all the criteria enumerated in the conventional lists emerged here as component parts of final integration and of its oscillating modes of maturity. This is why by now it has become superfluous to present the reader with the conventional lists of criteria. Moreover, by merely listing the criteria of maturity, one takes them out of context and actually misinterprets them. For, taken by themselves, these criteria cannot even function as criteria for maturity. Although most authors agree that the criteria of maturity are not independent of one another, but overlap and partake of each other in various ways, they fail to understand the true nature of this interdependence as the existential response to the *logos* which sets all things apart in their primordial unity of Being.

In addition, a mere listing of the criteria reduces psychology to the mere common sense approach in the depreciated sense of "the kind of understanding that everyone has of everything." "Everyone" knows that a mature person is independent, self-confident, and well-integrated. "Everyone" knows that to be mature is to be well-adjusted, to be successful, and to have things under control. And "everyone" takes it for granted that he understands the meaning of these "qualities" of the mature personality. Yet, "everyone" is deadly wrong.

For "everyone" is the subject of one's average everydayness, which Heidegger calls the "they," the "common man," *(das Man)* who is nobody, and yet everybody, though not as the sum total. (88, 164) In one's average everydayness, one reads the books *they* read; one sees the movies *they* see; one does the things *they* do; one thinks the way *they* think; one finds shocking what *they* find shocking. Nothing escapes the dictatorship of the *they.* The *they* is simply insensitive to what is fundamental, authentic, original, and unique. In the understanding of himself and his world, the common man relies upon sound common sense, which in turn appeals to self-evidence. In the matter-of-factness and self-evidence of his everyday world he understands himself as a thing among other things, endowed with properties or qualities. (88, 163–168)

It should be obvious by now that the common sense approach of "everyone" to the criteria of maturity is simply useless. Its criteria of maturity are listed out of context; they are a list of qualities that the mature person is supposed to possess, rather than his fundamental ways-of-Being-in-the-world. The common sense approach uses immature criteria for the testing of maturity. It even uses non-criteria. For, because of its inability to differentiate between existential ways-of-Being-in-the-world on the one hand, and mere qualities or properties on the other, it mistakes features such as success, talent, popularity, power, or fame for criteria of maturity. And, finally, the common sense approach, because of its inability to grasp maturity as an all-encompassing and experiential phenomenon, does not realize that any understanding of maturity or its criteria involves the whole of maturity, not only in thought, but also in reality. It does not realize that when one speaks of maturity, one is not dealing with static concepts or external standards that can be applied as criteria for the testing of a subject. It does not realize that any insight into maturity or its criteria is experiential and always internal to the reality of maturity itself.

Let me clarify this with the example of mature leadership. When one thinks of "leadership," one usually thinks in terms of administration, management, organization, government, control, commands, and power in the hands of state or Church officials. A leader is one who has power, executive ability, and skill in managing. A leader is one who directs or controls an army, a political or civic organization, one who can control, manipulate, and influence other people. This is how "everyone" sees it. It is obvious that this common sense understanding of leadership restricts itself to the impersonal level of functions, work, and organization, and rests on calculative thinking and controlling action.

As contrasted with this common sense view, the philosophy of mature leadership takes the authentic personality into consideration, and arrives at an insight which does justice to both the genuine meaning of maturity and the etymological sense of the term "leadership." A leader is one who shows the way, who allows one to go or to travel. The word leader is derived from the Old English verb *laedan,* which means making a person go, allowing him to travel, rather than to organize, to control or to manipulate. Now, it is precisely through the evocative power of personal maturity, which is both a creative process and co-Being-with-others, that one makes others go, that one allows them to become and gives increase to their Being. In other words, personal maturity, and not management, control, or manipulation, is the key factor in mature leadership.

This implies that mature leadership is first and foremost non-utilitarian rather than functional; leisure rather than work; celebration rather than organization; a Being value rather than a need value. Mature leadership is final integration as concelebration of one's ex-sistence within the realm of the ultimate concern, rather than a useful organization in order to serve any particular purposes. Mature leadership is listening to the essence of things, rather than getting things under control; it is sharing the charism of Being, rather than making blueprints; it is rejoicing in the world as happening rather than subjection to the serious ritualism of the world of total work.

It will be instructive to make a brief comparison between true leadership on the one hand and mere management on the other. Leadership is personal and deals with persons, whereas management is impersonal and deals with things and structures. Leadership can only be shared, requires the detachment of the saint, and is a mystery to be lived, whereas management can be delegated, requires the detachment of the spectator, and is a problem to be solved. Leadership has no particular aim, is non-utilitarian, and involved in the way of life of the ultimate concern. Management has specific objectives, is functional, and involved in particular concerns. Leadership is a fundamental way of co-Being-in-the-world, and the prerogative of every mature human Being. Management is a technique, a skill, and the prerogative of a special talent or an expert. Leadership is experiential, holistic, and sacred, whereas management is experimental, specialized, and profane. Leadership is inspirational, evocative, and has personal authority and influence. Management is administrative, organizational, and has functional authority and power. Leadership as a Being value is primarily celebration; it is open to mystery, inspiration, creative conflicts, and the unpredictability of the future. It works with creative imagination, but never with blueprints. It endures deferment, knowing that authentic ex-sistence is essentially unfinished business. Management, on the other hand, as a need value is primarily work. It demands clear objectives, accurate planning and blueprints, and wants to get things under control. Leadership does not impose its own will, but it creates an active union of wills. It enables others to make their own unique contribution to their shared historical adventure of the World-building Being-process. Management commands and gives orders. It has administrative and supervisory authority over the subjects of the organization, the party, or institution.

The radical difference between leadership and management is unmistakable. They are even on different levels of human ex-sistence. The distinctive criterion of leadership is letting-become, letting-dwell, or letting-be. Leadership, therefore, receives its directives from the *logos* and is found on the personal level. The distinctive criterion of management is functional organization. Management, therefore, receives its directives from functional and logical thinking, and is found on the functional level. In the mature personality, however, there is no separation between these levels. In other words, mature leadership is the interplay of leadership and management, of inspiration and administration, of celebration and work. Leadership as mere work is not mature, and as mere celebration it does not work. In the mature personality, the pendulum is constantly swinging between celebration and work. Mature leadership, therefore, holds together the usual world of work and management and the unusual world of wonder and celebration in the prophetic distance of their primal conflict.

This conflict is not the kind of conflict or tension that requires physiological discharge, nor is it a conflict in the pathological sense of the term. On the contrary, this conflict is an existential conflict which Heraclitus calls "the father of all things." For this unity in diversity, this conflict of opposites, is the source of all creative dynamism. Says Thomas Clarke, "Humanity owes much to its great engineers and planners and builders, but it owes much more to its dreamers, its contemplatives, its mystics." (37, 164) A mature leader is a person in whom leisure and work, celebration and action, leadership and organization are harmoniously integrated into the final process of integration. This means that the empirical and objective criteria of sound management have to be integrated into the experiential and fundamental criterion of inspirational leadership. How does the mature leader achieve this difficult and precarious integration?

The achievement of final integration resembles the art of the artist infinitely more than the art of a technician. Similarly, the art of mature leadership is much more an artistic art than a technical art. Just as the artist, in one differentiated but undivided act, mobilizes his tools and techniques, and allows his inspiration to execute the work of art through them, so also the mature leader employs his administrative talents and managerial skills, allowing his inspirational leadership to become effective through them. Mature leadership is much more a matter of artistic creativity than of technique or correct procedures. The artist does not have a complete idea of his work of art before he brings it into being, but he discovers his creation in the very act of creating it. Similarly, the mature leader does not impose a blueprint on his community, but in the act of his creative leadership, he discovers the possibilities for the future.

The mature leader is never a distant outsider who imposes his will on the community. On the contrary, he leads his community as the conductor leads his orchestra, not by isolating himself, but by becoming his very Self in intimate integration with the orchestra. By putting his organizational talents and techniques at the service of the evocative and inspirational powers of his personal leadership, the mature leader creates at one single stroke, which is really a stroke of genius, a new world or a new community. It is a world or community that holds together the world of work and organization and the world of celebration and personal leadership in the creative conflict of their fundamental symbolism. The mature leader composes his leadership as an artist composes a poem or a symphony. One could also compare the artistic creativity of the mature leader with the activity of a magnet which rearranges in one single stroke a heap of iron filings.

The criteria for mature leadership cannot function as criteria until they are integrated into the over-all and self-validating criterion of final integration. It is not until one applies the criteria within the experiential context of this self-validing criterion of maturity itself that things begin to fall into place. It is in the light of the fundamental aspects of final integration that one understands why mature leadership is educational, edifying, reconciliatory, therapeutic, sacramental, and thought-provoking. It is in the light of mature leadership as a response to the transcendent World of Being that one understands why a true leader is not so much concerned about his own position, his own dignity, or his own power over other men, but rather with the promotion of a common cause. Mature leadership involves the leader with his entire ex-sistence. He leads with his mind, his heart, and his hands. Yet, the mature leader is not overanxious or arrogant, but rather relaxed and humble. For he realizes that it is not he in his mere humanness who inspires and influences people, but rather his surrender to transcendent reality, his response to a gift. This is why he considers listening and silence more important than organization and management. Mature leadership is not deadly serious, but rather playful, for the leader enjoys in himself the interplay of work and celebration, of the world as institution and the World as Event.

THE QUESTION OF MATURITY IN PERSPECTIVE

At the beginning of this study, questions were raised about mature adulthood. These questions were asked within the usual objectifying way of thinking, with its reductive analysis which breaks up the human person into elementary units. However, no amount of research within this objectivistic, dualistic, and fragmented perspective would yield the data one was looking for. The questions about mature adulthood impelled one to ask fundamental, i.e., philosophical questions concerning the essence of man, and the unity of the human personality. It was found that man's essence is to ex-sist, and that his authentic ex-sistence is to be a participant in primordial Being. This philosophical insight has several important implications for an understanding of the maturity question.

In the first place, the question as to what man is can only be asked as part of the question of Being. And since the question of Being as the ontological mystery is a question that encroaches upon its own data, or is a self-questioning question, the question as to what man is, too, is a self-questioning question in man, rather than a question about man. It is a question man is, rather than a question he has. Consequently, the true question of maturity, the question as to what man's authentic co-Being-in-the-world is, is also a self-questioning of the mature personality, rather than a question *about* maturity as a questioned object (problem). The genitive "of maturity" in the question of maturity is at once both a subjective as well as an objective genitive. The usual question *about* maturity as a problem to be solved is asked within the wrong perspective. This very asking of the question remains outside the very phenomenon in question. Maturity is a mystery to be lived, not a problem to be solved. The question *of* maturity can only be truly asked within the perspective of holistic or existential thinking.

To say, however, that maturity is a mystery to be lived, is not to say that one cannot give answers to a self-questioning question. But it does say that the answers cannot be final in the sense of an accomplished fact. And here is another important implication of the philosophical understanding of man as a participant in primordial Being. Man "essentiates" by becoming who he is, by progressively presenting his true Be-ing in the presence of the inexhaustible mystery of Being. Man's essence is a progressive Self-definition within the primordial question of Being where every answer returns as a deeper question. This is why Heidegger says, "the determination of the essence of man is never an answer but essentially a question." (89, 143) Personal maturity is the progressive Self-questioning of authentic ex-sistence within the context of the primordial question of Being. This is why Heidegger's statement about the nature of answers given to fundamental questions fully applies to any answer given to the question of maturity. "The answer," he says, "to the question, like every genuine answer, is only the final result of the last step in a long series of questions. Each answer remains in force as an answer only as long as it is rooted in questioning." (91, 70)

The question of maturity, therefore, can never be answered with perfect finality. Maturity cannot be encapsulated in the fixity of a static definition. Maturity begins in the phenomenon of wonder, the primordial question of Being. But it never leaves this primordial question behind. Maturity *is* wonder in the inexhaustible process of its dialectical self-manifestation. It is primordial wonder that keeps the life of the mature personality open, dynamic, and in touch with the birth-process of Being. It is primordial wonder that keeps the question of maturity in the proper perspective, and at the proper distance between the self-less world of Lockean empiricism and the world-less self of Leibnizean rationalism. It is primordial wonder that prevents the mature personality from becoming stagnated, fragmented, and immature. Wonder is the oldest question of maturity, and at the same time it is always the youngest question asked by every mature personality. Wonder keeps the mature personality within the eschatological tension between his always "already" and his perpetual "not yet." The life of the mature personality is a creative waiting, a sense of expectancy, which infinitely transcends the merely chronological concept of life expectancy in meaning and richness. At every instant, he waits for something more, something deeper, truer, better, more wonder-ful, yet to come.

Man's mature response to Being is ever in process; it must constantly be worked out anew. One cannot author life with a single act, once and for all. According to Hanley and Monan, "it is one of the lessons of maturity that one's understanding of the rich experiences of labor and leisure, of other persons, of democracy, of sorrow and joy, are not exhausted in a year or a decade. These experiences are nourishment for a lifetime to one who remains permeable to their influence." (77, 87) Maturity is a lifelong happening, and "everything that happens," says Rilke, "keeps on being a beginning." With regard to the question of maturity, there are only beginners, whether they are first beginners or advanced beginners. And since each true question concerning maturity gathers in its own way the whole of maturity, it should be said that in each answer the whole of maturity is at stake. In answering the question of maturity, every step means a new beginning of the whole; one does not build step by step on results that have been achieved once and for all; one does not draw conclusions from established premises. In answering the question of maturity, every move re-defines the whole of maturity; every reflection remains open to new incursions of experience; and the whole of the answer is already a question for the future.

Furthermore, the fact that I raised the question of maturity in the context of existential thinking, rather than within the usual framework of objectifying thinking, made these investigations radically different both in purpose and scope from the traditional experimental approach in psychology. Let me merely mention some of the most important implications of this difference in perspective. The initial question about mature adulthood did not remain the chief concern throughout the book. The perceptive reader must have noticed that I gradually lost interest in "adulthood" altogether, and even ceased to employ the term. The reason is, of course, that adulthood, as a measurable quantity, is exclusively accessible to objectifying thinking, and that its importance for an understanding of personal maturity is negligible. Even the etymology of the terms "adult" and "mature" is relevant in this respect. The term "adult" is derived from the Latin *adultus,* which is the past participle of *adolescere* denoting "to grow to maturity." The term "adult," therefore, connotes an end point, an accomplished fact. The term "mature," on the other hand, connotes process and fulfillment. It is derived from the Latin *maturus,* meaning "completely developed, early, fully aged, ripe" (i.e., ready for reaping and eating). The very question of maturity underwent a radical change of perspective. I was no longer concerned with the problem of mature adulthood. Instead, I started to reflect on the mystery of the mature personality in the existential sense of the term.

The shift from objectifying thinking to existential thinking entails a shift from reductive analysis to existential analysis. Reductive analysis breaks up the human personality into elementary units which it can investigate independently. Existential analysis, on the other hand, starts from the primary data of human ex-sistence, namely the original unity of his co-Being-in-the-world. Existential analysis tries to uncover the structural characteristics of man by performing its analysis within the original unity of the primary data. Reductive analysis cannot reconstruct the original unity of the mature personality, whom it does not perceive to begin with, out of simple elements or fundamental units. (Hence the conspicuous absence of any comprehensive study on the subject.) For the objectifying thinker, the only way to arrive at a unity of the mature personality is to artificially construct it. The existential thinker, on the other hand, does not have to arrive at this unity, because he starts from it as a primordial gift. He merely has to respond to this gift, and to deepen and differentiate it in an unending process of Self-questioning and Self-defining. One wonders, indeed, if not a good deal of psychopathology can be understood as shipwrecked attempts at constructing a mature identity to compensate for the lack of a given identity.

The fact that one doesn't "construct" maturity implies that the an-. swer to the question "How to become mature?" will never be found in a how-to-do-it manual. Since maturity is man's response to the happening and the inspiration of the *logos,* and, therefore, to that which occurs without prevision and is unpredictable, no one can make either himself or anyone else mature. What Pieper says about "happiness" applies equally, and for the same reason to maturity. "We are," he says, "whenever happiness comes our way, the recipients of something unforeseen, something unforeseeable, and therefore not subject to planning and intention. Happiness is essentially a gift; we are not the forgers of our own felicity." (171, 25) Moreover, since maturity is all-encompassing, experiential, dynamic, and unique, it is not an object, a blueprint, or a technique that can be handed over to man as a thing. Yet, since man is essentially a participant in the event of Being, every human being has within himself the capacity and the tendency, latent if not evident, to grow towards maturity. What can we do to become mature? Hugh Downs put it aptly where he says "we can never enjoy the fruits of maturity by reaching out for them." (48, 134) And elsewhere, "The oblique approach is more clearly indicated. It may be more a matter of stepping back—relaxing—to let something already within our nature operate unhindered." (48, 192) No legislation, no organized educational effort, no school system, no social planning will accomplish the task of "making" humanity mature. Unless it "happens" on the personal level, it will not happen at all.

Another important implication of the emphasis on the existential perspective of investigation is the fact that one comes to understand the traditional topics of developmental psychology in their fundamental meaning and unity as manifestations of the birth of the Being-process in man. The developmental stages and crises that encompass the entire human life, and not merely the earlier years, are existential stages and crises in the birth of the Being-process. By understanding these phases in the light of primordial Being, and not merely as biological or psychological stages, one attaches greater importance to personal maturity than to the first five years of human development. This also means that one puts greater emphasis on the creative element in human development than on the merely mechanical, chain-reaction type of causality. Fromm confirms this view when he says, "To be creative means to consider the whole process of life as a process of birth, and not to take any stage of life as a final stage. Most people die before they are fully born. Creativeness means to be born before one dies." (5, 53) And since this birth-process of Being is a continuity in discontinuity, man never outgrows any stage, but rather integrates it into higher and deeper stages. The mature personality is not one who has outgrown infancy, childhood and adolescence, but rather one who has not silenced the infant, the child, and the adolescent in himself.

Another implication of a philosophical understanding of the question of maturity is that one does not have a maturity concept in the strictly scientific sense of the term. Maturity, as the self-actualization of man's co-Being-in-the-world, eludes any abstractive and objectifying kind of thinking. But one does have an existential and experiential awareness of maturity. This awareness can be twofold. One can have maturity awareness as an implicit, spontaneous, unreflected, immediately lived experience of authentic co-Being-in-the-world. This is not a knowledge one arrives at through inductive or deductive reasoning, or through any amount of research. On the contrary, this maturity awareness is the primary datum and starting point of any possible reflection on the meaning of maturity. One must *be* mature to have at least this implicit awareness of maturity. It *is* maturity *as* the Self-revelation, as the natural light *(lumen naturale)* of Being in man. This maturity awareness is a cognition of Being, rather than a deficiency cognition. And as such, it is a criterion of maturity and a peak-experience, characterized by mystery, awe, inspiration, uniqueness, ecstacy, creativity, enthusiasm, gratuitousness, etc.

This implicit maturity awareness is not the prerogative of talented or formally educated people, but of every mature personality. Formal education or special talents cannot be equated with personal maturity. The learned and the mature are not synonymous. Indeed, some highly educated people may demonstrate some closed, fixated, or even infantile features in their personality. On the other hand, a person without any formal education may exhibit a truly mature personality. A "simple housewife" (a term invented by immature professionals) may be more mature than a well-known college professor. A mature personality does not need an explicit or thematic awareness of maturity in order to be mature. Yet, an explicit, existential reflection on the question of maturity, since it is experiential and involves the very being of the questioner, will definitely contribute to the growth of his personal maturity.

The mature personality actualizes his authentic ex-sistence, and lives in accordance with the *logos.* But doesn't this insight result in a boring uniformity, in subjecting people to one, approved way of being mature? And doesn't this contradict the actual richness and diversity one finds in mature people? This would only be an objection, of course, as long as one translates *logos* with "logic." To be a person is to be a unique Self-presence to the whole of Being *(logos).* And the mature personality is a unique interplay between a unique person and a unique cultural and physiological inheritance. A person is mature, not when he has found the approved way of being mature, but when he paves his own way to authenticity. There are no typically mature personalities; there are only typically fixated personalities or immature adults. The mature personality actualizes himself in all the dimensions of his ex-sistence at the same time: as a unique Self-presence to the whole of Being; as a representative of his culture; as belonging to a certain socio-economic class, a certain sex, a certain age group, etc. According to the well-known words of Kluckhohn, every man is in some respects like no other man, in some respects like some other men, and in some respects like all other men. This means that the mature personality is one who is ever open to experience, to the variety and richness of reality, to the diversity of life. He is a living dialogue with all the dimensions of his ex-sistence, and as a result, he is ever growing, always changing, never static. The mature personality has a genuine feel for life, and lives life as an inexhaustible adventure. There is, of course, not one correct way to be mature, any more than there is one correct way to love or to be happy.

But haven't I tried to describe some kind of Utopia? How many people even come close to this ideal of perfect maturity? Again, it is obvious that what is speaking in these questions is "the psychopathology of the average." If the large majority of the world population has not arrived at what one calls personal maturity, then the whole issue has no statistical significance and can be conveniently overlooked. It is precisely within the perspective of existential thinking that one has been able to expose the radical inadequacy of both the merely statistical approach and the perfectionist interpretation of maturity. I have repeatedly shown that, for two reasons, personal maturity is never perfect. In the first place, maturity is an inexhaustible process, and never an accomplished fact. Secondly, maturity is essentially involved in the primal conflict with its opposite, i.e., with immaturity as "not yet" mature, and immaturity as fixation, disorder, sickness, evil, and disintegration. In other words, immaturity is an essential constituent of maturity. The mature personality is always in the process of freeing himself from immaturity. Hugh Downs puts it aptly where he says: " 'Mature' and 'immature' are not either-or propositions. They form a continuum that we can tackle a step at a time. There is a ladder out of the pit, a door in the dungeon." (48, 219) Allport's study of the criteria of maturity arrives at the same conclusion. "All the criteria we have reviewed," he says, "point to an ideal seldom, if ever, achieved. The sturdiest of personalities have their foibles and their regressive moments; and to a large extent they depend on their environmental supports for their maturity. Yet it is perfectly clear that some people . . . lead lives far closer to this ideal than do others." (4, 282–283)

And, finally, the shift from objectifying thinking to the existential approach has its implications even for an understanding of bodily maturity. Usually the end of growing and the presence of the reproductive capacity are regarded as criteria for the maturity of the body. This is valid, of course, as long as one restricts oneself to biology, physiology, and anatomy. For these are objectifying sciences that exclusively deal with what Merleau-Ponty calls the "body-object." However, in one's multidimensional openness, one is present to the body too. The body is not *a* body, a body-thing, or a body-object, but a lived body, a place where one appropriates one's world, a body-subject (Merleau-Ponty). In the surrounding world, the body-subject is the embodiment of the *ego*, which relates one to the environment as a whole. Within the existential perspective, the body-subject becomes mature when it is integrated into the mature personality, when it becomes the dwelling place of the mature person. Only when one's body-subject and one's personal Self-presence to the whole of Being enter into the primal conflict of their fundamental symbolism can the body be regarded as mature. The mature human body is not the body that has ceased to grow, and that is capable of reproduction, but the body that has become a fundamental symbol. This is not the body that re-presents maturity, but the body that allows personal maturity to take place, that makes it actually present. The mature body is the language that allows maturity to speak for itself.

If I have truly answered the question of maturity, it is because I have entered the true questioning. Since every fundamental answer always returns as a deeper question, the present answers are already future questions. To be mature and to understand maturity is an unending task sustained by the willingness to be born everyday.

BIBLIOGRAPHY

1. Allers, R., *Character Education in Adolescence*, 1950.
2. Allport, G., *Personality*, 1937.
3. Allport, G., *Becoming*, 1955.
4. Allport, G., *Pattern and Growth in Personality*, 1961.
5. Anderson, H., ed., *Creativity and its Cultivation*, 1959.
6. Arasteh, A., *Final Integration in the Adult Personality*, 1965.
7. Arthus, A., *Ceux que l'on Nomme: les Grandes Personnes*, 1969.
8. Barrett, W., *Irrational Man*, 1958.
9. Beets, N., *De Grote Jongen*, 1954.
10. Berdyaev, N., *The Meaning of the Creative Act*, 1962.
11. Bergson, H., *Creative Evolution*, 1944.
12. Bergson, H., *The Creative Mind*, 1946.
13. Bergson, H., *The Two Sources of Morality and Religion*, 1956.
14. Bertocci, P., and R. Millard, *Personality and the Good*, 1963.
15. Binswanger, L., *Being-in-the-World*, 1963.
16. Blair, A., and W. Burton, *Growth and Development of the Preadolescent*, 1951.
17. Blanton, S., *Now or Never: The Promise of the Middle Years*, 1959.
18. Boelen, B., *Eudaimonie en het Wezen der Ethiek*, 1949.
19. Boelen, B., *Existential Thinking*, 1971.
20. Boelen, B., "The Fallacy of Perfect Adjustment," in *Modern Myths and Popular Fancies*, 1961.
21. Boelen, B., "Human Development and Fixations in Moral Life," in *Proceedings ACPA*, Vol. XXXV, 1961.
22. Boelen, B., "The Maturity Concept as a Basic Factor in the Problem of Authority," *Humanitas* I, No. 2, 1966.
23. Boelen, B., "The Question of Ethics in the Thought of Martin Heidegger," in *Heidegger and the Quest for Truth*, ed. M. Frings, 1968.
24. Boelen, B., "Developmental Aspects of the Teaching of Philosophy," in *Proceedings ACPA*, Vol. XLVII, 1973.
25. Buber, M., *I and Thou*, 1958.
26. Buber, M., *Between Man and Man*, 1961.
27. Bugental, J., *The Search for Authenticity*, 1965.
28. Bühler, Ch., *Das Seelenleben der Jugendlichen*, 1927.
29. Bühler, Ch., *The First Year of Life*, 1930.
30. Bühler, Ch., *Der Menschliche Lebenslauf als Psychologisches Problem*, 1959.
31. Bühler, K., *Die Geistige Entwicklung des Kindes*, 1924.
32. Buytendijk, F., *Woman*, 1968.
33. Calon, P., *De Jongen*, 1953.
34. Carr, E., *What is History?*, 1961.
35. Chesterton, G.K., *Orthodoxy*, 1959.
36. Chorus, A., *Zuigeling en Kleuter*, 1947.

37. Clarke, T., *New Pentecost or New Passion?*, 1973.

38. Cole, L., *Attaining Maturity*, 1944.

39. Cole, L., *Psychology of Adolescence*, 1959.

40. Coleman, L., *Understanding Adults*, 1969.

41. Cox, H., *The Secular City*, 1965.

42. Cox, H., *The Feast of Fools*, 1969.

43. de Beauvoir, S., *The Second Sex*, 1961.

44. de Beauvoir, S., *The Coming of Age*, 1973.

45. Deeken, A., *Growing Old*, 1972.

46. Dondeyne, A., *Contemporary European Thought and Christian Faith*, 1958.

47. Doniger, S., ed., *Becoming the Complete Adult*, 1962.

48. Downs, H., *Potential*, 1973.

49. Eliade, M., *The Sacred and the Profane*, 1961.

50. Eliens, P., *De Volwassen Man*, s.d.

51. Emerson, R.W., *Essays, First Series*, 1865.

52. Erikson, E., *Youth: Change and Challenge*, 1963.

53. Erikson, E., *Childhood and Society*, 1963.

54. Erikson, E., "Identity and the Life Cycle," (Selected Papers), *Psychological Issues*, 1, Monograph 1, 1959.

55. Fink, E., *Vom Wesen des Enthusiasmus*, 1947.

56. Frankl, V., *The Doctor and the Soul*, 1960.

57. Friedenberg, E., *The Vanishing Adolescent*, 1968.

58. Fromm, E., *The Art of Loving*, 1956.

59. Fromm, E., *Man for Himself*, 1969.

60. Fromm, E., *The Sane Society*, 1969.

61. Fromm, E., *The Revolution of Hope*, 1971.

62. Gardner, J., *Self-Renewal*, 1965.

63. Garrison, K., *Psychology of Adolescence*, 1956.

64. Gesell, A., *The First Five Years of Life*, 1940.

65. Gesell, A., and F. Ilg, *The Child from Five to Ten*, 1946.

66. Gesell, A., F. Ilg, and L. Bates Ames, *Youth*, 1956.

67. Ghiselin, B., *The Creative Process*, 1952.

68. Ginott, H., *Between Parent and Teenager*, 1969.

69. Goffman, E., *Asylums*, 1961.

70. Goffman, E., *Stigma*, 1963.

71. Goldbrunner, J., *Holiness is Wholeness*, 1955.

72. Goldbrunner, J., *Individuation*, 1956.

73. Goldbrunner, J., *Cure of Mind and Cure of Soul*, 1958.

74. Gottlieb, B., *Understanding your Adolescent*, 1957.

75. Guardini, R., *Die Lebensalter: Ihre Ethische und Pädagogische Bedeutung*, s.d.

76. Hadfield, J., *Childhood and Adolescence*, 1962.

77. Hanley, K. and J. Monan, *A Prelude to Metaphysics*, 1967.

78. Harding, R., *An Anatomy of Inspiration*, 1948.

79. Häring, B., *Christian Maturity*, 1967.

80. Harris, S., *The Authentic Person*, 1972.

81. Havighurst, R., *Developmental Tasks and Education*, 1952.

82. Havighurst, R., *Human Development and Education*, 1953.

83. Heath, D., *Explorations of Maturity*, 1965.

84. Heidegger, M., ed. W. Brock, *Existence and Being*, 1949.

85. Heidegger, M., *What is Metaphysics?* in *Existence and Being*, ed. W. Brock, 1949.

86. Heidegger, M., *On the Essence of Truth*, in *Existence and Being*, ed. W. Brock, 1949.

87. Heidegger, M., *Kant and the Problem of Metaphysics*, 1962.

88. Heidegger, M., *Being and Time*, 1962.

89. Heidegger, M., *An Introduction to Metaphysics,* 1959.

90. Heidegger, M., *The Question of Being,* 1958.

91. Heidegger, M., *Poetry, Language, Thought,* 1971.

92. Heschel, A., *Who is Man?,* 1966.

93. Hofstadter, A., *Truth and Art,* 1965.

94. Hollingworth, L., *The Psychology of the Adolescent,* 1928.

95. Horney, K., *Neurosis and Human Growth,* 1950.

96. Huizinga, J., *Homo Ludens,* 1950.

97. Hurlock, E., *Adolescent Development,* 1955.

98. Hurlock, E., *Developmental Psychology,* 1959.

99. Husserl, E., *Ideas,* 1952.

100. Huxley, A., *Brave New World,* 1960.

101. Jahoda, M., *Current Concepts of Positive Mental Health,* 1958.

102. James, W., *The Varieties of Religious Experience,* 1942.

103. James, W., *Essays in Pragmatism,* 1949.

104. Jarrett, J., *The Quest for Beauty,* 1957.

105. Jaspers, K., *Man in the Modern Age,* 1957.

106. Jaspers, K., *General Psychopathology,* 1963.

107. Jaspers, K., *Way to Wisdom,* 1964.

108. Jaspers, K., *Philosophy,* 1969–1971.

109. Jersild, A., *Child Psychology,* 1954.

110. Jersild, A., *The Psychology of Adolescence,* 1963.

111. Jolivet, R., *Introduction to Kierkegaard,* 1950.

112. Jourard, S., *Personal Adjustment,* 1963.

113. Jourard, S., *The Transparent Self,* 1964.

114. Jourard, S., *Disclosing Man to Himself,* 1968.

115. Jung, C., *Modern Man in Search of a Soul,* 1933.

116. Jung, C., *The Integration of the Personality,* 1939.

117. Jung, C., *The Development of Personality,* 1954.

118. Jung, C., *The Undiscovered Self,* 1957.

119. Keen, S., *Apology for Wonder,* 1969.

120. Kierkegaard, S., *Concluding Unscientific Postscript,* 1944.

121. Kierkegaard, S., *Stages on Life's Way,* 1945.

122. Kierkegaard, S., *Concept of Dread,* 1946.

123. Kierkegaard, S., *Either/Or,* Vol. I, 1949.

124. Kierkegaard, S., *Either/Or,* Vol. II, 1949.

125. Kierkegaard, S., *The Sickness unto Death,* 1951.

126. Kinsey, A., *et al., Sexual Behavior in the Human Male,* 1948.

127. Kraft, W., *The Search for the Holy,* 1971.

128. Kraft, W., *A Psychology of Nothingness,* 1974.

129. Kübler-Ross, E., *On Death and Dying,* 1969.

130. Laing, R., *The Divided Self,* 1960.

131. Laing, R., *The Politics of Experience,* 1971.

132. Langer, S., *Philosophy in a New Key,* 1942.

133. Langer, S., *Problems of Art,* 1957.

134. Lee, D., *Freedom and Culture,* 1963.

135. Lepp, I., *The Psychology of Loving,* 1963.

136. Lersch, Ph., *Aufbau der Person,* 1956.

137. LeShan, E., *The Wonderful Crisis of Middle Age,* 1974.

138. Levinas, E., *Totality and Infinity,* 1969.

139. Luijpen, W., *Existential Phenomenology,* 1969.

140. Macquarrie, J., *Three Issues in Ethics*, 1970.

141. Marcel, G., *The Philosophy of Existence*, 1949.

142. Marcel, G., *Being and Having*, 1949.

143. Marcel, G., *Homo Viator*, 1951.

144. Marcel, G., *Metaphysical Journal*, 1952.

145. Marcel, G., *Man against Mass Society*, 1952.

146. Marcel, G., *The Mystery of Being*, Vol. I, *Reflection and Mystery*, 1960.

147. Marcel, G., *The Mystery of Being*, Vol. II, *Faith and Reality*, 1960.

148. Marcel, G., *Creative Fidelity*, 1964.

149. Maslow, A., *Motivation and Personality*, 1954.

150. Maslow, A., *Toward a Psychology of Being*, 1962.

151. May, R., *Man's Search for Himself*, 1953.

152. May, R., *Love and Will*, 1969.

153. May, R., Angel, E., Ellenberger, H., eds., *Existence*, 1959.

154. Mead, M., *Coming of Age in Samoa*, 1949.

155. Mead, M., *Male and Female*, 1962.

156. Merleau-Ponty, M., *Phenomenology of Perception*, 1962.

157. Merleau-Ponty, M., *Sense and Non-Sense*, 1964.

158. Mounier, E., *The Character of Man*, 1956.

159. Moustakas, C., ed., *The Self*, 1956.

160. Murphy, G., *Personality*, 1947.

161. Muus, R., *Theories of Adolescence*, 1962.

162. Nixon, R., *The Art of Growing*, 1964.

163. Oger, H., *La Crise de l'Age Adulte*, s.d.

164. Otto, R., *The Idea of the Holy*, 1960.

165. Overstreet, H., *The Mature Mind*, 1949.

166. Piaget, J., *Judgment and Reasoning in the Child*, 1959.

167. Piaget, J., *The Language and Thought of the Child*, 1959.

168. Piaget, J., *Psychology of Intelligence*, 1960.

169. Piaget, J., *The Child's Conception of the World*, 1960.

170. Piaget, J., *The Child's Conception of Physical Causality*, 1960.

171. Pieper, J., *Happiness and Contemplation*, 1958.

172. Pieper, J., *Leisure, the Basis of Culture*, 1960.

173. Pieper, J., *In Tune with the World*, 1965.

174. Pikunas, *Psychology of Human Development*, 1961.

175. Pressey, S., and R. Kuhlen, *Psychological Development through the Life Span*, 1957.

176. Remplein, H., *Die seelische Entwicklung in der Kindheit und Reifezeit*, 1954.

177. Richardson, W., *Heidegger*, 1963.

178. Rideau, E., *The Thought of Teilhard de Chardin*, 1965.

179. Riesman, D., *The Lonely Crowd*, 1950.

180. Rogers, C., *Client-Centered Therapy*, 1951.

181. Rogers, C., *On Becoming a Person*, 1961.

182. Rogers, C., "A Counseling Approach to Human Problems," *The American Journal of Nursing*, Vol. 56, No. 2, 1956.

183. Roscam Abbing, P., ed., *Volwassenheid*, 1968.

184. Rümke, H., *Levenstijdperken van de man*, 1958.

185. Sadler, W., *Existence and Love*, 1969.

186. Salinger, J., *The Catcher in the Rye*, 1951.

187. Sartre, J-P., *Being and Nothingness*, 1966.

188. Saul, L., *Emotional Maturity*, 1947.

189. Scheler, M., *Man's Place in Nature*, 1960.

190. Scheler, M., *Formalism in Ethics and Non-Formal Ethics of Value*, 1973.

191. Schneiders, A., *Personality Development and Adjustment in Adolescence*, 1960.

192. Schwarz, O., *The Psychology of Sex*, 1958.

193. Sheehy, G., *Passages*, 1976.

194. Sonnemann, U., *Existence and Therapy*, 1954.

195. Sorokin, P., *The Crisis of our Age*, 1941.

196. Spicker, S., ed., *The Philosophy of the Body*, 1970.

197. Spiegelberg, H., *The Phenomenological Movement*, 2 vols., 1960.

198. Spranger, E., *Psychologie des Jugendalters*, 1953.

199. Stace, W., *Time and Eternity*, 1952.

200. Stone, L.J., and J. Church, *Childhood and Adolescence*, 1957.

201. Strasser, S., *Phenomenology and the Human Sciences*, 1963.

202. Sullivan, H., *The Interpersonal Theory of Psychiatry*, 1953.

203. Symonds, P., *The Dynamics of Human Adjustment*, 1946.

204. Teilhard de Chardin, P., *The Phenomenon of Man*, 1959.

205. Teilhard de Chardin, P., *The Future of Man*, 1964.

206. Tillich, P. *The Courage to Be*, 1952.

207. Tillich, P., R. Kimball, ed., *Theology of Culture*, 1959.

208. Tournier, P., *The Meaning of Persons*, 1957.

209. Tournier, P., *Learn to Grow Old*, 1971.

210. Toynbee, A., *Civilization on Trial*, 1948.

211. Van den Berg, J., *The Changing Nature of Man*, 1961.

212. Vander Kerken, L., *De Goede Mens en zijn Gebreken*, 1957.

213. Van Kaam, A., *Religion and Personality*, 1965.

214. Verhoeven, C., *The Philosophy of Wonder*, 1972.

215. Vycinas, V., *Earth and Gods*, 1961.

216. Waters, J., *Achieving Maturity*, 1949.

217. Watts, A., *Nature, Man and Woman*, 1960.

218. White, R., *The Abnormal Personality*, 1964.

219. Wijngaarden, H., *Hoofdproblemen der Volwassenheid*, 1952.

220. Woodworth, R., and D. Marquis, *Psychology*, 1949.

INDEX

Abstraction: nature of, 70–71; spirit of, 166

Adjustment: defined, 145; fallacy of perfect, 143–45; inadequacy of traditional definition, 143; in late adolescence, 107–10; traditional definition, 143

Adolescence: *see* Early adolescence; fundamental meaning, 55; *see* Late adolescence

Adulthood: etymology, 199; vs. maturity, 1, 130

Adult personality: change of emphasis, 113–14; vs. mature personality, 113; stage of, 113–15

Aesthetic phenomenon, 97–98

Allport, G., 4, 11, 30, 175, 182, 183, 203

Angyal, A., 142, 183

Animism: defined, 38–39; in early childhood, 38–43; and magic, 38–42

Anxiety: in crisis of autonomy, 31; in early adolescence, 95–96, 106; vs. fear, 31; in the negative stage of adolescence, 84

Aquinas, Thomas, 9

Aristotle, 9

Authenticity, meaning of, 8

Authoritarianism, vs. permissiveness, 32–36

Authority: as co-authority, 158–59; functional, 159; fundamental meaning, 158; mature, 159; as obedience, 159

Autocracy, 160

Autonomy, crisis of: fundamental meaning, 28–32; symptoms, 27

Associative play, 51–52

Asynchronous growth, principle of, 58

Bally, G., 148

Beauty, 97–98

Beauvoir, S. de, 122

Behavior: authentic, 153–54; ethical, 154; etymology, 153

Being, and beings, 6

Being, primoridial, 6, 8, *passim; see also* Wonder

Birth: as existential crisis, 15–21; fundamental meaning, 18–21; as a lifelong process, 14–17

Blair, A., 68

Bodily maturity, 203–4

Body changes: existential significance of, 60–61; psychological significance of, 59–60; in pubescence, 57–59

Body-object: vs. body-subject, 57; changes in pubescence, 57–59

Body-subject: vs. body-object, 57; changes in pubescence, 59–61

Boredom, existential, 77, 80–81

Bugental, J. 144

Bühler, Ch., 77

Burton, W., 68

Church, J., 44, 46, 50, 51, 65, 69, 73, 91

Civilization, 148–49

and authentic temporality, 150–51; an authentic way of Being-in-the-world, 136, 137; as authority, 158; as being composed, 181–82; as being well-balanced, 149–50; of the body, 203–4; and civilization, 148–49; as conscience, 160–61; as creativity, 151–52; criteria, 4–5, 87, 105, 135, 136, 143, 190–94, 197; defined, 136; developmental task of, 133–34, 136, 138; *ego* vs. Self, 137, 138; emotional, 171–73; as ethical virtue, 155; etymology, 130, 200; and existential analysis, 4; fidelity to principles, 154; as final integration, 134–39; its finite manifestations, 138–39, 152–53; as a gift, 137–38, 154, 164; as a gift of Self, 164; historicity of, 148, 150, 154, 165; as holiness, 139, 187–90; as holistic thinking, 139, 174–82; as an ideal, 138; as integrity, 139, 153–73; and intimacy, 169; as love, 161–65, *see also* Love; as mental health, 139, 182–86; and motivation, 169–70; as mystery, 138; as normality, 86, 183; as obedience, 159; as peace, 139, 165–68; as playful seriousness, 147–48; as primal con-flict (sym-bol), 141–42; as a process, 133, 134, 136, 138, 142, 154, 158, 165, 174, 187, 191; as psychological integration, 139–52; the question of, vii, viii, x, 197–204; the question of definition, 135; and reductive analysis, 3–5; as response to the *logos*, 134, 136, 137, 138, 149, 152, 153, 154, 159, 174, 183, 187, 202; and self-assertion, 135; and self-consistency, 145–47; as self-definition, 136; single, over-all criterion of, 136; and spontaneity, 169–70; never stereotyped, 145–46; transcending dichotomies, 168–73; as uniqueness, 91, 202–3; as a unitary phenomenon, 134

May, R., 3, 85, 90, 105, 166, 190
Mead, M., 86
Mental health: compared with peace, 183; and conflicts, 184; contrasted with mental illness, 185–86; defined, 183; as final integration, 139, 182–86; as personality health, 184
Merleau-Ponty, M., 57, 169, 203, 204
Monan, A., 199
Muus, R., 86
Mystery: defined, 7; vs. problem, 7

Naming mania, 31–32, 41–42, 181
Negative stage of adolescence: anxiety (in Kierkegaardian sense), 84; basic features, 76–78; educational problems, 78, 81–84; existential boredom, 77, 80–81; fundamental meaning, 76, 78–81; as a limit-situation, 79; as nihilation *(néantisation)*, 82–83; nothingness as "no-thing-ness," 78; doesn't listen to reason, 81; its sudden appearance, 80
Nicknames, 63–64
Nietzsche, F., 91
Nixon, R., 87, 109, 110, 137, 138
Nooneurosis, *see* Existential neurosis
Normality: defined, 86, 183; misconceptions of, 182

Objectivity: abstractive, 37, 70–75; animistic, 37–43; realistic, 37, 43–47; semi-abstractive, 54
Oger, H., 116, 117, 126
Openness, as presence to Being, 8
Original perception: as aesthetic perception, 98–99; vs. classifying perception, 179; in early adolescence, 94; as primordial wonder, 94, 176–78
Otto, R., 188

Parallel play, 51
Pascal, B., 188
Peace: as dwelling, 167; as final integration, 165–68; fundamental meaning of, 166; and "the spirit of